ALSO BY RICHARD ENGEL

War Journal: My Five Years in Iraq

*A Fist in the Hornet's Nest: On the Ground in
Baghdad Before, During and After the War*

TWO DECADES IN THE MIDDLE EAST

RICHARD ENGEL

AND THEN ALL HELL BROKE LOOSE

SIMON & SCHUSTER

NEW YORK   LONDON   TORONTO   SYDNEY   NEW DELHI

Simon & Schuster
1230 Avenue of the Americas
New York, NY 10020

First Simon & Schuster hardcover edition February 2016

SIMON & SCHUSTER and colophon are
registered trademarks of Simon & Schuster, Inc.

For information about special discounts for bulk purchases,
please contact Simon & Schuster Special Sales
at 1-866-506-1949 or business@simonandschuster.com.

The Simon & Schuster Speakers Bureau can bring authors to your live event.
For more information or to book an event contact the
Simon & Schuster Speakers Bureau at 1-866-248-3049
or visit our website at www.simonspeakers.com.

Interior design by Ruth Lee-Mui
Maps by Paul J. Pugliese

Manufactured in the United States of America

7   9   10   8

Library of Congress Cataloging-in-Publication Data is available.

ISBN 978-1-4516-3511-9
ISBN 978-1-4516-3513-3 (ebook)

For Mary and Henry

CONTENTS

PROLOGUE 1

ONE 23

TWO 49

THREE 69

FOUR 89

FIVE 109

SIX 127

SEVEN 149

EIGHT 171

NINE 191

EPILOGUE 211

Acknowledgments 221

Index 223

PROLOGUE

MOST OF THE NATIONS OF THE MIDDLE EAST CAN BE DIVIDED INTO THOSE WITH long histories and no oil, and those that have lots of oil and very little history. With a few notable exceptions, both groups share a common feature: they were cobbled together by outsiders. The borders of the modern Middle East were drawn by Europeans after the First World War with no regard for the interests or backgrounds of the people who inhabited it. The lines that separate Jordan, Syria, and Iraq were mostly drawn by England and France a century ago. Before that, for the first thousand years after the explosive birth of Islam, interactions between what has come to be known as the Muslim East and the Christian West were limited and often hostile. The Middle East was a mystery to Westerners. Pilgrims and priests occasionally visited the Holy Land, eager to walk in Jesus's footsteps, but few had much interest in the people who lived in the wider region. Early Christians generally envisioned the Muslim Prophet Mohammed as a sinister pretender, a false prophet who spread his faith by the blade of a scimitar. Some medieval Christians thought Mohammed was a spurned pope who created his own domain and credo like the Fallen Angel.

In Dante Alighieri's early fourteenth-century *Divine Comedy*, in the *Inferno*, Canto XXVIII, Dante actually meets both Mohammed and Ali, the patriarch of Shia Muslims. It is a gruesome encounter. The two Muslim leaders are condemned to the eighth circle, ninth sub-circle, of Hell. For Dante, Hell was like a prison with cell blocks set aside for different types of offenders. Dante put Mohammed and Ali in the level of Hell reserved for "sowers of religious divisiveness."

Since Mohammed and Ali were considered dividers of religious unity—that is to say they threatened the unity of Christians—their punishment was to have their flesh torn apart. It was poetic justice: the dividers were to be themselves divided. Mohammed was split with a sword down his middle. Every time he healed, a demon would flay him open again. Ali has his face cleft in two. Mohammed's punishment was acted out in the 1911 silent movie *L'Iinferno*, the first full-length Italian feature film. It was far more graphic than the cartoons of Mohammed that have run in European newspapers, triggering reprisals from Islamic radicals.

Equally, the early Muslims of the Middle East wanted nothing to do with the West, discounting it as a land inhabited by

Christians who were too stubborn or too stupid to accept Allah's final and complete message to mankind, as revealed to Mohammed and written down by his companions in the Koran.

The two worlds' main interactions were the Crusades and the taking of hostages to sell for ransom or to enslave at the oars of merchant and pirate ships. It's no accident that most of the historic towns along the coasts of Italy and Greece were built high on hilltops and surrounded by walls. The inhabitants were terrified of being captured by Muslim pirates. Sicilians still sing folk songs about the evils of the *saraceni*, the Saracens, one of several names Europeans used to identify their Muslim enemies. Spain's most famous author, Miguel de Cervantes, was himself enslaved by Barbary Pirates for five years until a ransom was paid. The few Westerners who did venture into the lands of the "Mohammedians" were pilgrims or, later, adventurers, foreign agents, and treasure hunters who usually went home to write books about the dark-eyed women cloistered in harems and the antiquities they stole or bought from locals who placed little value on pre-Islamic rocks.

Everything changed with the First World War. The Middle East was reorganized, redefined, and the seeds were planted for a century of bloodshed. The Islamic world, led at the dawn of the twentieth century by the failing Ottoman Empire, had made the fatal choice of joining the losing side. The Ottomans, under the rule of a group of reckless and cavalier reformers called the Young Turks, sided with Germany and Kaiser Wilhelm II, the vainglorious emperor who dreamed of being the conqueror of Europe and the mythical Middle East like his idol, Napoleon, but similarly ended up making a mess of both. After nine million were dead in the trenches, the Ottoman Empire was no more.

The Russian tsar, who joined World War I with visions of taking control of Constantinople and unfettered access to the Mediterranean, wasn't around to claim his share of the slaughtered goose. The Russian Empire had collapsed in wars with the Bolsheviks, leaving England and France to feast on the Ottoman carcass. They carved out mandates and anointed kingdoms.

Lebanon, a Christian enclave on the Mediterranean coast, was of special interest to France. Many French crusaders had passed through the Lebanese cities of Tyre and Sidon on their way to Jerusalem. Syria, once one of the most important of the semiautonomous Ottoman regions, went to France as well, although much reduced in size. The British took Jordan as their special project—then called Transjordan—a "desert kingdom" that had never existed. Further south, Sunni Muslim Wahhabi fanatics aligned with Ibn Saud, a warrior chief from a desert outpost in central Arabia, and conquered what is now Saudi Arabia with their unbending religious zeal and British-supplied guns.

Egypt, the greatest of all the Middle East's ancient empires, was a British-run show as well, largely administered from the UK's embassy on the Nile and the bar of the Shepheard's Hotel. Iraq was a jigsaw puzzle, a forced combination of three Ottoman provinces, each dominated by a different ethnic or religious group: the Kurds in the north, Sunni Arabs in the center, and Shiites in the south. The British began suppressing revolts in Iraq almost as soon as they took charge of their jumbled creation.

The tiny Gulf States of Kuwait, Bahrain, Qatar, and the United Arab Emirates were considered of little consequence, convenient ports on the way to India, populated by a smattering of pearl divers and camel drivers. These little kingdoms were left to local emirs who later became among the world's richest men when oil was discovered under their sands.

The most problematic of Britain's new responsibilities, the child who cried loudest at night, was Palestine, promised to the Jews as a homeland without informing the Palestinian inhabitants that their farms and villages were part of the deal.

The mandates and European-advised kingdoms muddled along until Europe decided to attempt suicide again in World War II. After that, France and England had neither the money nor the political will to remain as the Middle East's shepherd. The United States became the region's new godfather.

The Eisenhower Doctrine in 1957 promised Middle Eastern countries economic and military aid in times of crisis. The Carter Doctrine specifically vowed to protect the Persian Gulf. The United States saw the Middle East as a battleground in its global struggle against Soviet communism. Cold War politics, support for Israel, and access to oil determined policy toward the Middle East.

A new generation of Arab leaders emerged under the American umbrella, a crop of Arab nationalists and autocrats. But they were paper tigers. While their leaders shouted over their state-controlled radio stations about Arab unity and Muslim power, the Arab states were serial losers in wars against the tiny Jewish state of Israel, losing Palestine in 1948 and then, in a single week, large chunks of Egypt, Jordan, and Syria in 1967. Only the strongest of the Arab despots survived these humiliations. They became the Middle East's strongmen. They were secular, nationalist, corrupt, and without exception brutal to their own people. Their names became synonymous with their nations: The Assad family in

Syria. Egypt's military men: Nasser, Sadat, and Hosni Mubarak. Tunisia's "Little Mubarak," Zine Al Abidine Ben Ali. Libya's flamboyantly bizarre colonel Mu'ammar Gadhafi. Iraq's gangster thug Saddam Hussein.

Over the years, I met many of them. Saddam had a terrifying gaze. I wanted to take a step back when he looked me in the eye. Even though I saw him through a glass screen in a courtroom where he was facing a death sentence, he still looked like a man who meant business and seemed as if he could order your death with no more concern than knocking the ash off his cigar. Gadhafi, who I saw in Tripoli just months before he was killed, seemed like a washed-up, strung-out rock star, eyes hidden behind sunglasses, his face hanging and tired, but he had a commanding enough presence to draw crowds of adoring, mostly female, fans. Mubarak, who I saw often at press events at his palace in Cairo, was initially considered to be a competent ruler, but with age increasingly seemed like a stubborn old man surrounded by generals in tight uniforms and civilian advisors in bad suits. When I met the second president from the Assad clan, Bashar, at his palace overlooking Damascus, he looked awkward and had the detached air of a rich kid who grew up abroad and had no feeling for his people or concern for their lives.

These were some of the big men who inherited the state system carved out of the Middle East after World War I and the brief mandate period that followed it. They were powerful enough to recover from their countries' losses to Israel. They were part of the system the United States depended on for decades to keep a volatile and religious region of rich governments and poor people in line, and to keep the oil flowing. In the end, however, the big men were all undone by a fatal combination of their own poor management and the actions and inactions of two two-term US administrations: Presidents George W. Bush and Barack Obama.

For twenty years, I watched the rise and fall of the big men, and the chaos that followed their demise. This was the slice of the Middle East's history I witnessed firsthand.

When I arrived in the region in 1996, Mubarak, Ben Ali, Saddam Hussein, Gadhafi, and the other big men were untouchable institutions. They were the embodiments of the states they ran. They were called al-Rais, an Arabic derivation of "the head," and without them the body didn't dare to move. Insulting al-Rais in public would get you fired or arrested. It was a crime for fishmongers in Egypt and Iraq to wrap their Nile perch and red mullet in newspapers that had the presidents' photograph on them. It was understood that big men stole and appointed their children and wives to high-profile and well-paid charities and political posts. The people were under-educated and under-employed, but the states held together, maintained a cold peace with Israel, and kept producing oil and shipping it out.

Of course, all the big men had rivals. They were all opposed by Islamic dreamers and fundamentalists. Islam has never accepted a division of church and state. For Islamists the distinction is nonsensical and heretical. In their eyes, Islam is a perfect system handed down by Allah himself through his chosen vessel with specific instructions on how men and women should manage their daily lives. So why wouldn't states also use it to administer their affairs? If Allah dropped a user manual from heaven, shouldn't all humans and their leaders read it and follow it? The big men imprisoned and tortured their Islamist rivals. Gadhafi locked them in Abu Salim Prison where in 1996

7

guards massacred 1,200 inmates. Bashar al-Assad's father, Hafez, killed an estimated twenty thousand residents of the city of Hama in 1982 to crush an uprising led by the Muslim Brotherhood. Saddam is thought to have massacred over one hundred thousand Shiite rebels after the 1991 Gulf War, although the exact number may never be known. He imprisoned Sunni fanatics too. Guards punished them by drilling perfectly round holes in their shins with power drills. I've seen the scars. Saddam imprisoned anyone who exhibited the slightest hint of religious radicalism. It was considered seditious and disloyal, which made the accusations by the Bush administration that he was in league with Osama bin Laden to plot and execute the 9/11 attacks so preposterous. Saddam was a murderous tyrant, but Islamic al-Qaeda–style radicals came to Iraq because of the US invasion and not, as the Bush administration claimed, the other way around.

The Middle East I knew under the big men was angry, oppressed, and rotten to the core. I like to think of the Middle East back then as a row of decaying houses that looked ornate, impressive, and sturdy from the outside but were full of termites and mold. Like hollowed-out trees, the states that looked strong from the outside could be toppled by a slight push. President George W. Bush gave them a hard shove. Through six years of direct military action, by invading, occupying, and wildly mismanaging Iraq, the Bush administration broke the status quo that had existed since 1967. He knocked over the first house. In the years that followed, Obama, elected by a public opposed to more adventurism in the Middle East, broke the status quo even further through inconsistent action.

President Obama encouraged uprisings in the name of

democracy in Cairo, turned his back on Mubarak, supported rebels with force in Libya, and then wavered on Syria. Red lines were crossed. Promises were broken. Trust was lost. The combined impact of Bush's aggressive interventionism and Obama's timidity and inconsistency completely destroyed the status quo. The United States didn't create the Sunni-Shia conflict: it began over a millennium before the Declaration of Independence. The United States didn't create ISIS: its brand of backward intolerance and violence has been a part of wars in the Islamic world since the earliest days of the faith and helped found modern Saudi Arabia. The United States isn't responsible for giving the Kurdish people a state or denying them one. Although everyone in the Middle East tends to blame Washington for everything from car bombs to the weather, the United States isn't responsible for the woes of the Middle East. But like old houses that were barely standing, Washington's actions and missteps pushed them off their foundations and exposed the rot within, unleashing the madness of the Iraq war, the bloodbath in Syria, Libya's post-Gadhafi anarchy, and ISIS.

I have watched the Middle East in a momentous transition. I saw a historic turning point. For twenty years, I saw the big men at their prime, and chronicled their downfall and the mayhem that followed. It took from 1967 to 2003—over three decades—to build the big men. It took a decade—2003 to 2013—to destroy them. I suspect a new generation of big men will return. No people can tolerate chaos forever. Dictators will offer a way out and many of the exhausted and brutalized people of the Middle East will accept them, and I suspect Washington will as well.

MOROCCO, 1987. I GUESS THAT'S WHEN IT ALL STARTED. I WAS THIRTEEN AND staying with my parents at La Mamounia, a glamorous hotel in Marrakech. My father worked on Wall Street, and I had a comfortable upbringing. We traveled a lot.

Each morning the staff put copies of the *International Herald Tribune* in embroidered bags outside guests' rooms.

One evening, while waiting for my parents to come down for dinner, I passed the time reading the *Herald Tribune*. I was entranced. It was the first time I had been exposed to international news. Not just breaking news such as earthquakes and wars and diplomatic breakthroughs, but also news of art fairs in Paris and theater in London and opera in Italy.

I remember sitting on a staircase, next to a horse carriage. My mother came down the stairs, typically all dressed up—there was a bit of another era in my mother. And she said, "The *Herald Tribune* is based in Paris. I can imagine you working for it."

I thought, That's it. I want to live in Paris and I want to write for the *International Herald Tribune*. I'll have an apartment overlooking the Champs-Élysées, and I'll wear a white suit and smoke cigarettes out of a bone holder. That was the vision.

While at Stanford, I decided that vision would be my life. I was drawn by the romance of it, by the prospect of traveling to new and exotic places, by sitting in an apartment overlooking the city and writing dispatches about intrigues and politics and spies and damsels and all the rest.

The core of the vision never changed, but the venue did. As my college graduation approached, I asked myself, Where is the place to be? It's not 1936, so I don't want to go to Paris. It's not 1986, so I don't want to go to Eastern Europe. It's 1996. What's going to be the story of my generation? I thought it would be either China or the Middle East. I assumed China would be a business story, and I wasn't much interested in business stories. I thought they were a little bit boring and would keep me chained to my desk. So I settled on the Middle East.

I had mixed feelings about Stanford and felt cooped up in Palo Alto, but I'll give it this: my international-relations classes got me thinking about the world geopolitically. With the Cold War over, the United States was the dominant hegemonic power, as my professors liked to say. And in a unipolar world, clashes between cultures, regional and religious groups would be the big foreign stories. That made the Middle East the biggest story.

I pulled out a map and traced the countries with my finger. Iraq? Saddam Hussein was in power and journalists couldn't do much there. Jordan? Not much going on, and not an exciting place to be. Syria? Similar problem to Iraq. Jerusalem, Israel, and the West Bank? I thought Israel was an interesting possibility, but the country was already flooded with journalists, and I thought I would have a hard time finding fresh stories.

That left Egypt. It was the biggest country in the region, and I didn't think many journalists were there. It also had the great value of simply being Egypt, with the pyramids and the whole pharaonic history, which I love.

So a few weeks after graduating, I embarked on the dream that began taking shape when I was a kid. I arrived in Cairo in June 1996 with two suitcases and about $2,000 in my pocket. My apartment was in a seven-story walk-up in a neighborhood called Mit Ouba on the Giza side of Cairo. It was as barren and dirty as a flophouse, with almost no furniture and nothing on the walls. Dust was everywhere, a fine dust that gets between your teeth, in your eyes and nose, the kind of dust you can't get rid of. When

I sat on the sofa, dust rose like a cloud. Several of the windows had no glass. I covered them with cardboard in my forlorn battle against the dust. And this was one of the bigger and better apartments in my building.

President Hosni Mubarak's state didn't really have much reach in Mit Ouba. I never saw black government cars or soldiers or even police. The narrow alleys were filled with children and trash, piles and piles of trash. I couldn't understand why people didn't pick it up. Cigarette packs, empty potato chip bags, and cookie wrappers swirled in the hot, dry air. Sheep stood tethered, splotches of pink painted on their fatty tails to show they'd been inspected and deemed halal. Goats munched on plastic bags. This was the meat Egyptians could look forward to.

The water came in a trickle because the building was only supposed to be five stories and the top two were illegal. So naturally the owner didn't buy an extra pump to push the water up the last two flights. When the water did arrive, the pressure was insufficient to use the handheld shower piece. I had to hold it almost to the ground to get any water out of it at all.

The building lacked central gas, and air-conditioning was an impossible dream. Everyone had a gas canister for his or her stove, and when the man who sold the canisters came by in his donkey cart, he would bang on them with a wrench. So when you heard his metal drum, you'd run downstairs and get him to install a fresh canister.

I came into my apartment one time and found six guys from the building cooking on my stove. They didn't even seem surprised when I walked in. They kept cooking and tactfully made something for me while I sat down at the table.

When they'd finished cooking their meals, they cleaned the

dishes, thanked me very much, and took their food back to their homes. I guess they figured that a single foreigner had gas to spare. It was actually a pleasant evening, a good opportunity for me to practice my Arabic on them. I didn't feel as if they were exploiting me in any way; it was just the idea of borrowing salt taken one step further.

There was no crime in Mit Ouba, which amazed me. I had a computer and a fax machine in my apartment, but I left it unlocked. Everyone in the building left his or her apartment unlocked, not that people had much to steal. I never heard of anyone being mugged. I never heard about a rape, but I wouldn't have anyway. Victims were often married off to their attackers.

I went out on the streets dressed as a foreigner, and my light complexion made me stand out even more. I usually had money in my pockets, certainly more money than the local guys, who had little or no money in their pockets. But I was never accosted, never threatened in any way.

All the people in the neighborhood had debts, including me. Everyone kept a tab at the local grocery store. You paid for the canned meat (appetizingly called "luncheon meat"), cookies, oil, soap, and so on at the end of the month, or whenever the grocer decided the debt was too big for him to carry. It depended on the reliability of the customer. I usually got to around one hundred pounds, which back then was worth about $35, before the grocer started asking for money. The idea of the tab was to give people time to get over the hump until payday. If someone was late paying his debt or disputed the amount, a cleric was called in, oaths were sworn on the Koran, and the matter was settled.

Egypt was a hard place to run, perhaps beyond the capabilities of any government. Back then around 60 million people lived on a tiny slip of green that zigzagged up the Nile River like a crack in the desert. People drank from the Nile and dumped sewage in it too. The education system was abysmal. What kept it all together was Islam. Islam was the solution, or at least that's what the Muslim Brotherhood was selling. The Brotherhood was a political and religious organization that was officially illegal. President Mubarak let the group work in the open so the government could monitor its activities. The Brotherhood took a strict religious line and effectively ran most of the schools, factories, and trade unions. It operated a parallel government, funded with donations from its 2 million members.

If you were a foreigner in Cairo in 1996, you could forget about privacy. You were never alone. Everywhere you went, people would come up and start talking to you. Some of it was just curiosity—about the United States and why I came to live in Egypt. Sometimes people were also trying to drum up business. If a man was a plumber, he'd talk to me for a little while, then he'd let me know if I needed a plumber, he was my guy. No one was ever hostile to me. The people were wonderfully welcoming and often invited me into their homes. These encounters taught me a lot about the country and helped me learn Arabic quickly. Within a few months I was holding basic conversations and felt comfortable with the language after the first year or so.

The more religious people wanted to talk about Islam and invited me to convert. I became a "devout" Muslim by osmosis. I didn't pray or believe, but in Mit Ouba you had to act Muslim. Language was culture out loud. I learned Arabic the way it was spoken in Mit Ouba. Every sentence began with "If Allah wills it" or "By the grace of Allah." When a shopkeeper wished me *salaam alaikum,* "peace be with you," I learned to answer with the forced poetry of "and peace be upon *you*, and the mercy of Allah and His blessings." I mumbled "In the name of Allah" before taking a sip of water. If I hiccupped, I said, "Praise Allah."

For two years, I almost never spoke to an Egyptian woman, unless she sold bread or vegetables, but even those precious interactions—exchanges of produce and crumpled currency—were limited. There was never any physical contact. No hands on the shoulder, no hugs, and certainly no Parisian-style double kisses between *jeune femme et homme.* Even when the old, veiled woman who sold sprouting onions and parsley from a wet blanket handed me change, I was careful not to touch her fingers. The rules were clear without an explanation. I don't know what the protocol was for sitting next to a woman. I never sat next to one.

In college, back in the States, if I was with a group of guys and an attractive woman came into the room, her presence would change the air, change the way the men interacted with one another. That's a good thing. It's the spice of life. But in Egypt they were afraid of that. It was like putting a contaminant in the water. Women are Eve. Women are to be protected and also to be feared; their sexuality is dangerous and can make you have impure thoughts and act in an impure way. You can lose control.

The result was a kind of social fraternity, a world composed almost entirely of men. In exchange for celibacy and seclusion, the fraternity was safe and even gentle. Men didn't curse. They seldom raised their voices and were elaborately generous, especially with food. It was impossible to eat on a bus because you had to offer more than half of whatever you had to the person next to you. You were obliged to tear your sandwich and put it in his hands. He was obliged to refuse and say, "May Allah preserve you." "May Allah preserve *you*," you had to say, and close his hands around the half sandwich.

Shortly after I arrived in Cairo, I applied for a job with the *Middle East Times*, a weekly owned by the Reverend Moon's Unification Church. This good, feisty paper covered news, sports, and culture, and a page or two of society news. It was the same kind of paper that was put on our doorknob in Marrakech, but on a much smaller scale, written for diplomats, tourists, visiting businessmen, and expats.

The *Times* didn't have any openings, but the publisher said he would keep in touch. Six months later, he called me at my apartment and asked if I was looking for work. When I said yes, he invited me to his apartment that night and offered me a job. The salary was $1,000 a month, in cash. I accepted at once and asked when he wanted me to start. "How about tomorrow?" he replied.

When I got to the office, I quickly understood the rush. The place was virtually empty. The publisher had fired a popular editor in chief, and the staff had walked out in protest. The only people left were an Egyptian sportswriter, a few accountants and advertising managers, and a Sudanese reporter. I called all the stringers the remaining staff knew and asked them to write something, just about anything would do. Somehow we managed to put out a paper with sixteen pages, half the usual number. I stayed on as news editor and chief reporter. I started writing about Islamic groups and the Muslim Brotherhood, subjects that would define my working life for the next twenty years.

One night, I invited a man and his son to my apartment. Before my guests arrived, I took a taxi to Zamalek, the ritzy neighborhood where most of the expats and diplomats lived. I bought imported ravioli and spent the next several hours mincing garlic and dicing tomatoes. It felt good to be doing something familiar. The falling of the knife relaxed me immensely. I bought a bottle of nice Italian olive oil for $10. It smelled clean and earthy and far from Cairo.

My guest was a writer for a religious newspaper. He showed up with his son, who looked about six. I served them cheese ravioli in my homemade tomato sauce. I'd lived in Sicily for a year in high school. I make good sauce. It was still steaming in the plastic bowl when I brought it out. The boy was disappointed. My Arabic was just good enough so that I could follow him. He wanted meat. He thought since he was eating out, and with a foreigner, that there would be meat.

"I want *kofta*," the boy whined. In Egypt, *kofta* is grilled minced lamb. His father looked at him, horrified at his behavior, and tugged his arm in a way that showed he wasn't joking.

"Can't you see this man is very poor? Now eat your potatoes. We'll have *kofta* at home."

After the meal, the man thanked me with pity in his voice. He too didn't care much for my ravioli. He barely touched them. The boy maybe took one bite. But my poverty endeared me to the writer, a member of the Muslim Brotherhood. He introduced me to the "family."

The Muslim Brotherhood's headquarters was a small apartment in El Manial, on an island straddled by the Nile near Zamalek. I waited in a big chair as fat men in oversize suits looked suspiciously at me until I was given an audience with Mustafa Mashhur, the Brotherhood's murshid, or supreme guide. I was interviewing Mashhur for the newspaper.

We talked about Afghanistan. He supported the Taliban,

which had just taken over Kabul, but he said they were making some mistakes. Girls should be educated, but kept at home as mothers and nurturers. He told me about Jews and how their religion was holy and godly, but that as individuals they were crafty warmongers and land thieves. He said sex was good and should be enjoyed, but that veils were needed because men and women couldn't contain their carnal natures. Female circumcision—in which a girl's clitoris is dug out of her vagina with a razor—was good too, he said, provided it was done safely. Israel had to be destroyed, but he didn't think Egypt should attack right away. He was an extremist preaching moderation. He supported hateful nonsense, but he always dialed it back a few degrees. It was the Brotherhood's way of pretending—and believing—that they were moderates.

Meeting Mashhur was my secret handshake. After that, I had access to the bureaucrats and government offices that made Cairo creak along. The men I met were all members of the Brotherhood. They were the middle managers in this country of tens of thousands of middle managers.

Cairo was, and remains, an ugly, cement-colored, park-free city, dotted with a few bewildering, mind-expanding splendors that make the whole place manic and magical. There was always noise, dirt, and exhaust, the honking of horns and the screeching of brakes.

My Brotherhood contacts made life easier for me. They held the ubiquitous stamp required for every inane piece of paperwork. They kept the giant logbooks in government offices. When I needed to renew my residency permit at the Mogamma, the government administration building in Tahrir Square, I didn't have to wait in line with all the Sudanese refugees. I knew a guy who knew a guy. The Brotherhood, as the name promised, was a family. I wasn't a relative, or even a distant cousin, but I was in its orbit. In Mafia terms, I wasn't a wiseguy, or a made guy, but a trusted guy, a friend of the family's.

I became obsessed with the Brotherhood and their hit-and-run battles with the thugs from Amn al-Dawla, the State Security service. I wrote about the Brotherhood every week. The expats and diplomats loved it. I was their inside man. The members of the Brotherhood loved it too. I was their window to the outside. This was before the Internet was a big thing. I was invited to the Brotherhood's *iftar* dinners, at which they broke their Ramadan fast. The Brotherhood called me whenever their members were arrested or there was a symposium at *Al Shaab*, a religious and socialist newspaper. Printed in blue ink, the paper ran cartoons of Jews with pointy ears, blood dripping from fangs, and swastikas on their foreheads. The Zionists had been transmogrified into National Socialists. The symposiums at *Al Shaab* were usually about Gaza or the Al-Aqsa Mosque in Jerusalem and how the West was raping both of them. America was the new crusader, blinded and tricked by Jews and their lobby in Washington.

It wasn't long before the government started to wonder what the hell an Arabic-speaking twenty-four-year-old American kid was doing hanging around with the Brotherhood. I was followed constantly and my phone was tapped. I could hear men listening to my conversations. They must have been smokers, judging by their coughs. Sometimes I heard clinking, like a tiny glass bell somewhere in the background. The agents from Amn al-Dawla were stirring their tea.

I grew to hate talking to members of the Brotherhood. Their minds were a cage of their own creation. Their pronouncements were always the same. Everything wrong with Egypt and their lives was somebody else's fault. The world wanted to keep Muslims down so they wouldn't restore the caliphate and take over civilization again. Jews were bloodsucking cheats, scorned even by their own prophets. America was afraid of Islam's greatness. There was a plot against Islam because the plotters knew if Allah's will—as written down in the Koran—was truly carried out, the capitalist-Zionist system of American hegemony would be destroyed.

The Brotherhood's diatribes against Israel, women, gays, and the Elders of Zion made me nauseated. Sometimes I would rush to one of the many casinos in Cairo to drink whiskey and play blackjack until dawn. I needed to escape the caged mind. I wanted to deliberately do something the Brotherhood wouldn't like. Gambling and drinking felt like streaking through a football stadium. I made more money at the blackjack tables than I did as a journalist. I was an über-infidel, and my nose was under the Brotherhood's tent.

THE BROTHERHOOD'S LOGO IS TWO CROSSED SWORDS WITH A KORAN FLOATING between the blades. Beneath the swords is a single phrase, "And Prepare," a quote from the Koran on "the spoils of war." The full quote is "And prepare against them whatever you are able of power and of steeds of war by which you may terrify the enemy of Allah and your enemy and others besides them whom you do not know [but] whom Allah knows. And whatever you spend in the cause of Allah will be fully repaid to you, and you will not be wronged." The two-word slogan is an instruction to the brothers to prepare for battle against Allah's enemies.

By the 1990s, President Mubarak was in his late sixties and had already become an old fool. His main concern was making the army rich and loyal. He let the Brotherhood dominate the mosques. Worst of all, he let the group infect the Egyptian mind with its hateful nonsense.

The revolution Egyptians needed wasn't for political power and democracy, but a revolution in thinking, a revolt against the Brotherhood's bile. Egyptians needed to strip away the conspiracy theories, anti-Semitism, and litany of victimization that passed for education. Sometimes I thought the only way to fix Egypt would be to drop books on it. Open the bomb doors of B-52s and let Kant and Locke, Hemingway and Gloria Steinem, rain from the heavens. But the big men let the Brotherhood and extreme Wahhabi clerics pollute their people's minds. It kept them angry with the West, Israel, Washington, and an international American-Zionist conspiracy instead of blaming their leaders for the nation's pathetic performance on the global stage. The Arab world of the big men was a deliberately stupid place.

For decades, Egypt—and every autocracy in the Middle East—was obsessed with controlling the media. Anything that had the potential to influence crowds, including newspapers and movies, was censored. I knew how rigorous the process was because I met frequently with an Egyptian censor. Every week we had to submit a proof of the *Middle East Times* to the censor before going to print. We had to finish writing on Wednesday night so the proof would be on the censor's desk Thursday morning. The censor got back to us Thursday afternoon so we could make the required changes and catch a flight to Athens, where we printed the paper. The next day the newspapers were shipped back to Cairo to go on sale. We printed in Greece so the newspaper would be classified as a foreign publication. If we printed in Egypt, we would have been considered domestic press, which was even more tightly controlled.

The censor was proud of his job and felt he was doing us a favor by allowing our little import scam. He even agreed to sit for an interview, in which he denied there was any censorship in Egypt. I ran the interview under the headline "Censor Denies Censorship in Egypt." Luckily, he missed the irony.

Sometimes the censor would cut a few sentences. We would fill the extra space this created by making the advertisements a little bigger. If an entire article was cut, however, we'd have to run a blank space. I thought it would be amusing to print photographs of President Mubarak in the white spaces where the articles had been removed. Not everyone got the joke. Some of my friends thought I was overcome by Egyptian patriotism. We decided instead to run a caption in the white space stating, "The article here was removed by the censor." The censor demanded that we stop. We stopped for a few weeks, but then went back to it.

By then I had learned that the rhetoric of the Brotherhood and Al-Gama'a al-Islamiyya (or Islamic Group, a party that advocated the most austere form of Sunni Islam) was only the outward manifestation of deeper rage that could not be sated by praising Allah and extolling virgins who smelled like mangoes. This rage could only find expression in violence, as I learned when my phone at the paper rang on the afternoon of September 18, 1997, two days after my twenty-fourth birthday.

1

CAIRO | JULY 2013

An iconic image of Cairo's Tahrir Square. The relatively small, tented protest camp at the center of the square swelled with up to a million demonstrators shouting "the people want to topple the regime."

CAIRO | AUGUST 2013

Islamist supporters of the Muslim Brotherhood chose the location for their protest badly. Many of the locals who lived around the Rabaa al-Adiwya mosque supported the coup against the Brotherhood. Here several residents hang a photograph of the coup leader, General Abdel Fattah el-Sisi, on the gate of the mosque where the protest was based.

2

3

CAIRO | AUGUST 2013

Egyptian security forces claimed they were shot at by Islamist protesters and returned fire, killing many in the side streets around the Rabaa al-Adiwya mosque at the edge of Cairo.

CAIRO | AUGUST 2013

In reporting on wars and uprisings, like here during the crackdown on Islamist protesters in Cairo, we are often confronted with images too graphic to show on American broadcast television, like this man shot in the torso. We try to take images that evoke what happened without being offensive to our viewers, like pictures of feet or even bloody clothing.

4

CAIRO | AUGUST 2013

The aftermath of the Rabaa crackdown. Bodies of Islamist protesters were gathered in mosques. Volunteers put blocks of ice on top of the bodies, which melted into the carpet under everyone's bare feet.

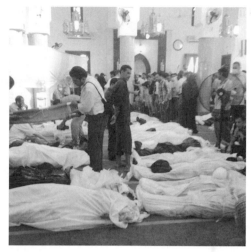

CAIRO | AUGUST 2013

After the Egyptian military overthrew the Muslim Brotherhood in a coup, Islamists set up a protest camp around the Rabaa al-Adiwya mosque on the edge of Cairo. They hoped it be would be like the Tahrir Square protests and that the world would back them. They were mistaken. Estimates of the death toll when Egyptian security forces broke up the protests range from 800 to several thousand.

7

GAZA | JULY 2014

Israel flattened Gaza City's al-Tufah neighborhood, claiming it was a Hamas stronghold. Palestinians called it collective punishment.

GAZA | JULY 2014

Gaza City's Shifa hospital was packed with children injured by Israeli bombs. The UN claimed its refugee shelters were repeatedly attacked despite having informed Israeli authorities of their locations.

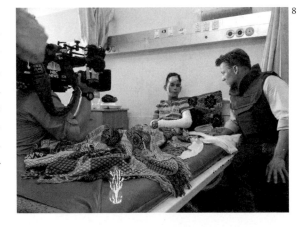

8

IRAQ | 2014

Television crews were a conspicuous presence during elections in Iraq. These moments were hailed by Washington of proof that democracy was spreading in Iraq, but ended up establishing a system of Shiite dominance that Sunnis resented, fueling civil war.

YEMEN | OCTOBER 2012

The old city of Sana'a in Yemen is a cultural and architectural gem, one of my favorite places in the Middle East. Unfortunately, I was there on this trip to interview Gregory Johnsen, an author and expert on Islamic radicals who explained how the militants were digging in as Yemen lurched from unrest to civil war.

11

LIBYA | AUGUST 2011

The Libyan rebels closing on Tripoli were overwhelmingly supportive of western journalists, believing our coverage had helped protesters topple President Hosni Mubarak in Egypt and would also help them overthrow Col. Mu'ammar Gadhafi. Crowds sometimes gathered when I did live television broadcasts.

12

LIBYA | AUGUST 2011

As anti-government rebels, backed by NATO air strikes, moved across Libya, the front lines shifted by the day, sometimes great distances. Reporters moved with them, moving on or retreating as the battles ebbed and flowed. Here we stopped for a live report.

TURKISH-SYRIAN BORDER | NOVEMBER 2014

Getting into Syria from Turkey often meant climbing over something—a fence, crops, or in this case the wall of a farmer's home. ISIS had taken over much of the Kurdish town of Kobane and was threatening to capture the rest. We went into the half-occupied town to see the Kurdish fighters who were brave enough to stand up to ISIS.

KOBANE, SYRIA | NOVEMBER 2014

The main market street in the Syrian town of Kobane, destroyed in fighting between ISIS and a Kurdish militia. After receiving American air support, the Kurds retook Kobane, the first major defeat of ISIS on the battlefield.

SYRIA | AUGUST 2013

The Syrian war created millions of refugees and many others, like these people, who were displaced from their homes but couldn't leave Syria because
they couldn't afford the risky and uncertain journey to Turkey or Europe.
By the fourth year of the conflict, half of all Syrians were out of their homes.

ONE

THE OFFICES OF THE *MIDDLE EAST TIMES* WERE IN THE ZAMALEK NEIGHBORHOOD of Cairo, on an island in the Nile. Zamalek was a cosmopolitan oasis, with nineteenth-century apartment blocks and villas. It was known for its restaurants and cafés and was a favorite of European expats. You could go into a restaurant in Zamalek, find a waiter who spoke English, and get a beer and Western food.

When the phone rang at midday, one of our tipsters said there had been a shooting on a tourist bus in front of the Egyptian Museum. The museum is in Tahrir Square, the busiest part of downtown, the Times Square of Cairo. The newspaper was a short hop away. You go across one bridge and you're almost there. I jumped

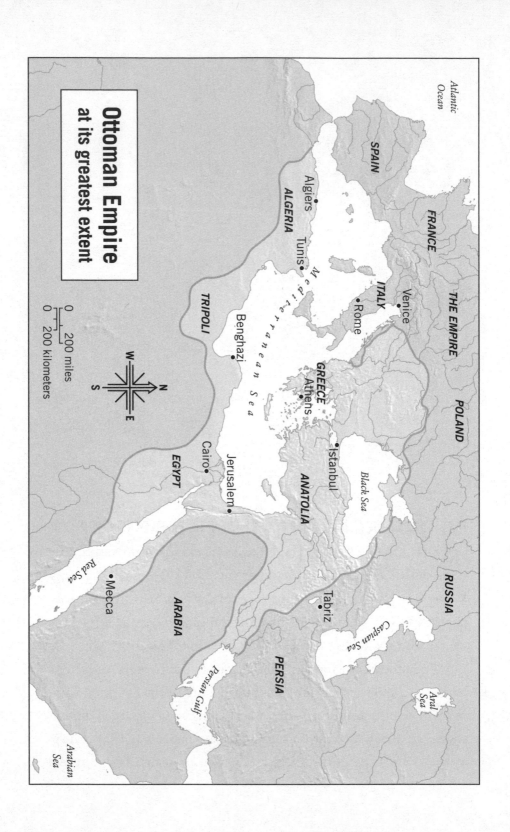

Ottoman Empire
at its greatest extent

0 — 200 miles
0 — 200 kilometers

Atlantic Ocean

SPAIN

FRANCE

THE EMPIRE

POLAND

RUSSIA

Algiers

ALGERIA

Tunis

Mediterranean Sea

ITALY

Venice

Rome

GREECE

Athens

Istanbul

Black Sea

ANATOLIA

Tabriz

Caspian Sea

Aral Sea

PERSIA

TRIPOLI

Benghazi

EGYPT

Cairo

Jerusalem

Red Sea

Mecca

ARABIA

Persian Gulf

Arabian Sea

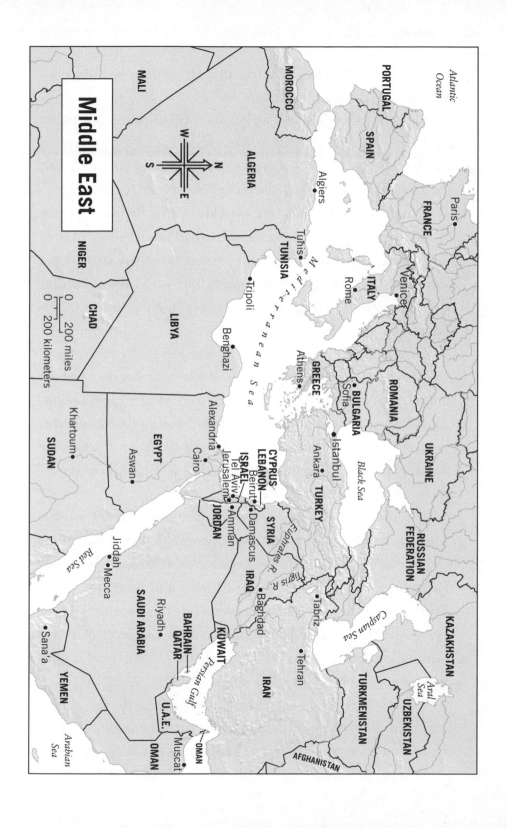

Middle East

MALI
MOROCCO
PORTUGAL
SPAIN
Atlantic Ocean

N
W — E
S

NIGER
CHAD
ALGERIA
•Algiers
FRANCE
•Paris

TUNISIA
•Tunis
ITALY
•Rome
Venice

LIBYA
•Tripoli
M e d i t e r r a n e a n   S e a
•Benghazi

0   200 miles
0   200 kilometers

SUDAN
•Khartoum
EGYPT
•Alexandria
•Cairo
•Aswan

Athens•
GREECE
Sofia•
BULGARIA
ROMANIA
UKRAINE

Istanbul•
Ankara•
TURKEY
Black Sea
RUSSIAN FEDERATION

CYPRUS
LEBANON
ISRAEL
Beirut•
Tel Aviv•
Jerusalem•
Damascus•
JORDAN
Amman•
SYRIA
Euphrates R.
IRAQ
Tigris R.
Baghdad•
Tabriz•

KAZAKHSTAN

Red Sea
•Jiddah
•Mecca
SAUDI ARABIA
Riyadh•
BAHRAIN
QATAR
KUWAIT
Persian Gulf
IRAN
Tehran•

Caspian Sea
TURKMENISTAN
Aral Sea
UZBEKISTAN

•Sana'a
YEMEN
U.A.E.
OMAN
•Muscat
OMAN
Arabian Sea
AFGHANISTAN

in a cab and arrived five minutes later. Our tipster had been fast because the attack had just happened.

The scene was chaotic. The bus was still burning. The police and soldiers had their guns drawn but hadn't put a cordon around the bus. They were still looking for the attackers. I got on the bus and looked down the rows of seats and didn't see any blood.

I just saw people who were melted to their Styrofoam seats. Fat was dripping off them because they had literally been roasted alive. Some were dead on the floor because when the attacker got on the bus, he killed the driver, opened fire with his assault rifle, and then started lobbing Molotov cocktails. Nine German tourists were killed.

It was so senseless. These people were just going to the Egyptian Museum. They had done nothing wrong. It was the opposite of a crime of passion. It was a calculated crime to achieve a political objective. The militants wanted to hurt the Egyptian government by scaring tourists away. By killing Christian tourists the attackers could also claim they had struck a blow against the infidels.

This was the first time I had come face-to-face with the other side of fundamentalism. The fundamentalism that I saw in my neighborhood was sexist and misogynistic and small-minded, but it wasn't violent. It was giving and loving and brotherly. It was about helping the poor, and since everybody was poor, that meant everybody helping everybody. There wasn't the kind of urban meanness you find in many American cities. It was as if a farm community had been transplanted to the city.

The attack on the bus showed the dark side of the fundamentalist mentality—the rage, the anger, the hate, the feeling of being left behind by history, the sense that Islam was under attack and needed to defend itself. The gunmen at Tahrir Square, and the terrorists who have gone on murderous rampages since then, see themselves as vigilantes for Islam. In their twisted minds, they are serving the greater glory of Islam.

Two months after the Cairo museum attack, assailants dressed as security guards and armed with automatic weapons and knives approached the Temple of Hatshepsut, the queen pharaoh, in Luxor in southern Egypt. They went on a forty-five-minute killing spree in the temple, mutilating many victims with machetes. Four Egyptians and fifty-eight tourists, including thirty-six Swiss and ten Japanese, were killed. The savagery was breathtaking. The gunmen shoved leaflets identifying themselves into the mouths and wounds of victims. As they fled to the hills, one terrorist was wounded by police, then shot dead by his compatriots. The five other attackers, taking refuge in a cave, machine-gunned themselves to death rather than be captured.

I count Tahrir Square and Luxor as the first al-Qaeda–style attacks. They were savage attacks, what terrorism experts and security officials would later call "spectacular." They were designed to be both brutal and headline grabbing. Within months, in February 1998, Osama bin Laden, Ayman al-Zawahiri, and three compatriots announced a "jihad against Jews and crusaders." That August, hundreds were killed in simultaneous bombings of US embassies in Kenya and Tanzania.

I had been looking into the militant groups and started digging deeper after the Luxor attack. The name that kept coming up—this was before the declaration of jihad—was al-Zawahiri. An Egyptian surgeon from a prominent family, he had lived in an affluent neighborhood of Cairo called Maadi before going off to

Afghanistan to fight with bin Laden. He was bin Laden's right-hand man and became al-Qaeda's leader after bin Laden was killed in 2011.

I think of bin Laden as an angry historian. He was quite widely read and thought a lot about what he was doing and why. He was eloquent and soft-spoken. He didn't come across as bloodthirsty. He was a bit effeminate in his mannerisms and in his speech. His speeches were hard to understand because they were so full of poetry. He obviously thought of himself more as a philosopher and spiritual guide than as someone who mixed explosives.

The anger of people such as bin Laden came from what they witnessed in their own lives, but it also had deeper roots. It dated to AD 610, when the Archangel Gabriel came to Mohammed and roughly demanded that he "recite" Allah's dictation, which the Prophet did for twenty-three years. These words from Allah were written down by his followers (Mohammed was illiterate) and collected in the Koran. Islam offered an appealing message: that all men are equal in prayer, humbled together in communal submission, rich and poor side by side. Mohammed kept the rites of the new faith simple and conversion easy. He asked for five daily prayers, a weekly gathering with a short sermon, partial fasting for a month each year, and a once-in-a-lifetime pilgrimage to Mecca, called the hajj, for those who could afford it.

From the beginning, Islam also provided the foundation for an empire. Unlike Christianity, Islam had no concept of what in more recent times became the separation of church and state. Islam expanded by conquest as well as by conversion. The early Muslims were hardy and effective fighters, attacking in small bands and retreating into the desert. After Mohammed's death,

Islam spread rapidly into the Persian and Byzantine empires despite internecine strife that resulted in the assassination of three of its first four caliphs, the "successors" to Mohammed and rulers of the faithful. Those early assassinations led to the split between Sunnis and Shiites, battle lines drawn fourteen centuries ago that US troops would encounter, and help reignite, in Iraq. There is no distinction between modern and ancient history in the Middle East. No region is more obsessed with its own past. Islam began as a force to be reckoned with, and Muslims have longed to return to their former glory.

Christianity, by contrast, spent three centuries in the shadows, dodging Rome's irregular but sometimes massive persecutions. Its fortunes began to change in 312 when Emperor Constantine the Great embraced the Christian God as his protector and then, in an audacious and revolutionary move, not only legalized Christianity but made it the empire's officially favored religion. He moved the seat of his empire from Rome to Byzantium, soon to be renamed Constantinople (which became Istanbul after it was conquered by a Muslim-led army in 1453). Through divisive councils and synods, Christianity refined and established itself over the next several hundred years.

In the eighth, ninth, tenth, and eleventh centuries, the Islamic world was a main center of culture and civilization. It was a leader in astronomy, algebra, and poetry, experiencing a golden era as Europe sank into the Dark Ages. While Vikings were plundering Europe, Muslims were translating Aristotle, building libraries, and developing surgical procedures. Muslims today know about this golden age and are nostalgic about it. There are costume dramas about this period on television in the Arab world every Ramadan. They are extremely popular.

The Crusades, waged intermittently from 1095 to 1291, but which continued in waves for centuries after that, were military campaigns sanctioned principally by the Roman Catholic Church to reclaim the Holy Land. American students barely learn about the Crusades, but they are essential to understanding the wars of the last decade.

As Islam spread after Mohammed's death, Muslim armies began to threaten the great eastern Christian empire founded by Constantine, Byzantium. Constantine founded Constantinople and with it the seat of Christian Rome in AD 330, but within only three centuries Islam was already challenging it. Byzantium tried to fight back, but the armies of Islam were winning. By the end of the eleventh century, Byzantium was so weakened and frightened by the growth of its Muslim neighbor that the emperor in Constantinople reached across the Mediterranean to ask fellow Christians in Europe to come to their rescue. By now European Christians were pulling themselves out of the Dark Ages and were in a position to help. Those wars, launched by Europe to save Byzantium and free Jerusalem from Muslim occupation, were the Crusades. They were ping-pong wars, some won by Christians, others by Muslims. From a Muslim perspective, modern wars launched by Christian powers into Islamic lands are still considered Crusades because they reflect the same basic East vs. West, Islam vs. Christianity, power struggle. When President Bush said he was launching a crusade after 9/11, many Muslims took his words at face value. The medieval Crusades left both Muslims and Christians politically and militarily exhausted. But the worst was yet to come. The two sides were about to be blindsided by a people from the harsh plains of Asia. The Mongol invasions of Genghis Khan and his descendants came like tidal waves. Constantinople was saved by negotiations and its three layers of walls, but Baghdad wasn't as fortunate. In 1258, the Mongols sacked Baghdad and executed the caliph. Several accounts say he was rolled in a rug or put in a sack and trampled by horses. Others say he was strangled or locked in a cell and starved to death.

Mosques and libraries in Baghdad were burned. Estimates of the number killed range from one hundred thousand to eight hundred thousand. The Mongol armies pursued a scorched-earth strategy. If Muslims surrendered, their cities were spared. If they resisted, every living thing was destroyed. The destruction of Baghdad ended the classical Muslim empires established by Mohammed's successors. The Mongols killed the first and most glorious Arab caliphate.

From the debris left by the Mongols, new Muslim empires rose, absorbing both the shattered Arab caliphate and emasculated Byzantium. It was the time of the House of Osman, the Ottomans as they came to be known, a Turkish Muslim tribe. For six hundred years, the Ottomans, "the Turk," as they were called in Europe, would rule Islam's most extensive empire. The Arab caliphate was weakened by the Crusades and killed by the Mongols. The Turkish Ottomans picked up the pieces and forged a massive Islamic empire.

The Ottoman Empire grew so powerful that it was finally able to deliver on Mohammed's prophecy and capture Constantinople for Islam. The Ottoman sultan Mehmed II camped just outside Constantinople's walls. He fought with the conviction that the world should have only one leader, him, and one religion, Islam. Once again, Constantinople's triple wall was its greatest defense. Mehmed had engineers tunnel under the walls to collapse them from below. He forged massive cannons to blast through. Finally, the walls of Constantinople, and with them all of Byzantium, came crumbling down. In May 1453, Mehmed entered Constantinople as conqueror, the title by which he's still remembered. He was only twenty-one years old.

The victorious Muslim armies turned Hagia Sophia, Christendom's most monumental church, into a mosque. Minarets were added. The axis of the floor was even shifted so that it faced Mecca instead of Jerusalem. It would be as if St. Peter's were realigned so that its altar faced Saudi Arabia. Constantinople, seat of the Christian Roman Empire for more than a millennium, was now the capital of the Islamic Ottoman Empire.

As the Ottomans grew stronger and the eastern Mediterranean more hostile, Europe began to look for new territory and new markets. They turned their attention west, searching for a new world. In 1492, just forty years after the fall of Constantinople, Columbus landed on America's shores.

But the Ottoman Empire was mainly agrarian and was steadily undone by technology and debt. The Ottomans never had an industrial revolution. By the eighteenth and nineteenth centuries, Europe had developed steam engines, trains, cotton mills, and factories. The Ottomans desperately wanted European technology and exports, and they borrowed heavily to get them. They ended up leveraging their empire into the poorhouse. By the 1900s, the Ottoman Empire was effectively run by European creditors and foreign embassies based in the upscale neighborhood of Pera, on a hilltop overlooking Hagia Sophia, the long-lost church.

As World War I approached, the empire was clearly dying. In 1908, a mysterious group of men who came to be known as the Young Turks pushed aside the tyrant Sultan Abdul Hamid II, turning him into a figurehead. The Young Turks were nationalists who worried that the European industrial powers were heading for war and that once it was over, the winners would carve up the Ottoman Empire.

They were absolutely right. The Young Turks were desperate to find a European ally. The empire was too big, and too strategic, standing right between Russia, Germany, Britain, and France, to stay neutral. The Young Turks reached out to Britain and France, but were rebuffed. Britain didn't think the Ottomans, crippled with foreign debt and lacking a modern army, could offer much help in the war effort. The Young Turks ultimately made what would be the worst decision in the Ottoman Empire's six-century history. In October 1914, they entered the war in alliance with Kaiser Wilhelm II, the German emperor and king of Prussia. In short, they chose the losing side in a war that was to redraw the borders of what was then much of the known world.

After the war, at Sèvres, France, and other conferences, European leaders divided up the Ottoman Empire into the modern Middle East. Ottoman provinces were re-formed and cobbled together into states. The region was carved up with little regard to ethnic, religious, or territorial concerns. The flawed and cavalier treaties of World War I explain to a large degree why the Middle East remains unstable and angry today. Every Muslim schoolchild is taught this arc of history and resents it: Islam's golden era of the Arab caliphate, the Crusades, the Mongol devastation, the rise of the Ottomans, World War I, the carving up of the Middle East by Europe, and the poverty, weakness, and wars in the Muslim world of the last century. This is the basic and sad narrative taught at every mosque, and it has the benefit of being broadly accurate. Osama bin Laden preached this arc of history as well. He obsessed over it. His solution for changing it was to attack the West's greatest power, the United States, the modern crusader, bring it down, and push history's reset button so Islam could rise again.

There is a problem of course with this general historic narrative. It blames every problem Muslims face on the West. Another way of explaining the Middle East's chronic instability for the last century is that the Islamic world, which embraces all Muslims as brothers and sisters, has failed to adjust to the nation-state system that replaced the empires that rose and fell but dominated civilization until World War I.

Even carefully drawn borders after the First World War would have been problematic in a region that had no concept of nation states or parliaments. But the European victors made a total hash of it. Ethnic minorities were divided and put in different states. The Kurdish people were scattered among five nations. Syria was reduced to a tiny fraction of the powerful Ottoman province it once was, even more insulting since it had once been a capital of the early caliphate. Iraq was cobbled together with different Sunnis, Shiites, and Kurds and given almost no access to the sea. A Jewish entity was established by mandate in Palestine (it became the state of Israel in 1948). World War I and the treaties and promises made by Europeans after it left the Middle East hopelessly divided.

The Arab caliphate, which had survived the Crusades only to be destroyed by the Mongols, had been reborn with the Ottomans. Now in the modern era, while Americans landed men on the moon and Western science sequenced the human genome, the house of Islam was in pieces and humiliated, the shrapnel from a giant explosion, the afterthought of victorious European powers. This great decline is the basic grievance in the Middle East. It is why Osama bin Laden went to war with the West. It is why the United States has been able to do little to stop Islamic radicals who see nation-building as an attempt to reinforce a foreign system, trickery under the banner of democracy.

Ironically enough, the United States had almost nothing to do with the age-old conflict between Islam and the West. The founding of Constantinople, the birth of Islam, and the Crusades occurred centuries before North America was even colonized. The United States was only peripherally involved in creating the borders of the Middle East after World War I. This centuries-old conflict was not America's fight, but Washington blundered into it and chose to make stabilizing the Middle East its main foreign policy objective.

After World War II, and especially during the Cold War, the United States became the guardian of Middle East stability. Islamic fundamentalists believe the United States has been policing a Middle East full of divisions that were deliberately put there to keep the region weak, keep Israel secure, and keep pro-American autocracies in place in Egypt, Saudi Arabia, and, until 1979, Iran— in short, to keep Muslims locked in a nation-state system that thwarted the rightful destiny of Islam. The fundamentalists were convinced that it was Israel and the Jews who really understood this game, using American muscle to keep Islam at bay.

I think of bin Laden as a violent and angry historian, but he left major gaps. In the Muslim world according to bin Laden, the Ottomans hardly count. Islamic fundamentalists look back almost exclusively to the Arab caliphate, particularly its early years. Those who see history as bin Laden did are generally called Salafi Muslims. Those who want to act like bin Laden to change the system through violence are called Salafi jihadis. Al-Qaeda is a

Salafi jihadi movement. Salafism is Islam as Allah recited it, and jihadi means "through war," so it is a militant movement seeking an "originalist" form of Islam and willing to use force to get there. Salafism is often associated with the Wahhabi movement, an equally austere branch of Sunni Islam that arose in the early part of the eighteenth century. Wahhabis dominate Saudi Arabia, the paymaster and invisible hand behind many political machinations in the Middle East.

In Cairo, living among the Muslim Brotherhood, Salafi dreamers, and seeing the horrors of what Salafi jihadis did at the Egyptian Museum and in Luxor, I delved deeper into the political side of the Islamic movement. I came in contact with a group called Tabligh wa Dawa. *Tabligh* means "to inform" and *dawa* means "to call," so roughly speaking the name of the group is "inform and call." It's a Salafi group, not violent but strict in its adherence to the words of Mohammed. It conducts Islamic patrols to *inform* Muslims when they are straying from the Prophet's teachings and *call* them to the righteous path.

I wanted to get to know these people because they have the same mind-set as violent fundamentalists. If someone from al-Qaeda sat down with members of Tabligh wa Dawa, they would agree on everything except how to get from A to B. They would agree on the fundamental narration of history: that Islam was perfect and that the caliphate was destroyed by the Mongols, reborn under the Ottomans, destroyed again by the Europeans, and locked into submission by a nation-state structure enforced by America and Israel.

As far as getting from A to B, a leader of Tabligh wa Dawa would say, "There's nothing we can do about it, let's just go to the mosque and pray for better days." Bin Laden would have replied,

"No, we're going to knock down buildings, we're going to pull planes out of the sky, and we're going to kill tourists, and we're going to do whatever it takes to bring down the infidels." Only a tiny portion of Muslims agree with bin Laden's tactics, but many millions understand the world vision he's talking about.

So I arranged to go out with a Tabligh wa Dawa patrol. We met at night on a street corner in old Cairo. They were dressed in white with short *jellabiyas*, which are a kind of pajama dress. They also had turbans with long tails hanging from the back. They looked a little like nuns, except for their beards. And they were the most polite, soft-spoken people you'd ever meet. "Hello, brother. How are you, brother?" Everyone's a brother. "Oh, it's so good to see you." If one of them had a dollar, he'd give you half and then tell you for an hour why Islam requires Muslims to be generous and share.

They were religious fanatics but gentle. That's the kind of Islam they wanted to project. They would go up to people who were drinking or smoking and try to win them over with kindness. "Oh, my brother, how can you do this to yourself? Come and have a sandwich with us. And then let's go to the mosque and pray."

I spent a night with these people going from coffee shop to coffee shop. The whole time they were trying to convert me because I was among them as a non-Muslim. "If I don't try and bring you to Islam," one of them told me, "you're going to go to hell, and then I'm going to go to hell too for not having tried to bring you into the faith."

During this conversation, he took out a cigarette lighter and told me to put out my hand. Then he lit the lighter and held my hand over it. It was hot and I pulled my hand away.

"No, no, no," he said, and put the lighter under my hand

again. "You see that? That's just a little, tiny fire and you pulled your hand away. It hurt."

"Yes, it did."

"Well, how about if you're in the fires of hell for eternity and they're burning you for eternity, how would you deal with that?"

I was trying to stay in their good graces so I played the game a bit. "Well, that would be terrible. I couldn't handle that."

"Well, if you come to Islam, not only will you not have this hellfire, you have virgins when you die, dark-eyed virgins who are waiting for you in heaven." It was a perfect fantasy and quite sexualized.

Their vision of heaven had a lot of sexualization. Heaven was the antithesis of Egypt. It was sweet smelling, the water was clean, there was no garbage, and beautiful virgins were everywhere. I got along well enough with the Tabligh wa Dawa and started spending a lot of time with them because they were a window on the fundamentalist world. It wasn't violent, but all you needed to do was pull the switch. They were almost comically gentle, but completely saw the world in black and white, right and wrong. If they were convinced something was against Allah, it wouldn't take much for them to kill. That's what bin Laden did, he made Salafis into jihadis and turned them on the United States.

I left the *Middle Eastern Times* in 1998 and started freelancing for ABC, *The World* (a coproduction of the BBC and Public Radio International), and other news organizations large and small that paid my airfare and expenses so I could travel. My first trip to Saudi Arabia was an eye-opener, and it's worth recounting because the Saudis are so central to the problem of militant fundamentalism. In many ways, they are its father. Their Wahhabi vision is a form of Salafism, and it doesn't take much to push this intolerant and unforgiving ideology into bin Laden's way of thinking about permanent war with the West.

The Wahhabi movement began as a reaction to the Ottoman Empire. For one thing, the Ottomans weren't Arab. They were people from the steppes—Central Asians, Turkmen, and other non-Arabs. The Ottoman Empire was incredibly diverse with many Muslim converts from the Caucasus in high positions. The Ottomans at various times were also not especially strict Muslims. Some sultans wrote classical music and operas, which are prohibited by Islam. Other sultans—who also had the title of caliph or successor to Mohammed—even painted nudes. Some drank alcohol. Nearly all the Ottoman leaders failed to follow the Prophet's model of simplicity. The Ottoman Empire was lavish, as can be seen by a quick tour of the Topkapi Palace Museum in Istanbul. The hilt of the Topkapi dagger, the target of thieves in the movie *Topkapi*, is ornamented with three large emeralds. Two large candleholders are mounted with 6,666 diamonds. A gold throne is here, a gold bassinet is there, jewels are everywhere. The names of sections of the palace capture the lifestyle of the sultans: the Imperial Harem, Courtyard of the Sultan's Concubines and Consorts, the Courtyard of the Eunuchs. Mohammed probably would have felt out of place.

The Ottomans used to travel to Mecca and Medina for the annual hajj in enormous caravans. They would bring gifts for the mosques, or even encase parts of the Shires in precious metals. The displays of wealth enraged the local Wahhabis. The Wahhabis, by contrast, celebrated Mohammed, an illiterate grain trader who married a wealthy older woman but continued to live simply, eating dates and drinking camel milk. The Wahhabis embrace Mohammed's nomadic ethical system born of, and perhaps

39

appropriate to, the harsh deserts of Arabia, valuing loyalty, generosity, physical endurance, and hospitality, as well as bravery in battle, dedication to family honor, and insistence on revenge. For the Wahhabis the highest aspiration would be to live as if they were in the days of the Prophet, acting as much like the Prophet as possible, rejecting the trappings of modernity. The Wahhabi movement also began a pro-Arab movement. Mohammed was an Arab from Arabia. He spoke Arabic. That the lavish Ottoman sultans didn't come from Arabia and often spoke little Arabic were all the more upsetting to the Wahhabis.

The early Wahhabi movement was a puritanical and violent reaction to the Ottoman excesses, and it spread the way ISIS would two centuries later. In the first few years of the 1800s, the Ottoman Empire faced an insurgency in Arabia led by fanatical Wahhabis who attacked Ottoman convoys, killed Shiites and destroyed their shrines in Iraq, eradicated antiquities, and cleansed the region of minorities and others who didn't follow their interpretation of Islam. The insurgents were followers of Salafi cleric Mohammed Ibn Wahhab and tribal chiefs of the al-Saud clan. By 1805 the forces of this alliance had conquered Mecca and Medina and committed massacres at Karbala in Iraq. The Ottomans pushed back with the 1811–18 Ottoman Wahhabi War, led by the Ottoman's viceroy in Egypt. The Ottoman forces ultimately prevailed, expressing outrage by taking Amir Abdullah bin Saud to Istanbul to be executed. The Ottomans took revenge by forcing him to listen to music before he was hanged, beheaded, and had his heart cut out of his body. His head was on display in Istanbul for three days. This Saud-Wahhabi alliance was defeated, but it would rise again in the early twentieth century under Abdulaziz al-Saud, better known simply as Ibn Saud (son of Saud), who would become the founder of modern Saudi Arabia. Ibn Saud revived the zeal of the initial Wahhabi uprising with a fanatical fighting force known as the *Ikhwan*, the Brothers, not to be confused with the Egypt-based Muslim Brotherhood.

On the surface it is difficult to understand why strict Wahhabism would appeal to masses of Muslims. Like all austere faiths, it is hard to warm up to. People have tended to be drawn to religions they can touch and feel with exciting festivals, specialty foods, inspiring saints and martyrs, music, art, icons, shrines, and promises of salvation. Salafism, or its Saudi form, Wahhabism, offers none of these. In fact, it actively preaches the opposite. In Salafism and Wahhabism there can be no music. No mingling of the sexes. No art. No alcohol. No dancing. No shrines other than mosques. Only prayer and submission to Allah's unbending will. As a way of life, it is not much fun. I like to think of Wahhabis (or Salafis) as akin to the Amish. Clearly the Amish are innocent of the savage violence associated with many Islamic extremist groups, but I make the comparison only to point out that both believe in a literal and inflexible interpretation of an ancient text, rejecting modernity. But why do the Amish have little mass appeal and no influence in world affairs, while Wahhabism has spread far and wide across the Islamic world? The answer is location and wealth. The Wahhabis, once they aligned with the Saud clan, took control of Mecca and Medina, the centers of Islam, where every year millions of Muslims congregate for the hajj. By dominating the physical center of the faith the Wahhabis have been able to exercise an outsize influence on the world's 1.6 billion Muslims.

Then, in the twentieth century, Saudi Arabia struck it rich. For many Saudis, the oil under their feet was further proof of Allah's blessing, a gift to Mohammed's homeland and the custodians of his faith. The combination of the annual hajj and an effectively limitless budget pushed Saudi Arabia's interpretation of Islam, Wahhabism, all across the Muslim world. For the last several decades, Saudi Arabia has funded untold numbers of mosques and Islamic charities and trained and inspired thousands, if not tens of thousands of clerics, in what the Wahhabis like to call "pure Islam." Wahhabis don't like to be called Wahhabis, or Salafis either. They like to be simply called Muslims, as if there was no other interpretation than their own. With its location and fantastic wealth, Saudi Arabia has set the tone for modern Islam. The faith would likely be very different if Wahhabis had never taken over Mecca and Medina or if there was only sand in the Arabian Desert. To continue the thought experiment, imagine if the Amish controlled St. Peter's in Rome and the churches in Jerusalem and suddenly became wealthy beyond measure. It's likely their impact would be far greater than it is today.

Simply put, Mohammed was born in a land where the founding fathers of the modern state entered an alliance with a puritanical, ascetic movement whose influence became supercharged with the discovery of oil. But money also changed Saudi Arabia. Many modern Saudis believe in Wahhabism in principle, but they don't all follow it in practice.

One evening I went to a dinner party at the home of a Saudi prince, an elaborate affair, with lots of liquor, women without veils, various ambassadors and foreign guests, and sophisticated, Western-educated Saudis. We had lively conversations about the latest comings and goings in Paris and what exhibits were in New York. It could have been a dinner party in London. You would not have imagined you were in Saudi Arabia.

Another time I was invited to the home of a newspaper

publisher. The modern house, minimalist and sleek, had the latest-model Mac computer on a desk. I ended up leaving after several more men showed up to take a dip together in a hot tub. They told me about parties with drag singers and men jumping from the windows to avoid the religious police. The more time I spent in Saudi Arabia, the stranger I found it and the more it seemed to be in no position to tell the majority of the world's Muslims how to think and behave.

When you instill the intolerant mentality of Wahhabism in a country such as Egypt, the effect is dramatic. In Egypt people drink water from the same river where they dump their sewage and industrial waste, scrounging out a miserable existence in a broken economy and shop in trash-strewn bazaars. The pros-elytizers tell the Egyptians that things would be great if only the West didn't keep the Muslim world divided, if only the modern banking system devised by the Jews was torn down, if only the Arabs could restore the caliphate. The result, unsurprisingly, is anger and resentment against the West, sometimes of the murder-ous kind.

ANTI-SEMITISM WAS PERVASIVE IN EGYPT. IN CONVERSATIONS WITH PEOPLE ranging from members of the Tabligh wa Dawa and the Muslim Brotherhood to the local shopkeeper to a newspaper editor, Jews were depicted as aggressive and bloodthirsty schemers who perse-cuted Muslims. This view came through in the media, in cartoons, in schools. When pressed, Muslims denied it: "That's not true. We as Muslims embrace Jews as people of the Book. We accept them as part of our own ancestry as people of the prophets." But in real-ity, anti-Semitism was inescapable and oppressive.

Oddly enough, some of the anti-Semitism actually goes back to Muslims' insistence that Jews, Christians, and Muslims all worship the same God, which Muslims call Allah. It sounds very inclusive and inviting, a message that the great monotheistic religious are part of a single family, until you think about it. If there is only one God, Allah, then there is also an assumption that Jews and Christians don't understand him. According to the Muslim interpretation, Jews began to worship thousands of years ago until Allah sent Jesus to correct their ways. Christians then worshipped according to Jesus taught until Allah sent Mohammed with the final draft of his plan in the Koran. By saying Jews, Christians, and Muslims worship only one God—Allah—Muslims are saying Jews are using an old and outdated text that was improved by Christians, but that only Muslims have the full picture. This hierarchy of understanding formed the basis of much of how Islamic or sharia law dealt with religious minorities. Under the Arab caliphate and Ottoman Empire, Jews and Christians were tolerated, but were considered second-class citizens who were required to pay special taxes and were forbidden from holding high-level jobs and even from using certain materials reserved for Muslims. Muslims didn't force Jews and Christians to convert, but believed it was better to be patient and let them convert on their own. Muslims believed if they waited long enough, Jews and Christians would eventually come around and recognize Islam's superiority. It was just a matter of time.

Muslims in medieval Europe, however, generally faired far worse. Christians considered Muslims to be heathens, infidels, enemies, and deniers of Christ.

Homophobia was also rampant in the Middle East and just as entrenched. A male orgy may go on in a luxurious private home in Saudi Arabia, but, if the participants were caught, the punishment could be severe. In Egypt, I reported a story about the Queen Boat—that was its real name—which was the venue for a gay party on the Nile. The police arrested fifty or sixty men and subjected them to humiliating examinations with fingers and rulers to determine whether they had engaged in homosexual sex.

There was also a fear of witchcraft. I did a story on a group of young people in Cairo who had been hanging out in an abandoned house, drinking and listening to heavy metal. They were arrested and accused of being Satan worshippers because of the kind of music they were playing. Anti-Semitism, homophobia, fear of Satanism—these were part of the baseline mentality of the hard-line religious groups that took their theological cues from Saudi Arabia.

The pragmatists of the Muslin Brotherhood and the dreamers of Tabligh wa Dawa were fundamentalists, but they could manage in Egypt because they weren't violent. Things were different for the hard-core Egyptian jihadists. The jihadists were simply the Salafis, the Wahhabis, who'd decided prayer wasn't enough. They'd decided austerity and self-denial couldn't change the world. They'd need to fight. The jihadis, who should technically be called Salafi jihadis or Wahhabi jihadis, would join the holy wars in Afghanistan against the Soviets or help the Muslims suffering in Bosnia or oppressed by Russia in Chechnya, then come back home. But it became harder and harder for these groups to return because the government started looking for them.

The last thing the jihadists wanted was to end up in an Egyptian prison. I remember driving by prisons and actually hearing screams from inside. The military put on mass trials of twenty, forty, or sixty Islamists. The detainees were put in a holding cage, and they held up their Korans, shouting *"Allahu Akbar!"* and calling for an Islamic state. The court would hand out death sentences by the dozens. If a detainee was lucky, he got fifteen years, but fifteen years in an Egyptian prison is basically a death sentence.

The Saudis, and in some cases the CIA, had encouraged and funded their foreign jihads, and these men had seen combat, lived hard in the mountains, did what their religion asked them to do. Then they came home to Egypt and were rewarded with a death sentence. The result was the creation of a standing army of jihadis who couldn't go home. They would go on to found al-Qaeda, which became something of a jihadi veterans association. History is always obvious in retrospect, but in this case the rise of al-Qaeda should have been fairly easy to predict. Saudi Arabia, Pakistani intelligence, the CIA, and others used jihadis to fight Cold War battles in Afghanistan and elsewhere and the jihadis, believing they were helping Muslims, were happy to go. But when the fighters tried to return home, they faced the horrors of prison and torture, so they went underground and became an army of exiles eventually known as al-Qaeda. What did Pakistan, Egypt, or the CIA expect would happen if they directed jihadis at their enemies like cannons and then abandoned them? The cannons would fire on them.

In 1996 the Taliban took over in Afghanistan. The Taliban were mostly Pashtun tribesmen with their own history and goals. But their religious fanaticism, harsh treatment of women, and hatred of the West were almost identical to those of the Salafi jihadis. So it was only natural that the Taliban would provide a safe haven for bin Laden and his murderous band, which they did, starting in 1996. Al-Qaeda set up bases and training camps in Afghanistan. At last the jihadists' army of exiles had a home.

The world would be very different if Saudi Arabia had never struck oil. The wealth allowed the Wahhabis to set a harsh standard for Islam, while staying isolated from it themselves. A growing number of Muslim reformers say—at great physical risk to themselves—that Islam needs to evolve and rediscover more tolerant strains of the faith, schools of thought that were pervasive in Islam when it led the world in science, mathematics, and medicine. Instead, these days Islam is unfortunately mostly known for its anger, which is a tragedy for most believers of one of the world's longest-surviving and decent religions.

West Bank

Haifa

Sea of Galilee

•Nazareth

Mediterranean Sea

Jenin•

Netanya•

•Tulkarm

•Tubas

•Nablus

•Qalqilya

Salfit•

WEST BANK

Jordan River

Tel Aviv•

Ramallah•

Jericho•

Jerusalem★

Bethlehem

Dead Sea

Gaza•

ISRAEL

•Hebron

GAZA STRIP

| | Palestinian Control |

•Beersheba

N
W—E
S

JORDAN

0   10 miles
0   15 kilometers

TWO

MY LIFE AS A FREELANCER IN CAIRO WAS FUN AND INTERESTING, BUT ALSO A hassle. The term of art in the business for each of your client publications is "a string," which makes you, the freelancer trying to report for all these disparate outlets, a "stringer." If you're stringing for newspapers, you don't know if they'll ever pay you, and if they do, it might be three or four months later. By then you've written fifty articles for other people, and you have a devil of a time figuring who's paid you for what. Every freelancer, at least back then, dreamed of getting a staff job. So it was a no-brainer when Agence France-Presse (AFP) offered me a job in Jerusalem as its Palestinian-affairs correspondent. AFP paid me the princely sum of $24,000 a year, not much more than I was making in Cairo, but with health benefits, a small housing allowance, and the assurance that I'd get a check every two weeks.

It was snowing in Jerusalem when I arrived over New Year's weekend in 2000. The city looked beautiful, even peaceful. But that was before the Second Intifada, before the riots and clouds of tear gas, before "rubber" bullets knocked me down and left painful welts on my legs, before protesters and soldiers killed each other in gunfights, before a suicide bomb tore bodies apart in the market across from my house—and before I bribed an official to give me a "human shield" visa so I could get to Iraq before the US invasion.

I got married a few months before leaving Egypt. My wife had been my girlfriend at Stanford, and we rekindled the relationship when I was in Cairo. We moved to Jerusalem to start a new life in a new land. We settled in a handsome, three-story brownstone off Agripas Street. It was quite charming—you entered through a gate and walked down a narrow path rimmed with morning glories and jasmine—but it badly needed renovation. The roof leaked, and there was no proper heating. We put oversize kerosene lanterns by the bed at night and by our feet if we were sitting and reading. The lanterns heated up a tiny area, but the smell was pretty awful. I loved the location of the house. It was a twenty-minute walk to the Old City, and right across from the Mahane Yehuda, the city's main market for butchers, bakers, and fruit and vegetable sellers. I spent a lot of time browsing in the market—or at least I did before the suicide bombers came.

WE LIVED IN AN AREA CALLED NACHLAOT, A SORT OF BOHEMIAN ENCLAVE. ITS winding lanes had speakeasies with no signs on the doors and a couple of underground music clubs in basements. It had a New York City East Village feel, a beatnik vibe, and was quite cool. Now large parts of it are ultra-Orthodox. Our friends were almost all journalists. The expat community was nothing like the one in Cairo. Most of the Americans in Jerusalem had made aliyah, a Hebrew word meaning "ascent," which by Jewish custom means going to Israel. They were Americans who had decided to embrace Zionism and their Jewish heritage, and they were deeply involved in their temple groups. I was never able to break into their close-knit communities.

Part of my job at AFP was doing my own reports—interviewing people, finding features, turning out stories. But my main focus was running a dozen or so Palestinian reporters—in Gaza, in Nablus, in Tulkarm, in Ramallah, and so forth. Every morning at eight thirty I'd start calling them to find out what was going on in their areas that day and what had happened overnight. I kept checking in with them throughout the day. So if a big story broke in Ramallah, say, I would be on the phone a lot with my reporter there and write stories under his byline.

In Egypt I did a lot of local stories, even some restaurant reviews. Aside from my pieces on the attacks at Tahrir Square and Luxor, almost nobody outside the Cairo community noticed my work. In Jerusalem, with the Camp David Summit only months away, I was writing big international stories. I was part of the game. I had to be fast and couldn't afford to make mistakes. When I hit "send," the story went to Nicosia for a quick check by the editors there, then it hit the AFP wire in a minute, sometimes less. A mistake would go around the world in the blink of an eye.

51

The AFP bureau was in the Jerusalem Capital Studios (JCS) building, which was a media center mainly serving broadcast outlets (ABC, CNN, and BBC among others) because it had studios and satellite dishes. It was also a good location for wire organizations such as AFP because Israeli officials were always prowling the halls.

You didn't need to work too hard to get a comment from an Israeli official. You could work for a regional Danish radio station, and if you needed a comment at four in the morning, you could reach a senior official who might spend an hour being interviewed on your station. In Cairo, you couldn't find an Egyptian official to talk about anything, even something as innocuous as tourism. If you met an Israeli minister or deputy minister, he'd give you a cell phone number, if not his own, then one for his aide. It was answered twenty-four hours a day, and the official was authorized to give you a comment that, more often than not, was spicy, provocative, thought-out, and in English. I had never seen such a well-oiled PR machine.

The Palestinians were no slouches at this game either. You could call Saeb Erekat, the senior Palestinian peace negotiator, at midnight, and he'd pick up the phone himself and stay on the line for as long as it took to answer your questions. There was never a time when a Palestinian leader wasn't available. They had learned from the Israelis that they needed to be quick in getting out their side of the story. Ordinary Palestinians also seemed to be far more sophisticated than the Egyptians, who were apt to think that the capital of the United States was New York. I was a novelty to Egyptians, and they talked to me mostly out of curiosity. The Palestinians talked to me not because I was a foreigner, but because I was an American journalist, and it was important to them that I understood their history and their cause.

During my nearly four years in Cairo, I lived in the world of the Arab big men, leaders like Mubarak who saw themselves as the fathers of their nations and who were opposed by a complex web of Islamic groups. Over the next three years based in Jerusalem, I witnessed the death of the peace process. But I didn't know it was about to die when I arrived. Back then there was so much hope. There was a feeling that a peace deal would finally result in a two-state solution and the creation of an internationally recognized state called Palestine with clear borders, passports, and maybe even a small army.

One of my first stories was about Palestinians designing their own currency. This was six months before the Camp David talks in July 2000. I was talking to the Palestinian negotiators and advisors every day—Erekat, Hanan Ashrawi, and Yasser Abed Rabbo—and they sounded optimistic even though they knew that a lot of big issues still needed to be resolved.

At that time, relations between the Israelis and the Palestinians on the West Bank were governed by the Oslo II Accord, an "interim agreement" signed in Taba, Egypt, in September 1995, and reinforced by the Wye River Memorandum, signed three years later in Maryland. These agreements, temporary and highly legalistic, were aimed at establishing a status quo that would allow Israelis and Palestinians to live together until "final status" negotiations could resolve the more complicated questions as part of a comprehensive peace plan.

Life under Oslo II was highly regulated and lawyerly. The agreements established three administrative designations for

Palestinians living in the West Bank. The three categories were determined by behavior not geography, and the map of the West Bank was a kaleidoscope of colors. Access to each area was restricted by Israeli checkpoints, which numbered six hundred at one stage.

Area A, which was under full Palestinian control, covered only 3 percent of the land area but included eight cities important to the Palestinians, among them Bethlehem, Ramallah, Jericho, Nablus, and 80 percent of Hebron. These areas were off bounds to Israelis except in security emergencies. Area B covered roughly one-fourth of the West Bank and included 440 Palestinian villages and no Israeli settlements. It was under Palestinian civil control but responsibility for security was shared by the Israelis and Palestinians.

Area C, which included all the Israeli settlements and encompassed 70 percent of the West Bank, was under full Israeli control.

It was a strange system in which Palestinians had different rights depending on where they lived. In Area A, Palestinians theoretically controlled their own destinies, but only within that space. A areas were like tiny islands of Palestinian autonomy. B areas were even stranger because Palestinians were governed by both their own leaders and the Israel government, and it was never clear who ran what. In C areas Palestinians were theoretically under full Israeli control, but didn't enjoy the same rights as Israeli citizens. The system was a mess, but it was all supposed to go away once a "final status" deal was agreed to.

The A-B-C zones amounted to a good-behavior system. If an area showed it was stable and secure, it could move up a rung, from C to B or even B to A. In other words, if the Palestinians showed they could run a place peacefully and successfully, the Israelis were supposed to give them more autonomy. But the process was slow, and even a minor infraction, or alleged infraction, could knock a whole village down a rung.

The "final status" talks at Camp David brought together Israeli prime minister Ehud Barak, Palestinian Authority chairman Yasser Arafat, and President Clinton. The negotiations were supposed to tackle the hard issues and end up with a two-state solution that would supplant the complicated A-B-C system, which required a law degree to understand. The core issues of the "final status" talks hinged mainly on Palestinian refugees and their right of return, redrawn borders, and the Old City in Jerusalem—in other words, what the Palestinian state would look like, who would live there, what its capital would be, and how the two sides would handle the religious sites in the Old City.

The talks sometimes seemed like an exercise in hairsplitting, but how the hairs were split could have profound consequences. The negotiators would spend days talking about "control" versus "sovereignty"—that is, who would control the land as opposed to who actually owned it. These distinctions took on outsize importance when applied to what Jews consider their holiest site and call the Temple Mount and Muslims call the Noble Sanctuary or Al-Aqsa compound in the Old City, Islam's third holiest site.

After two weeks of talks at Camp David, on July 25 the negotiators started discussing the issue of how to handle the Old City, a tiny 220-acre parcel encompassing four quarters (Muslim, Jewish, Christian, and Armenian) and on its east side the rectangular-shaped Temple Mount/Al-Aqsa compound. The Palestinians were ready to give up the "right of return" to land captured by the Israelis in return for reparations of roughly $30 billion, to be raised mainly by the United States. The two sides reportedly agreed that Jerusalem would be the capital of both Israel and Palestine. While the final borders had not been settled, they could be resolved with some land swaps. But agreement on the status of the holy sites in the Old City remained out of reach. These were the last days of the Clinton administration and, as is often the case, the political clock ran out before a historic resolution could be reached.

Whether an agreement could have withstood events on the ground in Israel is an open question. When Camp David unraveled, the conservative Likud Party smelled political blood and started hammering at Barak and the Labor Party as weak and prepared to give away the store.

The internecine squabbling turned deadly after September 28, 2000, which marked the beginning of the Second Intifada, Arabic for uprising. The revolt was sparked when Ariel Sharon and a Likud delegation visited the Temple Mount. It's hard for many Americans, even regular churchgoers, to appreciate the religious passions stirred by the Temple Mount, which is a raised plateau buttressed on its west side by what is known as the Wailing Wall. The Wailing Wall, also called the Western Wall, is believed to be the last vestige of two Jewish temples that once stood on the spot. Three sacred Islamic structures—the Al-Aqsa Mosque, the Dome of the Rock, and the Dome of the Chain—were built between AD 685 and 705 on the ruins of the temple site. Muslims who pray on top of the Temple Mount can look down and see Jews worshipping at the Wailing Wall. The Jews below can look up and see Muslims worshipping on land where their temples once stood. It is a religious conflict set in stone.

It is also hard for Americans to appreciate the passions stirred by Sharon. Regarded by some as Israel's greatest field commander, he's a tough-guy hero to many Israelis for his assault of the Sinai during the 1967 war and his encirclement of the Egyptian Third Army in 1973, widely viewed as the decisive moment in the Yom Kippur War. To Palestinians, though, he is evil incarnate because of his role in the Lebanon War, in which he failed to stop the massacre in 1982 of thousands of Palestinians and Lebanese Shiites in the Sabra and Shatila refugee camps. Israeli troops encircled Sabra and Shatila and illuminated the sky while pro-Israeli Christian militiamen (the Phalanges) entered the camps and slaughtered hundreds, perhaps thousands, of Palestinians.

In September 2000, Sharon went on top of the Temple Mount, with an entourage, walking through the area where Muslim mosques have stood for centuries. Sharon's stroll was his way of showing "we're in charge here." It clearly signaled to the Labor government that the Likud Party was preparing a political challenge. More importantly, it was an unmistakable provocation to the Palestinians. Overnight, the dream of two peoples living peaceably in adjacent states gave way to a nightmare of urban combat between Israeli armed forces and Palestinians.

Many Israelis then, and equally true now, scarcely saw the Palestinians as human. Despite the interim peace accords, the Israelis did everything possible to make the Palestinians' lives miserable. The streets in Palestinian areas controlled by Israelis were potholed and the trash often wasn't picked up. If you were in Palestinian East Jerusalem, you struggled to get a taxi to Jewish West Jerusalem. If you wanted cable television, the YES Network, an Israeli company, wouldn't come to your home. To pay bills, Palestinians in East Jerusalem had to go to West Jerusalem. West Jerusalem, by contrast, was like a European capital. Shops were on every corner, with clean and safe streets lined with restaurants

serving international cuisine with fine wines and espresso afterward.

Because I was covering the Palestinians, I frequently went
through the Qalandia checkpoint en route from my home to the
West Bank, where I would go to Ramallah, Nablus, and other Palestinian areas outside Jerusalem. I had West Jerusalem plates on
my little car and Israeli press accreditations, so it usually took
me between ten minutes and half an hour to get through the
checkpoint. It was managed by a half dozen Israeli soldiers—boys
and girls, really. A line of hundreds of Palestinians waited to get
through, and it would take them hours, often sitting by the side
of the road in the hot sun. The Israeli soldiers at the checkpoint
spoke only a few words of Arabic, and when they encountered
people whose papers weren't in perfect order, they were curtly dismissive. With their palm down, they flicked their fingers outward,
as if to say, "Get away from me." The Palestinians would have to
go to the back of the line and wait another hour or two to talk to
another soldier. At first I wondered how so few could control so
many, but I came to understand that the Palestinians knew that
reprisals would be swift and severe if they stepped out of line.

After Sharon's visit to the Temple Mount, violent clashes
broke out between the Palestinians and Israeli soldiers. I watched
many of them in Ramallah, about a forty-five-minute drive from
my home, depending on how long it took me to get through the
Qalandia checkpoint. The clashes began like the confrontations
in the First Intifada, which lasted from 1987 to 1993 and resulted
in the deaths of 160 Israelis and 2,200 Palestinians. Typically some
Palestinian boys would start throwing rocks at the Israeli soldiers,
who would respond by firing rubber bullets at them. (Rubber
bullets aren't as benign as they sound. They're slugs or marbles

encased in a thin layer of hard rubber or plastic. They were designed to cause contusions and hematomas, without being lethal, although shots to the head can be fatal. I was hit several times, mostly by ricochets. They still left enormous welts and sometimes knocked me down.)

These face-offs took place in areas no longer than a football field and considerably narrower. The scene usually unfolded like this: A road would be blocked by two Israeli jeeps with eight Israeli soldiers in helmets and flak jackets. A hundred yards away, Palestinian boys would throw stones that usually fell short of their target. Occasionally they rushed forward to get within throwing range. The Israelis would try, usually without success, to disperse the crowd with tear gas. Then they would fire rubber bullets, aiming primarily at legs, but not always. A boy would get hit in the head and be dragged away by his friends. An emotional scream would pierce the air. Another boy might sneak around the Israeli flank and toss a Molotov cocktail at a jeep. Or some older Palestinians would take potshots with live ammunition from a nearby building.

Things would then get deadly fast. The Israelis would replace their rubber bullet magazines with live ammunition and start firing. Instead of fifteen or twenty Palestinians injured by rubber bullets, five or ten or even fifteen Palestinians might wind up dead. That day or the next morning, there'd be a funeral. The funeral would turn into another protest. Kids would throw stones, then Molotov cocktails. Then someone would fire live ammo, and the Israelis would respond in kind. Another five or ten Palestinians would get killed. Then there'd be another funeral, and the cycle would begin anew.

I remember sitting at home in February 2001, with a pile of

newspapers in front of me, thinking that it was a month of grim foreboding. On February 6, Sharon trounced Barak in the Israel elections. Ten days later, President Bush sent twenty warplanes to attack five air defense installations in Baghdad because of increased targeting of allied planes policing "no-fly" zones over Iraq that were imposed after the 1991 Gulf War. Bush had been in office less than a month, and 9/11 was still seven months away. Arab nations accused him of focusing on Iraq when the real Middle East crisis was the bloody showdown between the Israelis and Palestinians.

By this time, even before Sharon formally took office on March 7, 2001, the Second Intifada was gaining ugly momentum. Under Sharon it grew white-hot. The Israelis sent tanks into the West Bank and targeted Palestinian militants for assassination, often with helicopter gunships.

Disheartened by their casualties, demoralized that their protests were having so little effect and were barely getting noticed internationally, the Palestinians quickly turned to suicide bombings to get revenge. They formed secret cells to carry out the attacks. They knew they would still take a disproportionate number of casualties (more than three thousand Palestinians died in the four-year conflict, and about a thousand Israelis), but suicide attacks allowed them to strike back in a dramatic and terrifying way. The attackers would put nuts, bolts, and nails around their bombs to create shrapnel, sometimes coating it with rat poison (an anticoagulant to increase bleeding) or animal feces (to cause infection). Oftentimes the head of a suicide bomber popped off like a champagne cork and remained incongruously intact amid the carnage.

On April 12, a seventeen-year-old girl detonated a bomb

strapped to her body at the entrance to the Mahane Yehuda market across the street from my building, killing six and wounding one hundred and four. On May 18, a suicide bomber killed five Israelis and wounded forty others in a Netanya shopping mall. On June 1, nineteen young Israelis died in a suicide attack at a seaside discotheque in Tel Aviv.

With public outrage building, Israeli lawmakers on July 5 heatedly debated, but rejected, a proposal to kill Yasser Arafat with a massive military strike. Two weeks later six Palestinian activists in Arafat's Fatah movement were killed in an explosion at a refugee camp in Nablus. A day later in Nablus, an Israeli helicopter carried out a rocket attack on an office of the Palestinian militant group Hamas, killing eight.

The tempo of the violence was unrelenting. On August 9, a Palestinian suicide bomber hit a crowded pizza restaurant, killing fifteen and wounding ninety; the next day, Israeli warplanes launched a missile attack that leveled the police station in Ramallah. On August 12, a suicide bomber blew himself up in Haifa, Israel's third-largest city, wounding fifteen; two days later, Israeli tanks leveled the police station in the West Bank city of Jenin. An opinion poll published August 17 in an Israeli newspaper found Sharon's support dropping because he wasn't tough enough on the Palestinians—even though by that point some forty Palestinian political and paramilitary leaders had been assassinated without trial.

I was twenty-seven years old, still feeling young and invincible, as many young men do when they first earn the right to call themselves "war correspondents." Even so, the wave of random and violent attacks caused me to change the way I lived. Instead of leisurely strolls in the market across the street, I shopped quickly and purposefully. I began sitting in the rear of cafés, my back against the wall, because suicide bombers usually detonated their devices at entrances.

The peace process took its last breath, at least for a generation, in the spring of 2002. On March 27, in the Israeli coastal city of Netanya, a Palestinian suicide bomber disguised as a woman walked into a hotel dining room during the annual Passover seder. He detonated a suitcase filled with powerful explosives, killing 30 and wounding 140. Many of the victims were elderly, and some were Holocaust survivors. It was the highest death toll of Israelis during the Second Intifada.

Israel responded with Operation Defensive Shield, the largest military operation in the West Bank since the Six-Day War. The Israel Defense Forces began by putting Yasser Arafat under siege in his Ramallah compound, then invaded Tulkarm, Qalqilya, Bethlehem, Jenin, and Nablus. The Israelis captured every city in the West Bank except tiny Jericho. The A-B-C administrative districts were scrapped. In effect, the entire West Bank became a C area, and the gradual shift to Palestinian control came to an abrupt end. During Defensive Shield, according to the UN, 30 Israeli soldiers were killed and 127 wounded; Palestinian fatalities were put at 497, with 1,447 wounded.

Yasser Arafat was confined to his compound from the start of the Israeli incursion until May 2, when he was released in a deal brokered by the United States. He was greeted by cheering crowds. A diminutive figure (five feet two inches) with splotchy skin, Arafat had been much beloved by Palestinians, not only because he was a symbol of their cause but also because he was a prodigious fund-raiser. He traveled widely and usually returned with satchels of money. He spoke English quite badly, but loved to speak it anyway. He was gregarious and emotional and enjoyed meeting with journalists. He liked people and frequently embraced them and kissed them. I was kissed on the cheek by Arafat several times.

Arafat himself was never the same after his captivity in his compound. I think he had a nervous breakdown. He became much more aggressive, wore fatigues, and called himself General Arafat. He no longer met freely with journalists. He did phone interviews with CNN and a few other news outlets, hanging up if a journalist said something that offended him. He was angry and incoherent, and I suspect he was suffering from some form of dementia. His Palestinian Authority had been severely weakened, creating a vacuum filled by Hamas and other radical groups.

By this time I had left AFP and was doing freelance television work for ABC affiliates and the BBC World Service, as well as radio stories for *The World*, a coproduction of Public Radio International and WGBH in Boston. Newspapers and magazines were struggling, and I thought I'd have a longer and more lucrative career in television. AFP was stingy about covering the cost of the gas I needed to get around for work, while TV correspondents were chartering planes. I thought to myself, Now that's the world I'd rather be part of. I arrived in Jerusalem expecting to report on the birth of a new state, Palestine, instead I saw peace talks collapse, Sharon capitalize on their failure, walk through Muslim areas on top of the Temple Mount, and start a bloody conflict of stones, tanks, and suicide bombers. But unlike the First Intifada, the outside world, especially the United States, paid little attention to the Palestinians' second uprising. It was a sideshow after 9/11.

I watched the twin towers collapse on TV from my apartment in Jerusalem. I knew then that the story I was covering was over.

No one would care anymore about rioting Palestinians. In the Second Intifada, Palestinians lost what little control they had in the West Bank. After 9/11 they lost the West's attention. Washington had other priorities.

The Bush administration was fixated on Iraq from the start. It's been well documented how Iraqi opposition groups and American neoconservatives convinced the president it would be easy to topple Saddam. Bush naively believed Saddam's regime could be replaced by a democracy, which the president saw as the antidote to all political evils. The United States was also hungry for revenge, the military was primed for war, and congressional checkbooks were open. All that was needed was a casus belli, and weapons of mass destruction (WMDs) fit the bill.

IN JANUARY 2002, PRESIDENT BUSH HAD GIVEN IRAQ TOP BILLING IN HIS "AXIS OF evil," ahead of North Korea and Iran, and in June he launched Operation Southern Focus to degrade Iraq's air defenses. In September 2002, one hundred US warplanes attacked air defense installations in western Iraq. Congress authorized military action against Iraq in October. In November, the UN passed Resolution 1441 finding Iraq in "material breach" of the cease-fire terms that had ended the Gulf War in 1991. As 2002 drew to a close, the United States was clearly going to go to war with hundreds of thousands of troops. I thought to myself, Okay, this is going to be the place where I make my career. I decided to leave Jerusalem on the train for history's next station, which I thought would be Baghdad.

First I talked to my wife. Jerusalem had given her a false idea of what being a foreign correspondent was all about. It was a commuter conflict. In the morning I'd drive to a clash between the Israelis and the protesters, I'd get a whiff of tear gas and maybe a rubber bullet in the leg, and then I'd be home in time for dinner. Sometimes I'd go out to the clashes, come home for lunch, and go back out for more. But Iraq was a completely different situation. I'd be away for weeks or months at a time. Maybe years. I didn't know.

I had bought a house in Sicily, a place I had loved since high school. The house, in a picturesque town called Cefalù, on the north coast, had cost about $100,000. The money to buy it had mostly come from my blackjack winnings in Cairo. I told my wife I might be away for a long stretch, that things could get messy in Jerusalem, and that she might as well go to Sicily to oversee the renovations of the house since we were going to fix it up anyway.

That left me with the problem of getting a visa. The Iraqi Foreign Ministry assigned "minders" to foreign journalists, which was a labor-intensive undertaking, and many more journalists were seeking visas than there were trusted minders. As a result, the Iraqis were only giving visas to the major networks, and I was a lowly freelancer.

But I had a friend in Jordan who I felt sure could help me out. Beneath her party-girl exterior as a flamboyant, melodramatic shopaholic, she was a shrewd operator who understood the mysterious ways of the Middle East. She ingeniously suggested that I enter Iraq as a peace activist. The so-called Iraqi Peace and Friendship Society brought foreigners to the country to act as "human shields" who would be willing to station themselves at oil refineries, power plants, air force bases, and other strategic sites in hopes of deterring American attacks. The society imported dozens of peaceniks, career hippies, Muslim fundamentalists, and assorted do-gooders. My friend in Jordan suggested I could get in the queue with a friendly bribe to a Jordanian official, and she had a man in mind.

He was besotted with his three-year-old son and, like most Arabs, greatly fond of tea. I got on a flight to London, bought some high-quality toddler clothes and some cheap tea, and then flew to Amman. It did the trick. He gave me the required stamp without even looking at the rest of my passport, which would have identified me as a reporter.

Human shields didn't need the gear I required, so I had to smuggle it in. That meant hiring a driver with the right disposition and a car with enough room for a handheld video camera and satellite phone, a bulletproof jacket, a chemical/biological/radiological suit and gas mask, and atropine autoinjectors (an antidote for nerve agents). I strapped $20,000 around my ankle in a pouch that looked like an Ace bandage and stuffed my pockets with $20 bills, which work best for quick payoffs. The only highway to Baghdad cuts through Iraq's Western Desert, where bandits sometimes robbed cars.

I was in a fairly weak position, all things considered. I was in a car filled with illicit equipment, I carried a misleading visa, and I had no firm commitment from the news network I was working most closely with at the time, ABC News. But I was surprisingly calm as I hopped into the GMC Suburban in the middle of the night on March 5, 2003. Maybe it was the car's red racing stripes. Maybe it was the digitized verse from the Koran that played when the driver turned the ignition key. Or maybe it was because I was a kid and didn't know what a real war was all about. I was now about to go to what I saw as the third stop on the train of history in the Middle East. First was Cairo of the big men. Next was Jerusalem to see the end of the peace process. Now I was off to Baghdad to cover a war that would set in motion events that would tear down the status quo across the Middle East and unleash pent-up religious and ethnic hatred, creating a new generation of terrorists even more vicious than al-Qaeda.

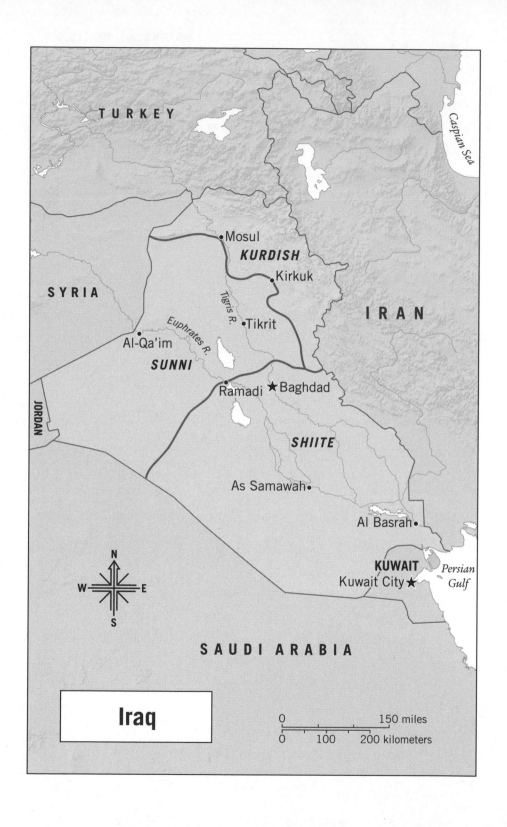

TURKEY

Caspian Sea

• Mosul
KURDISH

SYRIA

• Kirkuk

Tigris R.

IRAN

• Tikrit

Euphrates R.

• Al-Qa'im

SUNNI

JORDAN

Ramadi • ★ Baghdad

SHIITE

As Samawah •

Al Basrah •

KUWAIT
Kuwait City ★

Persian Gulf

N
W—E
S

SAUDI ARABIA

Iraq

0   150 miles
0   100   200 kilometers

THREE

WHEN WE ARRIVED IN BAGHDAD AT 4:30 A.M. ON MARCH 6, 2003, MY DRIVER, SAMI, parked the GMC in a lot in the Al Mansour neighborhood. I loaded my gear into a local taxi and started searching for a hotel. I knew only one thing for certain: I was not going to be a human shield. That made getting a reporter's visa my overriding concern.

Most journalists were staying at the Al-Rashid Hotel, the most luxurious and expensive ($150 a night) in Baghdad, but the place was crawling with Iraqi intelligence agents. Speaking in purposely broken Arabic, I asked the taxi driver to find me a small, clean hotel somewhere away from the center of the city. I landed at the incongruously named Flowers Land Hotel on a small side street. I rented a mini-apartment, with a kitchen, a living room, two small bedrooms, and two balconies facing the right direction, south-east, for me to pick up a signal on my satellite phone.

Baghdad seemed calm but the foreign journalists were edgy. No one knew how much firepower the United States and Britain would bring to bear, or even when the invasion would begin. The description of the American military strategy as "shock and awe" was designed to unnerve the Iraqis but it had the same effect on us journalists. Rumors swirled that the Pentagon was preparing to use electromagnetic bombs—e-bombs—that would knock out all computers and communications equipment, making it im-possible for the Iraqis to command and control their forces. An e-bomb would also knock out journalists, frying their laptops, satellite phones, and video uplinks. At the time, I supported the invasion on the grounds that Saddam Hussein was monstrously cruel to his people. I had been to Iraq several times and found Saddam's regime both terrifying and evil. Faced with the choice of supporting a policy that promised to eliminate that evil or one that left it in place, I thought the choice was obvious. I had no idea at the time how bad Washington would bungle it, how inept the Iraqis would be at managing their own affairs, and the hor-rible forces—the rot deep within the Middle East—that the war would ultimately unleash.

As the countdown to the bombing of Baghdad continued, I feared Saddam Hussein would round up Western journalists and kill us one by one to pressure the Americans to stop bomb-ing. Most journalists pulled out before the hostilities began. They would talk to each other and get themselves all worked up, then have panicky conference calls with editors and lawyers back in the States. I didn't have a home office so I missed all that. I had weighed the dangers before I went to Iraq and decided the risks were manageable. Beyond that, I was getting the chance to do what I had dreamed of doing: covering one of the pivotal moments in the Middle East, the story of my generation.

After settling in at the Flowers Land, I called Kazem, a low-ranking official at the press center, explaining my visa predicament. I reasoned that it was best to let the Iraqis know I was a journalist who broke the rules rather than have them catch me and accuse me of being a spy. Kazem, a bespectacled man in a three-piece suit, came to the hotel a few days later. Changing my visa wouldn't be easy, he said, but he would take it up with the head of the press center, Uday al-Ta'e.

I was surprised to learn that Flowers Land had a business center with an Internet connection. The Iraqis had blocked free e-mail servers such as Yahoo! and Hotmail, but Mohammed, a twenty-one-year-old hacker who presided over the center, made it his business to find free e-mail sites that had escaped the authorities' notice. He came up with several that apparently weren't on the government's radar and signed me up for one based in Moldova, a tiny country tucked between Romania and Ukraine.

I picked a man named Zarfar as my driver, mainly because he was forty, older than the other candidates. I felt that young drivers tended to be too opportunistic. Zarfar was just greedy. He also had a functioning but decidedly dumpy car, a 1986 Volkswagen Passat, that wouldn't attract attention.

I took Zarfar to lunch in hopes of putting a purchase on his trust and ended up with a bad case of food poisoning. I went to a pharmacy to buy some vitamin C. I assumed the pharmacist was a Christian, as many are in the Arab world, and I tried to break the ice with some casual talk about Rome. He told me he had an uncle in Milan who was a priest and that his own son was an aspiring soccer player who dreamed of playing professionally in Italy.

After ten minutes of small talk, I asked him how his business was doing, a routine question in the West but quite forward in Saddam's Iraq, where expressing opinions to foreigners was tantamount to treason. "Better than ever," he said. But what about the war? "Maybe there will be a war, maybe there won't be. Hopefully there won't be a war." His sixteen-year-old son came in, and I told him I'd get the address for the European soccer federation so he could inquire about trying out for a pro team. I promised to mail the letter after I left Iraq. I went back to the hotel and got the federation's address off the Internet. Then I returned to the pharmacy and waited for the other customers to leave. I gave the pharmacist the address and he invited me to the back room for tea.

"Do you think there will be a war?" he asked, offering me a Gauloises Blondes cigarette. I said I expected the conflict to begin soon. He said he feared Sunni extremists would use the ensuing chaos to harass Christians. I said I was concerned about foreigners once the war started, especially Americans such as me, and he said I could take shelter in his store in the event of trouble. That was how I found my first safe house.

As for Zarfar, he thought the war would make Iraq the richest country in the Middle East because of its oil and large number of educated people. He planned to buy a new car, and he had his eye on an apartment where he could take his eighteen-year-old mistress, a university student whose parents had hired him to drive her to and from campus—and got more than they bargained for.

But first, Zarfar said, he needed a decent pair of shoes. So we drove to a market downtown, where I shed my safari-style shirt and khaki trousers for a wardrobe that would make me look less like a foreigner. Most men in Baghdad dressed like Eastern Europeans, in low-quality dress shirts, slacks, and blazers in a variety of colors. I bought the local uniform, along with a bottle of black Just for Men hair dye.

After our shopping expedition, I asked Zarfar to hire me a policeman. Because of my visa problem, I thought it would be helpful to travel with someone who had police credentials to help us through the inevitable roadblocks. Zarfar managed to line one up, nonchalantly mentioning that the guy had a drinking problem. With an avaricious driver and a drunkard cop, I felt I was collecting the cast of characters for an updated version of Evelyn Waugh's *Scoop*.

At the press center and at the Al-Rashid Hotel, the reporters were cagey and withholding information from each other. Because they knew I spoke Arabic, some of them tried to wheedle tidbits out of me without offering anything in return. A few even seemed to take pleasure in my shaky visa situation. Journalists typically jockey for position before a big story, but I had never seen anything as competitive as this.

I had a low moment on March 11, when I secured a reporting visa only to have it taken away by the official who managed the day-to-day operations of the press center. I was then ordered to leave Iraq within three days. In a panic, I contacted Mohammed Ajlouni, ABC's longtime fixer in Jordan, who took care of everything from getting hotel reservations to finding drivers to scheduling interviews and then soothing bruised feelings if an interview turned ugly. He told me that Iraqi officials at their embassy in Amman were concerned about the exodus of journalists from Iraq and might be willing to issue reporting visas to make sure the war got covered. I left my gear in my hotel room, including what remained of my $20,000 emergency stash, and headed back to Jordan in yet another GMC Suburban. It was the biggest gamble of my Iraq venture: if I didn't get a visa, I wouldn't be able to get back into the country.

Ajlouni and I went to the embassy, and he was invited in while I cooled my heels in the reception area. A couple of hours later he returned with a reporting visa. On March 16, I wrote in my journal, "I'm back in Baghdad and finally in business. I drove to Jordan and back in the last 36 hours." Of course, I still didn't have a firm commitment from ABC News, and all hell was about to break loose. But at least I didn't have any kids, I thought.

When I went to the Al-Rashid, most of the journalists were pulling out or packing to go. Like the other networks, ABC was shutting down its operation. The network's chief producer in town told me the editors in New York had struck a deal with a British newspaper reporter to cover Baghdad during the war. I was furious. ABC eventually agreed to pay me a retainer and said I would split the reporting duties with the British journalist. ABC promised to pay me whether I stayed or left if I felt unsafe, a very professional way in which to take money out of the decision. Before the ABC guys pulled out, they gave me an extra satellite phone, a chemical/biological suit, a gas mask, and, most important, $10,000 in cash. I had already spent $10,000 on cars, drivers, rooms, generators, and fuel, so my ankle pouch was now fully replenished.

By March 17, the mood in Baghdad had abruptly changed. "It's as if the Iraqis are finally starting to realize that this new war is finally coming," I wrote in my journal. "There is now heavy traffic, almost all of it heading out of town. I've seen shop owners boarding up their businesses."

From seven hundred journalists at the beginning of March, the number had dwindled to about one hundred and fifty—print reporters, TV correspondents, photographers, cameramen, and support personnel. At the press center I encountered Kazem, who only a week before I had asked for help with my visa. "Why are you staying when everyone else is leaving?" he asked. I took a chance and replied in Arabic. Some journalists, I said, are as *samid* as the Iraqi people. *Samid* means "steadfast" and "brave" and is the adjective most often used by Iraqis to describe themselves. Kazem laughed and threw his arm around my shoulder.

Now that I had press credentials, I was assigned a minder, Abu Sattar, whose stocky build, square face, and thick mustache made him eerily reminiscent of Saddam Hussein. He took everything Saddam said as gospel, but fortunately he was lazy and careless, and I had no trouble losing him and going off on my own. I also met Ali, a nineteen-year-old who would become my trusted driver and friend. I told Zarfar I no longer needed him as a driver but would continue to pay him and his policeman pal. I rented them a two-bedroom apartment in the Dulaimi Hotel so they would be nearby in case of an emergency.

When I called ABC's foreign desk on March 18, I was told that President Bush was delivering a speech that night from the White House. I also learned that the British newspaper reporter had left Iraq, which meant I was ABC's only reporter in Baghdad. I viewed my elevated status with mixed feelings because of an e-mail I had received from my mother. "The time has come to leave, please. To hell with the networks, just get going and get out!!! I love you. Mom."

I listened to Bush's speech through my earpiece on a balcony above the press center. He gave Saddam and his two sons forty-eight hours to leave Iraq or face "military conflict." The president also called on journalists to leave Iraq, which sent chills down my back. I was scared as hell, a good deal less *samid* than before, but still determined to stay.

Militiamen from Saddam's Ba'ath Party, the only officially sanctioned political group in Iraq, suddenly took to the streets, brandishing Kalashnikovs. They set up checkpoints and guard posts on street corners. As I would learn later, the better-trained Republican Guards were positioned on the outskirts of the city, preparing to close a noose on American soldiers once they entered Baghdad. Channeling my fear into logistics, I hurriedly set up two more safe houses and equipped them with food, water, and generators. I now had four bolt-holes in case I needed to disappear. Ali was dismissive of the Ba'ath militiamen: "They won't fight," a surprisingly blunt statement from someone who had lived his entire life under the iron fist of Saddam Hussein.

Iraqi press officials ordered foreign journalists to move to one of the three state-run hotels: the Palestine, the Al-Rashid, or the Al Mansour. I chose the Palestine because it was across the Tigris River from the press center and other government buildings. I booked three rooms on three sides of the building so I could have different views of the city. The Palestine was rickety—it would sway when bombs exploded—and that wasn't its only drawback. It also housed upward of twenty-five Islamic extremists. One told me he'd come to Iraq to become a martyr. The radicals were mostly Arabs but with some Asians. Efi Pentaki, a Greek journalist who had the room next to mine on the fourteenth floor, said she recognized several of the men from a training camp for suicide bombers that she had visited a couple of weeks earlier. Iraq had indeed imported a strange cast of characters, from human shields to Islamic fanatics, anything to slow down the American invasion.

On March 19, before the ground assault began, Washington launched a type of preemptive strike, firing forty cruise missiles and dropping four two-thousand-pound "bunker buster" bombs on the Dora Farms complex in southern Baghdad, where Saddam was thought to be meeting with his sons Uday and Qusay. (It was later revealed the men were not there at the time of the attack.)

Not knowing the purpose of the attack, and expecting "shock and awe," I thought the first night was something of a dud. Saddam responded with a speech declaring that the "day of the great jihad" had arrived and accusing the United States and Britain of having "evil imperialist and Zionist intentions." It was typical Saddam bluster, but it increased my feelings of isolation and vulnerability. I was now in an enemy capital, under attack by my own government. If I got into trouble, help would not be coming.

The Information Ministry, which oversaw the press center, was bustling with activity the next day, and I was surprised at how normal everything seemed. My old minder had left Baghdad on "family business," and I was turned over to Abu Annas, a man of about sixty-five who was polite, dignified, and brave. His one weakness was his near-obsessive concern for the brown corduroy suit he wore nearly every day. Whenever faced with the choice between duty and possibly soiling his suit, he would invariably err on the side of corduroy.

Abu Annas took me to what would become daily briefings by the Iraqi information minister, Mohammed Saeed al-Sahhaf, who would end up as one of the most memorable characters of the invasion period. He had been a Ba'ath Party enforcer during

Saddam's rise to power, and he retained his brass-knuckles bravado. But mostly he became known for his over-the-top language and utter dedication to spreading mistruth. He referred to American soldiers as "desert animals" and swore they were many miles away even after they had breached Baghdad's city limits.

Like the other networks, ABC had switched to continuous live coverage, and I worked virtually nonstop. At first ABC described me as a freelance reporter, but after a few days I was being introduced on-air as "ABC's Richard Engel" or "our correspondent." It felt good to get my epaulets.

After a second night of bombings, which included several direct hits on the presidential compound across the Tigris, Ali arrived with the daily newspapers (which amazingly kept publishing through the twenty-one-day invasion), freshly baked diamond-shaped loaves of bread, salty farmer's cheese, and a carton of mango juice. Breakfast was pure bliss.

Later that day, the Iraqi government expelled CNN from Baghdad, and correspondents Rym Brahimi and Nic Robertson and their crews left in a fury. I doubt anything they said was more offensive to the Iraqis than my reports, but Uday al-Ta'e, the press center director, only watched CNN, Fox, and the BBC. With CNN gone, only two American television correspondents remained in the capital—me and Peter Arnett, who was working as a freelancer for NBC.

Shock and awe arrived on the overnight of March 21st to 22nd. As I wrote in my journal: "It was ten times the intensity of the first two nights. . . . I could feel the heat and wind of the blasts [from the other side of the Tigris]. . . . The bombs were falling one after another. It was like lightning hitting the ground, the fury of Thor and Zeus crackling with explosions."

After spending the night and into the next morning broadcasting, I took a few hours off to collect my thoughts and take Ali to lunch. The restaurant was crammed with customers, and the headwaiter had to search to find us a table in the back. The bombing started up again, with explosions all around us, in broad daylight, but no one in the restaurant even flinched. Iraqis seemed numb after a quarter century under Saddam's whip-hand rule. It was heartbreaking to see what a harsh dictatorship can do to the human soul.

In less than a week, I had grown almost inured to explosions and fires. Then something new caught my eye from my fourteenth-story perch at the Palestine Hotel—a plume of black smoke snaking hundreds of feet into the sky. Soon I counted twenty plumes rising around the perimeter of Baghdad. The Iraqis had set oil fires in an effort to "blind" satellites and drones taking reconnaissance pictures and trying to locate Saddam.

From March 21st to 25th, Iraqi forces in the southern port city of Umm Qasr put up an unexpectedly strong fight against British and American units, and the Information Ministry seized the battle as a propaganda tool. Iraqi television broadcast footage of American POWs, as well as "dead American, British, and Zionist forces." (ABC and other US networks did not broadcast the pictures and accused Iraq of violating the Geneva Convention injunction against exploiting prisoners. Al Jazeera and many European networks aired the pictures of the American captives.) Iraqi television also broadcast brief interviews with five American POWs, several of whom were bandaged. One was visibly shaken, apparently looking off camera for instructions, and another was interviewed in bed and in evident pain.

An enormous sandstorm hit Baghdad on March 26, the

largest *asifa* that Iraqis had seen in a generation, covering cars with what looked like orange snow. The black plumes of smoke and the orange-colored air created a surrealistic scene right out of Hollywood.

I was in a tense encounter that day in the al-Shaab section of northeast Baghdad. At least two missiles had hit a downscale commercial district, killing civilians. I was surrounded by an angry crowd shouting, *"Allahu Akbar,"* which is Arabic for "God is greater" but is customarily translated as "God is greatest."

The demonstrators could see I was a reporter because I was carrying a camera and a notebook, but they didn't know I was an American. I put on my best Egyptian accent, making sure to pronounce *j*s like *g*s, and used colloquial expressions the Iraqis would recognize from Egyptian TV shows and movies. The toughest barb came from a man who had the Arab genius for rhetorical questions: "If Americans didn't want to hit civilians, why did they hit civilians?" I suggested the strike was a mistake. All shook their heads, reflecting an attitude common among Arabs. They distrusted the American government but had absolute faith in American technology. For Iraqis who had seen cruise missiles turn corners to hit government buildings, it was inconceivable that al-Shaab could have been an accident.

That night, American and British warplanes finally bombed the Information Ministry. The Palestine now became the press's HQ—where we broadcast from, where we ate, where we slept. The hotel's Orient Express restaurant served the same meal every night: overcooked spaghetti with oily tomato sauce, broiled chicken, and soggy stewed zucchini. If this had been a subsistence war zone, I would have been grateful for the meals, but every day I passed markets brimming with ripe tomatoes, eggplant, fresh meat and poultry, and every kind of fruit imaginable. The Palestine was like a sleepover party with execrable catering, bombs exploding outside, and wary friends. All told at this point of the war, about a hundred foreign reporters, cameramen, and photographers were there, along with fifty minders.

Ali and I had a close call at a telephone exchange that had been destroyed by American bombs. Ba'ath Party members carrying Kalashnikovs surrounded us within minutes. They confiscated my press card and Ali's papers. To my surprise, the usually shy Ali was defiant, telling them I was a properly credentialed journalist and, by the tone of his voice, that they should buzz off. They said they were going to take us to a police station, and Iraqi security headquarters was the last place I wanted to be at this stage of the conflict.

I protested again that I was an American journalist. "If I see an American here on the streets of Baghdad, I could kill him," the leader of the group said. I replied that if he killed me, no one would tell the Iraqi people's story except reporters embedded with US ground forces. Then he asked if I really tried to tell the truth, and I responded with an Arab-style rhetorical question: "If I didn't want to talk to Iraqis and tell the world what they were thinking, then why would I be out on the streets—in Iraq, during wartime— talking to you?" He was trapped in his own argument. He let us go, and I mumbled to myself, *"Al-hamdu lillah"*—Thank God.

I was sick by now. I hadn't been getting much sleep, and my stomach—because of stress, the smoke in the air, and generally dirty conditions—was in turmoil. I also had a hacking cough that prevented me from finishing an interview with Tariq Aziz, Iraq's deputy prime minister. When the session broke up, Aziz handed me a glass of water, which I could barely hold. "American biological weapon," I joked to Aziz and his aide. We all laughed and I fell into another coughing fit as they left.

This sort of chummy attitude with officials from an enemy government proved the undoing of Peter Arnett a few days later. He had covered the first Gulf War so was in a better position than any other journalist to report on the invasion. But then he gave an interview to Iraqi state television in which he said the US war plan hadn't worked and questioned whether the American people supported the war. It was a propaganda bonanza for the Iraqis, and NBC fired Arnett a few hours later. Arnett told me the interview had been a case of bad judgment. "Richard, all I can say to you is be careful."

I felt badly for Arnett, who was rebuilding his career after he had been reprimanded by CNN in 1998 for a report he couldn't substantiate that US soldiers in Laos had used sarin gas in 1970 as part of Operation Tailwind. After he left, I was the last American television correspondent in Baghdad. I understood why most journalists left before the bombing began. What I've never quite grasped is why the networks didn't weigh the risks beforehand. Instead they spent millions preparing to cover the war from Baghdad only to pull out at the last minute.

In the days after the sandstorm, I could only *hear* the air war. The bombs thudding around Baghdad were in a blind spot—too far away for me to see, and far out of earshot of the reporters embedded with US troops. The Pentagon said at the time that it was going after the Republican Guards who had encircled the city, but I never felt the military told the full story of the bombings. In all likelihood, many of the Iraqi casualties occurred in these off-camera attacks.

The thunder of the bombs was a constant reminder that it

was just a matter of time before US tanks rumbled down Sadoon Street, Baghdad's main thoroughfare. I was beginning to worry that my safe houses weren't really safe. I came across a Sudanese television crew that had escaped the notice of the Information Ministry and had a house only a block away from the Palestine. They said I could stay with them in case of trouble. I wasn't sure their place was safe either, but it had the virtue of being close and easy to run to.

The power went out in Baghdad on April 3, and the mood of the city changed markedly. Residents finally faced up to the fact that an invading force was closing in. Stores and restaurants were locked tight, and the streets were virtually empty. I tried to stay outside as much as possible because I was nervous that the concentration of Westerners at the Palestine made an inviting target if Saddam decided to take hostages. I went to the market stalls to buy batteries, water jugs, and food, but I wasn't good for much else. The constant work and stress had left me exhausted. I was so wiped out that I slept through an appearance on *Nightline*. On April 4, I wrote in my journal, "There were many blank looks on people's faces. Baghdad is now a city without life." I probably had a blank look myself.

As it happened, April 4, 2003, was a decisive day. The US Army captured Baghdad International Airport after several hours of fierce fighting. Along with Umm Qasr in the south, this was one of the two times that the Iraqis had put up stiff resistance. Hundreds of Iraqis were killed in the fight. The US Army turned the airport into one of its main bases of operations in the capital.

The next day, the Americans conducted "thunder runs" with armored vehicles racing through the city to test Iraqi resistance.

On the morning of April 6, I was awakened by the sound of

breaking glass. At first I thought a bomb had exploded nearby, but then I saw a beam of light showing through a hole in the curtain covering the sliding door of my balcony. Someone had fired a round through my room, probably from street level; I could see where the bullet had lodged in the ceiling. I was confident that no one had been targeting me specifically, that it was just part of the growing mayhem. But I wasn't taking any chances. I moved from the fourteenth floor to another room I had rented on the twelfth.

Baghdad is divided in two by the Tigris. The US Army captured the western half of the city on April 7 while the Marines were fighting their way toward the eastern half—my half. The army couldn't cross the Tigris without the Marines because they would be spread too thin and risk getting cut off from the airport from the rear.

The war came to Baghdad most dramatically on April 8. The night of shock and awe early in the invasion had been spectacular, but it had a disembodied character that made it seem almost like going to the movies. On the eighth the military display was every bit as awesome, but the killing was being done by human hands in close combat. Tanks, automatic weapons, attack helicopters, and the A-10 Warthog attack fighter with its terrifying Gatling gun turned a city of 5 million into a battlefield.

The day was notable for two other reasons. It was the end of the Saddam regime as I had known it. Abu Annas and all the other minders left the Palestine Hotel that morning, never to be seen again. Uday al-Ta'e and his mercurial boss, Information Minister Mohammed Saeed al-Sahhaf, stayed until the end, but they were cut off from the regime and, in al-Sahhaf's case, detached from reality. It was also the day that the Third Infantry's tanks fired on the Palestine, killing two cameramen. A subsequent inquiry cleared the tankers and their superior of any wrongdoing, but I will always believe the decision to fire was reckless. The Palestine was on the Pentagon's list of protected sites, and the hotel was too far away—approximately a mile—to pose any danger to the tank.

The Marines finally arrived on April 9, cautiously fanning out from their tanks. Within a quarter hour, a crowd of curious Iraqis cautiously approached them. Some of the Iraqis at the front were bare chested and waved their white undershirts to show they didn't mean any harm.

This group of about two hundred people started pulling down Saddam's statue. They tied a rope around Saddam's neck but couldn't budge the mammoth statue, which was anchored in cement. Two blocks away, a company of Marines watched and waited. Doubtless aware that a large television audience was watching back home, they finally drove a Marine tank rescue vehicle—an armored personnel carrier with a crane to drag away damaged vehicles—to the base of the statue.

Several Iraqis jumped on the vehicle as a Marine looped a chain around the statue's neck. The atmosphere was electric, almost like a carnival, when the Marines pulled down the statue and Iraqis slapped their shoes on Saddam's effigy, a profoundly insulting gesture in the Arab world. Ali raced around capturing these iconic images on my handheld camera.

The Marines first covered the statue with an American flag, but quickly understood that this sent the wrong message and replaced it with an Iraqi flag. I put several Marines on camera as the crowd, composed of Shiite Muslims, chanted, "Yes to freedom and the fall of dictatorship!" Freedom and dictatorship fortuitously rhyme in Arabic. But they also yelled, "Remember and love Sadr," a reference to an influential Shiite cleric who had been killed by Saddam's agents in 1999.

I knew at once this was an ominous sign and said so in a live report on ABC: "As for the future of Iraq, about 60 percent of the population are Shiites, and the government of Saddam Hussein was Sunni. The Shiites in this group here are saying they want the next government to be a Shiite government, and they hope the Americans are going to support them. So this will be a tricky maze to navigate during the next period."

Saddam Hussein was finally hunted down on December 13, 2003. His feral sons, Uday and Qusay, had been killed by US forces five months earlier. I thought it was brave to remove Saddam and his horrific system of government, and I would have considered it just and even noble if it had been the main reason for invading Iraq. He certainly had enough blood on his hands. His regime had murdered thousands—hundreds of thousands if you included those who died in the ultimately pointless and victor-less war with Iran that lasted from 1980 to 1988. Another thirty thousand died in the Gulf War waged by the United States and thirty-three other nations in 1991 to reverse Iraq's military annexation of Kuwait. But as time passed I grew increasingly skeptical that the United States had a plan to manage Iraq. The Americans arrived with decisiveness and purpose but then seemed to improvise everything else. It was as if there was no plan at all to deal with Iraq after invading it. I was also suspicious of Washington's changing explanations as to why it went to war in the first place. President Bush's administration said the primary casus belli was destroying Iraq's weapons of mass destruction, which turned out to not be real but were seized upon by political hawks. The secondary reason offered up was that the war was needed to stamp out the

Iraqi regime's links to international terrorists, who only arrived in numbers *after* it became clear there would be a US invasion. Later the administration said it invaded Iraq to bring democracy and protect human rights. The casus belli was a moving target.

Back in the States, many people saw the capture of Saddam (he was hanged on December 30, 2006) as the end of the war. What it really was, although few appreciated it at the time, was the end of a chapter. The *war* lay ahead. To the chagrin of the United States—the president and Congress, military leaders, the general public—America would be stuck in Iraq for eight more years and the impact will still be felt for years to come. Saddam was the first of the Arab big men to go. He was knocked off his perch by Washington, which was odd since it was Washington that supported him in the war with Iran and chose not to remove him even after he invaded Kuwait. President Bush decided Saddam Hussein had to go to make way for the fantasy garden of democracy he wanted to plant in the Middle East. Saddam was one of the key leaders, horrible and brutal with psychopaths for children, who'd been holding up the house of the Middle East safeguarded by the United States since World War II. The others: Mubarak, Gadhafi, Ben Ali, and the Assad family, would soon face major challenges of their own. Their fall would unleash the religious fanaticism and ethnic hatred they'd been simultaneously containing and creating because of their horrific mismanagement, brutality, and corruption. The big men had incentives to both contain and maintain a permanent enemy. The dictators claimed that without them in charge, Muslim fundamentalists would take over. It would become a self-fulfilling prophecy.

FOUR

I SAW THE BLAST IN MY SLEEP, AN ORANGE FLASH SO BRIGHT THAT IT PASSED through my eyelids. My room at the Hamra Hotel in Baghdad was filled with smoke and dust and shards of glass. Several ceiling panels had crashed to the floor, and the door to the balcony had been ripped off its frame. A sharp piece of shrapnel about the size of an egg was melting the synthetic fibers of the cheap industrial carpet. I crept to the balcony and looked outside. Across the street I saw the twisted remains of a truck bomb outside the Australian embassy. Several cars were on fire.

Since I'd arrived in Iraq, I had been keeping a video journal, turning the camera on myself at emotional moments. I reached for the small camera and pointed it at my unshaven, tired, and wild-eyed face. It was January 19, 2005. My voice was shaky:

"When the explosions happened, I thought . . . finally this was it, that they had blown up a bomb in the basement. I thought when it exploded that—that they had done what they had been threatening to do." Which was to blow up our hotel. For Sunni fanatics, anyone was fair game—soldiers, policemen, women and children, journalists.

I had been gung ho when I came to Iraq nearly two years before. I felt bulletproof. But the constant gunshots, explosions, fear of kidnapping, dead bodies, the memory of a stray dog carrying a severed human head between its teeth—the savagery of it all had worn me down to a psychological nub. Too much adrenaline had coursed through my veins. I'd had too many bad mornings.

I looked back into the video camera. "Am I just lucky so far, and how much can you push your luck? When do you decide that this is just not worth it? . . . I am still cheating death. . . . It feels like you are trying to pull a fast one on history, that you are trying to get away with it, get out, sneak out, get information, and get back without being kidnapped or losing an eye or a limb.

"Today with this explosion, I got away with another little bit . . . but how many more times can you get away with it? I don't know."

I knew I was becoming paranoid. I saw danger everywhere. I had tied an escape rope to a drainage pipe off the balcony of my room at the Hamra. I would be ready if trouble came. I started dreaming, sometimes when I was sleeping but mostly when I was awake, about how I would be remembered if I got killed. Would I be reduced to a mention on the *Nightly News*, of interest for half a news cycle? Or if it was a slow week, a very slow week, maybe I'd be a three-day story?

Reporters go through four stages in a war zone. In the first stage, you're Superman, invincible. In the second, you're aware that things are dangerous and you need to be careful. In the third, you conclude that math and probability are working against you. In the fourth, you know you're going to die because you've played the game too long.

I was drifting into stage three. I couldn't connect with friends back home, and I couldn't relate to my wife. She couldn't understand why I wanted to stay in this awful place where people spent their days killing one another. She believed that life was for living and creating a family. Our marriage had been tottering for a year, and now we had decided to get a divorce.

My stage three jitters began nine months before, in April 2004, about a year after I left my contract job at ABC and signed on as a full-time correspondent at NBC. Instead of focusing on my personal life, I did what many men and women do, I buried myself in work. I read as much as I could about the Sunni and Shiite conflict. The more I read, the more concerned I became about what the United States had embarked upon. Washington had opened a Pandora's box that went back more than thirteen hundred years, to the schism over who would be the first caliph after the death of Mohammed.

One faction believed that the Prophet, lacking a male heir, designated his cousin and son-in-law Ali to carry on his work. His followers—the *shiat* of Ali, the "party" or "faction" of Ali— came to be known as Shiites. They believe that the inner meaning of the Koran can only be understood by intense study, and that members of the Prophet's family, the sayyids, are especially attuned to the message that Allah handed down to one of their own.

The other faction believes that caliphs should be chosen by consensus. They practice what is generally called an "orthodox" form of Islam, strictly following the words and sunna, or traditions, of Mohammed. They became known as Sunnis and now account for about 85–90 percent of Muslims in the world. Hard-line Sunnis don't even consider Shiite Muslims monotheists because they also worship Ali and his son Hussein (Ali's son by Fatima, who was Mohammed's daughter).

The faction we now call Sunnis prevailed in the selection of the first caliph, Abu Bakr, father of one of Mohammed's wives. Ali got his chance after the third caliph, Uthman, a venerated figure in Islam because he codified the Koran, was murdered by Egyptian extremists. Ali at first declined to follow Uthman as caliph, but Shia supporters prevailed on him to change his mind. He ruled the caliphate from the Iraqi city of Kufa near Najaf.

Ali faced two implacable enemies. In the north was the governor of Syria, Mu'awiyya, one of Uthman's relatives; in the south was one of Mohammed's widows, Aisha, who was also aggrieved by the death of Uthman. Ali, just like Uthman before him, was murdered in 661 by an extremist, allowing Mu'awiyya to quickly seize the caliphate and found Islam's first royal-like dynasty, the Umayyads, based in Damascus.

What began as a hereditary dispute was about to turn forever bloody. In 680, Ali's son Hussein raised a small army and set out to avenge his father. He confronted the forces of Yazid, Mu'awiyya's son and the second Umayyad caliph, on the plains of Karbala, an Iraqi city about forty-five miles northwest of

Najaf. What happened that day still lives vividly in the Shia imagination and explains the tension between Shiites and Sunnis, played out over a millennium in bloody encounters between the two sects.

Yazid's soldiers surrounded Hussein's tiny force of seventy-two now-legendary fighters. According to Shia tradition, Hussein and his men were slaughtered after a valiant fight. Yazid's soldiers beheaded Hussein and carried his head to Damascus. Reconciliation was now out of the question.

Shiites commemorate Hussein's death every year in Karbala, with an elaborate reenactment and crowds approaching 2 million. Their sense of grievance is exacerbated by their minority status in the Muslim world, where they represent a majority only in Iran (90–95 percent of the population), Iraq (60–65 percent), and Bahrain (60–70 percent).

That Saddam Hussein was a Sunni, a despot from a minority sect who reserved power and patronage for fellow Sunnis and who had slaughtered many thousands of Shiites, explains why the American invasion represented much more than the toppling of a tyrant. For the Shiites, it was both a political victory and a moment of religious ecstasy. The Americans, they believed, had helped complete Hussein's seventh-century mission and would eventually return them to power.

The shameless looting in April 2003 after the United States captured Baghdad showed that the United States faced enormous challenges in bringing democracy to Iraq, a backward, somewhat isolated country mainly known to Americans for the depredations of Saddam Hussein, its eight-year bloodbath with Iran, and its military collapse during the Gulf War in 1991.

Few associated it with their elementary-school lessons on the glories of Mesopotamia, "the cradle of civilization," between the Tigris and Euphrates Rivers.

On May 23, 2003, came the fateful decision by America's special envoy in Iraq, L. Paul Bremer III, to dissolve Iraq's army. Bremer issued his decree only a day after informing President Bush and the National Security Council, reportedly catching many high officials by surprise.

The decree, part of an effort to remove Saddam's Ba'ath Party from Iraq's politics, guaranteed the enmity of the country's military men, most of them Sunnis, who had enjoyed prestige and job security under Saddam. To the Sunnis, de-Ba'athification amounted to de-Sunnification. So it was not surprising that these men mainly from the military, who American officials called "regime dead-enders," set about inciting Iraqi Sunnis and foreign jihadists to attack Shiites and Americans.

The Shiites remained preternaturally patient, largely at the behest of their most senior cleric, the Grand Ayatollah Ali al-Sistani, who urged them to turn the other cheek. He had his eye on history. He remembered the mistakes of 1920, when Shiites led the successful revolt against the British only to see the Sunnis seize power. If the Shiites caused problems now, he believed, they would risk losing out again.

In any case, Iraqis were only briefly grateful to the Americans. The Sunnis were aggrieved, and the Shiites were itching to run the political show. Instead of becoming a beacon of democracy, Iraq turned into a political mosh pit. Upward of two hundred parties sprang up, each with its own disgruntled constituents. After two decades of submissive silence, Iraqis seemed to whine about everything, and the Americans were handy whipping boys.

US officials seemed stunned by the primitiveness of the place. Knowing that the Iraqi power grid would have to be rebuilt after the war, the military had been judicious in selecting targets, but then looters stole copper wires, switches, and other integral equipment—and the Iraqis blamed the Americans for not quickly switching the lights back on. The US military was untrained and unprepared to be Iraq's policeman. Abrams tanks were no help combating the lawlessness in Baghdad, which was recording seven hundred murders a month, fourteen times the number in New York City.

At first, we journalists could move around Iraq relatively freely. Ordinary Iraqis were eager to tell us about the brutality of Saddam's regime, sometimes pulling up their shirts to show us the purple scars left by tortures in his gulags.

Then came what seemed to be a trivial provocation. On March 28, 2004, US soldiers shut down the *Hawza*, a radical Shia newspaper, for printing lies, rumors, and incitements. It was the personal megaphone of Muqtada al-Sadr, a pudgy, utterly unprepossessing thirty-year-old Shia cleric with a hot head and a potent family name. His father and father-in-law were prominent ayatollahs. Both were assassinated by Saddam's regime, in 1980 and 1999, and they became known as "the first martyr" and "the second martyr." The "Remember and love Sadr" chants on the tank recovery vehicle pulling down Saddam's statue were, as I suspected, a sign of things to come.

Sadr sent his Mahdi Army into the streets, the first large-scale Shia revolt since the US invasion. Sadr wasn't listening to the more cautious Grand Ayatollah Sistani. At the same time, Sunnis were facing up to the loss of their monopoly on power and privilege. US troops for the first time were facing threats from both the Shiites they'd help bring to power and the Sunnis they'd displaced. The United States was now in the middle of a civil war. Three days after Sadr's Shia newspaper closed, Sunni gunmen in Fallujah, which had become the center of Sunni resistance, ambushed four American security contractors. Crowds pulled them from their SUVs, dragged them through the streets, doused them with gasoline, and set them ablaze.

Abu Musab al-Zarqawi, a Sunni jihadist of astonishing savagery, was already conducting a murderous bombing campaign, killing twenty-two at Baghdad's Canal Hotel in August 2003, including the UN special envoy to Iraq. He killed upward of 180 Iraqis in March 2004 in bombing attacks at Shia shrines in Karbala and Baghdad.

To achieve his goal of rivaling or surpassing Osama bin Laden, Zarqawi apparently decided that something more theatrical was needed to raise his macabre profile. On April 10, Nick Berg, a twenty-six-year-old freelance construction contractor from suburban Philadelphia, went missing in Iraq. He ended up in Zarqawi's hands to be used for what can be considered ISIS's first beheading video. Wearing a ski mask, Zarqawi stood behind Berg, unsheathed a butcher's knife, grabbed Berg by the hair, and sliced his neck as the American let out an agonizing scream. Zarqawi kept sawing away until he severed Berg's head, which he held up like a trophy. Zarqawi's group wasn't called ISIS then. The group would change names seven times over the next decade, but bloodlust and the strategic use of macabre videos would remain central to its group identity.

Zarqawi picked up the tempo of atrocities as 2004 wore on. He bombed Shia mosques during midday prayers, killed the odd government official, blew up Iraqis signing up for jobs in the army, and assassinated Shia clerics at a rate of two a week.

After the shuttering of the *Hawza* and the growing Sunni insurgency, it was open season on journalists. My NBC team started traveling in convoys of two vehicles or more so we would have a getaway car in case one was hit or broke down.

The bombing at the Australian embassy signaled that 2005 would be the year that the insurgency moved into full swing. The much-hyped parliamentary elections were scheduled for January 30. To hear American officials tell it, all Iraqis had to do was drop ballots into boxes and their miseries would be over. The country was abuzz over this supposed gift of freedom.

Trouble was, almost no one—including American officials; Prime Minister Ayad Allawi, the interim leader handpicked by the United States; and the UN, which organized the elections—saw how the political deck could be stacked. But Sistani and the *hawza*, a web of Shiite seminaries and clerics after which the radical Shiite newspaper was named, understood that it was a simple matter of turnout. Their ground game left nothing to chance: they told fellow Shiites that casting ballots was a religious duty. The Sunnis, feeling embittered and betrayed by what they saw as America's favoritism toward the Shiites, decided to boycott the voting. The decision would cut Sunnis off from power, alienate them, and play into the hands of fanatics like Zarqawi, but the boycott did have a certain logic to it. Sunnis had watched US forces topple their patron, Saddam Hussein, disband their beloved army, and watched the United States organize a vote that, because of their majority, could only help Shiites even more. Sunnis decided they didn't want to play the American game and would opt out. Under ordinary circumstances, an election probably would be fatally tainted if about a third of the population, including most members of one religious group, stayed away from the polls. But Washington didn't seem to care. It was enough that the elections took place as planned. It *looked* like democracy.

In the run-up to the voting, bin Laden anointed Zarqawi the "emir of Iraq," which made him the jihadist equivalent of a capo in the Mafia. Zarqawi reciprocated by renaming his group "al-Qaeda in Iraq." He also correctly predicted that the hated Shiites would carry the vote and "form a majority government that would control the strategic, economic, and security infrastructure of the state."

A curfew was imposed a week before the elections, and the turnout was high among Shiites. "Only" fifty Iraqis died while millions cast their ballots. Iraqis holding up their fingers stained with purple ink made for great TV. We had what looked like a good-news story for once. But it was only superficial. In truth, the elections laid the foundation for a long, drawn-out civil war.

One of my best sources told me that Sunni radicals had decided to form their own parallel state in response to the vote, with Zarqawi as president. It would be "an Islamic state with sharia as the law and the Koran as the constitution." The source said the insurgents were imposing their fiercely intolerant brand of Islam within days of the voting. Iraq was now one country divided into three nations, which I called Shiastan, Kurdistan, and Jihadistan.

After the bombing of the Australian embassy, I had begun sleeping on the floor, with my mattress flipped up on its side to serve as a shield. Because of the danger and the expense—and di-minishing interest in the Iraq war in Europe—the number of peo-ple chronicling the conflict had shrunk dramatically. Gone were the filmmakers and the freelancers sitting by the Hamra's pool, the stringers in string bikinis. It cost hundreds of thousands of dollars a month to support a full Baghdad bureau with armored cars, bodyguards, satellite phones, and local staff—too expensive for anyone except the large American television networks and major newspapers and magazines.

Life in Baghdad was dangerous but not entirely dreary. One night in March 2005, about thirty of the remaining Westerners put on a bash at the Hamra's Chinese restaurant. We were all young and single, or about to be single—emotional casualties of the conflict. The music was loud and we drank and danced a lot.

In this mostly grumpy and cynical crowd, Marla Ruzicka was a ray of sunshine. She was one of the few humanitarian workers left in the country, bouncing around the news bureaus to use the Internet and phones when we weren't busy. Ruzicka was tirelessly lobbying the US military to pay compensation to the families of civilians killed in the fighting.

Ruzicka and I left the party together and went to my room. It was one of the last times I saw her alive. She was killed by a suicide bomber a few weeks later on the way back from Camp Victory, the US military's headquarters at Baghdad's airport. When US sol-diers reached her, she was so badly burned that only a tuft of her blond hair remained. "I'm American, and I'm still alive," she told the soldiers. They tried to medevac her back to Camp Victory, but she died on the way.

I was emotionally flattened by her death. I kept seeing images of her in my hotel room, drinking cheap Lebanese wine and talking about life, love, and Iraq. I begged off doing the story on her death. I just couldn't reduce her to a two-minute news package, so another correspondent filed the report. Back in my room, I cried for the first time since I arrived in Iraq.

On May 3, 2005, three months after the parliamentary elections, Iraq's parliament finally swore in an elected prime minister, Ibrahim al-Jaafari, although the vote that brought him to power had clearly been flawed. His appointed predecessor, Ayad Allawi, had been an unabashed strongman. Jaafari was anything but. A small, soft-spoken man with friendly eyes, he was a Shiite scholar, an intellectual, and a sayyid, a descendant of the Prophet Mohammed, who preferred business suits to the black turban he was entitled to wear because of his bloodline. Jaafari had been the leader of an opposition party that had tried to kill Saddam. But by now Iraq was a jumbled mix of religious hatred with a large foreign occupying force, and it would prove impossible to govern.

When the curfew was lifted a week after the elections, the hunting season against journalists opened in earnest. I gathered the NBC team to go to a background briefing in the Green Zone on the new government, the governmental center of America's Coalition Provisional Authority. I pulled on my blue flak jacket and grabbed a notebook. Our British bodyguards checked the tires, gas, guns, and radios. I sat in the backseat of the lead car, an armored Jeep Cherokee. A chase car was twenty feet behind.

The British driver, incongruously named Bunny, noticed a BMW on our tail. It was weaving into traffic, pulling up close, then dropping back. "Somebody's playing with us," he announced, and we went on high alert.

Another bodyguard, who appropriately enough was riding

shotgun, loaded his AK-47 and put it on his lap. The BMW, which was carrying four men, suddenly pulled up next to us, probably to see if we were worth kidnapping. With their fast and slow driving, they were trying to see how many cars were with us and how we'd react to an ambush. My stomach turned sour with adrenaline and fear.

Bunny swerved into the BMW, trying to ram it off us. But the BMW was much more nimble than our armor-laden Jeep. It raced ahead and cut us off. A second car, a white Toyota, moved in from the rear, trapping us in between. The two cars then tried to squeeze us to the right, onto an off-ramp that would have put us in a run-down area where we would have been sitting ducks.

But Bunny had other ideas. He took a hard right and made as if we were trying to escape. It was a bluff. The BMW followed us, then Bunny hit the brakes, made an almost ninety-degree turn back toward the road, drove across the outgoing lanes, and jumped a center divider into oncoming traffic on the other side. He was going about eighty miles an hour and weaving between cars coming directly at us.

After several hundred yards, we finally reached a traffic circle that allowed Bunny to get with the traffic flow going in the correct direction. Then we spotted a third car gaining on us from the rear. Bunny hit the gas and sped back toward the bureau. The third car finally gave up the chase only when we drove up to the gate leading to the Hamra.

THE NEW GOVERNMENT THAT TOOK OFFICE IN MAY 2005 LIVED UP TO THE SUNNIS' worst fears. It was composed of former enemies of Saddam's Sunni regime, along with allies of Washington and the *hawza*.

The spring and summer of 2005 were a nightmare of murders, bombings, shootings, and kidnappings. Each day had the same bloody rhythm: mortars at dawn, car bombs by 11:00 a.m., drive-by shootings before tea, and mortars again at dusk. At night the death squads went to work.

Aside from the uprising by Muqtada al-Sadr, it was still a mostly one-sided civil war. The Sunnis, who had boycotted the elections, were determined to punish the Shiites and their American backers. Although there were intense battles in parts of Baghdad and in southern Iraq between US troops and the Mahdi Army, many Shiites refused to follow Sadr into war with the Americans. They agreed with the patient Grand Ayatollah Sistani that the US invasion was the biggest boost to Shiite empowerment in the region for decades, if not centuries. Sunni extremists, many of them loyal to Zarqawi, attacked American soldiers and Marines and Shiites everywhere—in mosques, markets, even at funerals.

They kidnapped and executed 150 Shiites in mid-April in Madaen, a town twenty miles south of Baghdad. That same week in Baghdad, there were fourteen car bombs, forty-two roadside bombs, and twenty-two shootings. The week after that, at least fifty-eight members of the Iraqi security forces, eighteen Western contractors, ten US soldiers, and one journalist were killed. The US military reported seventy attacks a day in Iraq. I was jittery and wired, and most of all strangely detached. I was deep into stage three, with inklings of stage four.

On August 31, as Hurricane Katrina was dissipating north of New Orleans, leaving devastation in its wake, Baghdad suffered its deadliest day yet. Several hundred thousand Shiites gathered in the ancient Kazimiya quarter in northern Baghdad for the annual pilgrimage to honor the eighth-century martyr

Musa al-Kazim, one of the twelve imams believed to be rightful descendants of Ali.

To get to Kazim's tomb, pilgrims crossed the Imma Bridge, a three-hundred-yard span that rose thirty feet above the Tigris. As they crossed that morning, the pilgrims were packed together so tightly that they could only advance by inches. Many were lost in religious ecstasy, crying and beating their chests to mourn the imam, whom Shiites believe was executed by Sunnis in 799.

Then someone cried out, "Suicide bomber!" The crowd panicked. In the ensuing stampede, terrified pilgrims ran in both directions, many colliding in the middle of the bridge. A side railing collapsed under their weight, and scores leaped into the water whether they could swim or not. Hundreds were trampled to death. More than a thousand died. Hundreds of pairs of sandals were scattered around the bridge, left behind when pilgrims made their desperate dives into the river. I was given all of seventy-five seconds to tell the story on the *Nightly News*.

Over the summer, Iraq descended into anarchy. I coped by spending six or eight weeks in Baghdad, then taking ten days off to go scuba diving. I never minded going back. Sometimes I wondered whether the war was warping me into a man my old friends wouldn't recognize.

At 8:12 a.m. on November 18, 2005, a white minivan pulled alongside the Hamra's blast barriers. When the van exploded, it blew a hole in the blast wall wide enough for the water truck that was following closely behind to drive through. The truck was packed with enough explosives to bring down the hotel and kill us all. But the attackers had put too much explosives in the minivan, so when it exploded it formed a ten-foot-deep crater in the street.

The water truck fell into the crater, which shielded the hotel from the worst of the blast. Even so, the NBC bureau was a mess. Computers, desks, and televisions were all smashed.

I was in Thailand, scuba diving, when the attack took place. I rushed back to the bureau and found that we had a personnel crisis. Producers and correspondents balked at coming to Baghdad anymore. Many of our London-based correspondents, who rotated through Baghdad most frequently, decided it had become too dangerous.

ABC was already facing a lawsuit by one of its former London-based correspondents, Richard Gizbert, who claimed he had been fired for refusing to go into the war zones in Afghanistan and Iraq. Gizbert was the father of two children and had covered the fighting in Herzegovina and Chechnya. That was enough for him. ABC claimed his refusal had no bearing on his dismissal, but a London court disagreed and gave him a $100,000 settlement. The decision and award were reversed in 2006.

While NBC never pressured me to stay, I gave the network an easy way to avoid a similar mess. I liked the Baghdad bureau and was willing to keep coming back. Just as police and fire sirens reminded New Yorkers they were home, the sound of car bombs reminded me I was in Baghdad, which had become home for me. I was like a battered wife who can't leave the man abusing her. I had moved into stage four and assumed, as a matter of math, that I was going to die in Baghdad. But still I wanted to stay.

The Constitution of Iraq was ratified on October 15, 2005, which left only one step in the US plan for bringing democracy to the country: the December 15 election of a permanent, 275-member Iraq Council of Representatives. The first election had been to select a committee to write the constitution and a prime minister to oversee the transitional period. This vote was to elect a parliament to run the country. The voting system had been adjusted to give more weight to the Sunnis, who planned to participate this time.

Sunnis expected to win 40–60 percent of the vote, which was unrealistic. Because of their long years in power, and their grandiose sense of entitlement, some Sunnis were convinced they comprised a majority of Iraqis, a self-deceiving mythology of arithmetic. They wound up with only 21 percent of the vote. They said the election was a fraud and blamed Iran, their ancient Persian and Shiite enemy, for rigging the vote. To them, Iran was the invisible hand, aiding its favorite Shia candidates. Zarqawi's group lashed out at fellow Sunnis for voting this time, accusing them of legitimizing a Shiite project cooked up by Iran and Washington.

Stressed-out by a year of violence and by covering the elections, journalists at the Hamra threw a New Year's Eve bacchanalia, drinking to excess, dancing wildly, and knocking over any furniture that got in the way. Two American reporters, from the same newspaper, started kissing at midnight and didn't stop until dawn. I danced a lot with Jill Carroll, a freelance reporter who wrote most of her pieces for the *Christian Science Monitor*. She was young, attractive, and idealistic—and one of the few freelancers left in Baghdad. She traveled alone with her translator, and many of us warned her that she was an easy target for kidnappers. A week later she disappeared. She was blessedly released, unharmed, after three months in captivity.

I may have been in stage four, but I wasn't completely crazy. At least eighty-six journalists had been killed in Iraq, more than in any other conflict since World War II, and another thirty-eight had been taken hostage. More would die in the years to come. I knew I had to limit my movements and take special care when I did go out. If I had to do an interview, I would first send an advance team of local toughs in black leather jackets to take GPS coordinates and map out possible escape routes. I also devised a beat system for our Iraqi staffers: One covered politicians, police, and hospitals. Another tracked Sunni insurgents and their activity on the Web. My trusted friend Ali took the Mahdi Army and Sadr City, a Shiite slum in Baghdad, because he was a fellow Shiite and lived nearby.

ON THE EVENING OF JUNE 7, 2006, ABU MUSAB AL-ZARQAWI WAS KILLED BY US Special Forces in a small cinder-block farmhouse in a village forty miles north of Baghdad. The troops had tracked Zarqawi's deputy, Abu Abdul Rahman, to the farmhouse, and an informant from Zarqawi's inner circle called US commanders to confirm that the al-Qaeda leader was inside.

Within minutes, two F-16 jets dropped two five-hundred-pound bombs on the farmhouse, demolishing the building and digging a twenty-foot-deep crater in the soft black soil beneath it. Zarqawi was still breathing after the airstrike. The blast threw him against a wall, breaking his leg, and into an adjacent field. He was put on a stretcher by US troops and reportedly died when he tried to move and was restrained. Rahman was among five others who were killed.

The military locked down the area for forty-eight hours to look for evidence. The forensic search turned up an intelligence treasure trove—memory sticks, phone numbers, Zarqawi's personal diary. Then the military flew a handful of reporters to see

Zarqawi's last hideout. As we circled the site, it was hard to see where the farmhouse had been. Not a wall was standing. All I could see was a crater surrounded by palm groves and wildflowers. It looked like a swimming pool filled with debris. Zarqawi's legacy, however, would continue. He would later be remembered as the founder of ISIS, who established its barbarous practices of beheadings and mass executions. Zarqawi the beheader set the bar for ISIS's brutality and its hatred of Shiites. He understood that the United States was disenfranchising Sunnis and used it as a powerful rallying cry. ISIS wouldn't have existed without the US invasion of Iraq. It was born out of the Sunnis' feeling of alienation, their belief that they'd been pushed aside—which, of course, they had been. Sunnis suffered a thirteen-century-old injustice with power stripped from them by Washington and given to Iraqi Shiites and their coreligionists in Iran. This grievance is at the core of ISIS ideology. Simply put, no Iraq war, no ISIS.

Two weeks after visiting Zarqawi's destroyed farmhouse, I moved to Beirut with the new title of Middle East correspondent and Beirut bureau chief, although I would keep rotating through Iraq for the next several years.

My promotion to bureau chief for NBC was beyond anything I had imagined when I went to Cairo in 1996 without a job. It finally felt like I was starting to realize my dream of making a name as a foreign correspondent. As for Zarqawi, he wanted to make a name as well as a jihadist in a league with bin Laden. It turned out his infamy was just beginning. He would redefine Islamic terrorism into something more brutal, more digitally connected, and more widespread than any of his radical predecessors.

In Lebanon, unbeknownst to me, another war awaited. Trouble seemed to follow me around. The late Tim Russert, my friend and the esteemed moderator of NBC's *Meet the Press*, once joked, "Richard, just don't come to Washington."

Of course I did come to Washington from time to time, and on one visit I met with President George W. Bush for ninety minutes. Since the invasion he had earned the equivalent of two PhDs about Iraq and the Middle East. He had done the reading, met the key players, and studied the reams of information that only a president gets. But I still didn't think he understood how to deal with the Arabs. I don't think he fully understood the forces he had unleashed. He certainly refused to admit he'd done anything to benefit Shiite Iran, even thought that was obvious. Under Saddam, Iraq was Iran's hostile and dangerous neighbor. Now Iraq was run by fellow Shiites, many of them directly loyal and answerable to Tehran.

"I'm sort of jealous," Bush said. "I'm envious of what you've been doing." He was referring to the chance to travel and explore, the adventurous side of my job. "Are you some sort of thrill seeker?"

"No, no thrill seeker," I said. "I don't like driving fast or bungee jumping. I just think this is important."

"It is. You ever been to Iran?"

FIVE

AFTER YEARS AS A WARTIME VAGABOND WITH NO OTHER HOME BESIDES A HOTEL room in Iraq, I saw my move to Lebanon as a new beginning, a chance to rebuild my personal life and, with my new title of Beirut bureau chief and Middle East correspondent, to cover stories beyond Iraq. I was sick of suicide attacks, bombed-out hotel rooms, and the fear that I was going to die in that godforsaken place.

I knew, even then, that the war in Iraq would set the tone for the region for years, if not decades, to come. Lebanon was an ideal listening post because it was so fragile, a mere sapling of a country that has survived by bending to the geopolitical winds of its neighbors and the great powers. If Iran became the region's

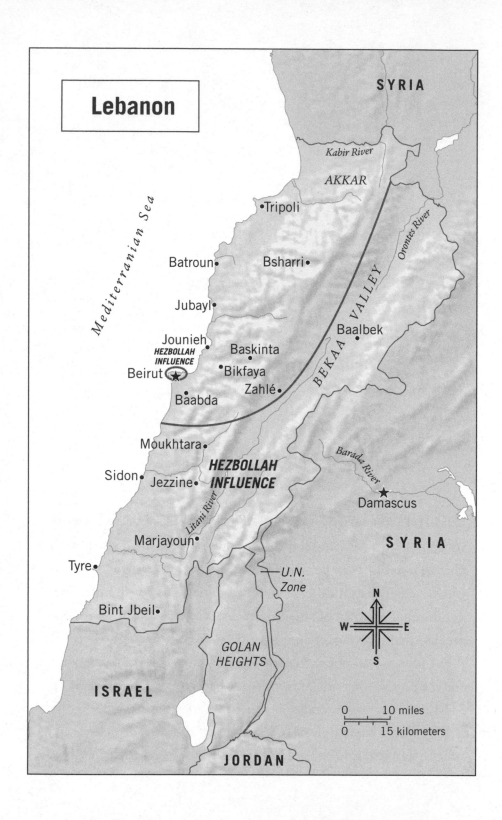

Lebanon

SYRIA

Kabir River

AKKAR

•Tripoli

Batroun•   •Bsharri

Jubayl•

Orontes River

Jounieh•
*HEZBOLLAH
INFLUENCE*
Beirut⭐   •Baskinta   •Baalbek

•Bikfaya

Baabda•   Zahlé•

Mediterranean Sea

BEKAA VALLEY

Moukhtara•

***HEZBOLLAH
INFLUENCE***

Sidon•   Jezzine•

Barada River

⭐
Damascus

Litani River

Marjayoun•

SYRIA

Tyre•

—*U.N.
Zone*

Bint Jbeil•

N
W——E
S

*GOLAN
HEIGHTS*

ISRAEL

```
0          10 miles
├──┼──┼──┤
0          15 kilometers
```

JORDAN

bully, or if Israel got twitchy, or if Sunni jihadists grew restive, or if democracy showed signs of life—I'd feel all those things first in Lebanon.

I also needed a home. I was divorced. I had no belongings. No framed photographs. No furniture. No place to put my books. Lebanon seemed like a perfect place to settle down for a while. It had recovered from its devastating civil war, and most important, it was at peace. It was urbane and socially relaxed with a vibrant nightlife, lovely women, and a perfect climate. While looking for an apartment, I stayed in the Mövenpick Hotel on the fabled Corniche. I could feel the tension draining out of me as I stood on the balcony and looked out over the Mediterranean.

I was watching Al Jazeera on June 25, 2006, when the story broke that the Sunni militant group Hamas had kidnapped an Israeli soldier and spirited him back to the Gaza Strip. Then the foreign desk at NBC in New York called to say the network had a correspondent working the Israeli side but needed someone in Gaza. I hopped a plane to Jordan and drove across the border to Israel, where I met with the soldier's father.

All countries take the kidnapping of their troops seriously. But it drives Israel absolutely crazy. It is an affront to every person. Almost everyone in Israel is or has been a soldier. There is total commitment to the principle "leave no man behind" because nearly everyone could be that man or woman. All men and women, except some Israeli Arabs and ultra-Orthodox Jews, serve in the military, and remain in the reserves. When a soldier is kidnapped, Israelis think of their own sons and daughters.

That was especially so in this case because Corporal Gilad Shalit came across as such a kid—skinny and awkward looking, with close-cropped hair and wire-rim glasses. Friends described him as a physics whiz, a soccer goalie, a quiet, nice boy who volunteered for combat duty.

Hamas was calling the shots in Gaza. In the 2006 parliamentary elections, it defeated Fatah, which had been founded by Yasser Arafat, and then drove out Fatah altogether. Hamas now asked for the release of Palestinian prisoners in exchange for Shalit. Israel keeps a lot of Palestinian prisoners in part for situations like this one.

I ALSO MET THE FAMILY OF A FIFTEEN-YEAR-OLD PALESTINIAN BOY ARRESTED FOR throwing stones. He was one of a thousand prisoners Hamas was demanding be released in exchange for Shalit.

The next day I made my way to Gaza, through the Erez Crossing, which is like crossing the river Styx. On one side is Israel, modern and clean with its LA attitude and beach culture—untucked shirts, flip-flops, girls with tattoos and pierced noses. To get to the Palestinian side, you walk nearly a mile through a tunnel with a metal roof and wire fencing on both sides. When you emerge, you feel as if you've stepped back fifty years. Trash and graffiti are everywhere. Bombed-out buildings stand like scarecrows.

I went to a small building where the Palestinian authorities are supposed to write down your passport information. Normally a man sits behind a desk with a log. Nothing is computerized. Not that it mattered: No one was at the desk. Hamas had just come into power, but was under attack and feared its border registration building would be bombed, so the place had been evacuated.

I arrived at night, dragging a suitcase with a flak jacket and helmet inside. I could hear explosions in the distance. I also realized I was standing next to a Hamas building and wanted to get away from it. I called our Gaza fixer, Wajjeh, who sent a van for the dangerous pickup. We saw no other cars on the road during the fifteen-minute drive to the center of Gaza City. The Israelis were bombing. I saw Hamas fighters huddled in small groups by doorways.

Israel had only turned over Gaza to the Palestinians the year before in keeping with the Bush administration's determination to plant democracy in the Middle East, on the shaky premise that democracies don't attack other democracies and that everything else would magically fall into place in the Middle East from there. So elections were held in Gaza, and the winner was Hamas, which promptly expelled its rival Fatah at gunpoint and kidnapped a soldier from democratic Israel.

Israel felt Gaza's thumb in its eye and decided it was time to send a strong message that would restore its aura of military invincibility and depose the Hamas-controlled government. The Israelis started bombing quickly and aggressively, hitting the centers of Hamas power—government buildings, police stations, and military outposts. Many Palestinians were killed. It was a big story, and I covered it extensively—until an even bigger one came along.

On July 12, Hezbollah, a Shiite extremist group in Lebanon, kidnapped two Israeli soldiers and killed eight others. News of the kidnapping was all over Palestinian radio and TV, and people in Gaza cheered in the streets. Dan Halutz, chief of the Israel Defense Forces, threatened to turn back "Lebanon's clock by twenty years" unless the kidnapped soldiers were returned. I knew Gaza would quickly become a sideshow to a much larger conflict.

Hezbollah was a far more serious adversary than Hamas. Backed by Iran, hardened by battles against the Israelis in southern Lebanon, Hezbollah was considered to be one of the most effective guerrilla armies in the world—dedicated, smart, disciplined, well trained, and creative. I suspected that Israel, even with its vaunted war machine, would have its hands full with Hezbollah in Lebanon.

Getting from Gaza to Beirut was not easy. They are close on a map, but worlds apart. At first light on July 13, I went back through the wormhole passage out of Gaza, drove to Tel Aviv, and flew to Jordan. (There are no flights from Israel to Lebanon; the two countries are still officially at war.) From Jordan I got a car to Syria. I then drove across Syria and got to the Syrian-Lebanese border at nightfall. The border was packed and chaotic with Lebanese fleeing into Syria. I had to get out of my car and walk the last half mile because traffic was such a snarl. I eventually got to the passport building, where I stood at the counter, frantically waving my passport in hopes of getting the border agent's attention. I knew the border would close at any minute, and I was desperate to cross before it did. I was finally stamped to exit Syria and enter Lebanon, one of the last people allowed in.

I changed to a Lebanese car and drove through the Bekaa Valley toward Beirut. The Israelis were already bombing the roads. The Bekaa is a Hezbollah stronghold, where many of its secret training camps are located. We drove with our lights out. Israel was targeting trucks to prevent Hezbollah from moving rockets from the Bekaa to the southern front along the Israeli border. After a white-knuckle drive I made it to Beirut just in time for the *Nightly News* (which broadcast live at 1:30 a.m. local time). The Israelis were already bombing the Beirut airport. I reported that Israel and the United States believed "that for decades Iran has used this airport to land 747s full of weapons and money for Hezbollah. Israel does not want the organization to be resupplied at this moment."

I could scarcely believe that my new home was engulfed by war before I even had time to find an apartment. It seemed that war followed me everywhere I went. In Jerusalem, the Second Intifada broke out nine months after I arrived. I went to Iraq believing that the United States would invade, and sure enough "shock and awe" lit up Baghdad. Then I moved to Beirut to get away from the killing, and two weeks later the Israelis were bombing an airport only five miles from my hotel.

Lebanese officials in the foreign media office (conspiratorial like most of their counterparts in the Middle East) thought my move to Beirut meant that I had advance warning that war was coming. They thought it was too much of a coincidence that NBC opened a bureau two weeks before the fighting started. Obviously it was happenstance, but it did change my opinion of human nature. I now saw war as a constant, akin to wildfires. They break out unless you work actively to prevent them. It's an atavistic thing, buried deep in our DNA.

The war in Lebanon was vastly different from the conflict in Iraq. The US approach in Iraq was to kill insurgents while also trying to win hearts and minds. The Americans conducted lots of limited raids and operations, and bomb and missile strikes were intended to be as "surgical" as possible. Iraq was a hit-and-run war. The Americans patrolled, gathered intelligence, then pounced. The insurgents blew them up whenever they could or responded by bombing soft targets like markets.

The Israelis weren't trying to win hearts and minds in Lebanon. Anything but. They set about flattening the south side of Beirut street by street and southern Lebanon village by village. The goal was to punish Hezbollah, and all of Lebanon, and teach them a lesson they would not soon forget. Israel had tired of the peace process. A new era in the Middle East had begun.

The war started amid misconceptions on both sides. The

exasperated Lebanese prime minister, Fouad Siniora, asked an aide to Hezbollah leader Hassan Nasrallah, "What have you done?" Hezbollah played only a small role in the Lebanese government, holding 14 of the 128 seats in parliament and 2 of the 24 cabinet posts, but it had more military muscle than Lebanon's armed forces. Siniora was assured that everything would calm down within a day or two. Nasrallah seemed to be gambling that Israel would settle for a prisoner swap. "We do not want to escalate things in the south," he said. "We do not want to push the region into war."

Israel, the warrior state, was for the first time being led by men, Prime Minister Ehud Olmert and Defense Minister Amir Peretz, who had no experience in military command. They relied on the advice of Dan Halutz, the first air force commander to become chief of staff of the Israel Defense Forces (IDF). Halutz believed the war could be won from the air, perhaps without any ground operations. Peretz thought the conflict would last ten to fourteen days. Olmert figured Hezbollah would sue for peace after a few days of aerial pounding. Most starry-eyed was Foreign Minister Tzipi Livni, who reportedly convinced herself that it would be over in twenty-four hours. They were all hopelessly and tragically wrong.

On the second day of the conflict, I did my stand-up on a hill overlooking Beirut's airport, which was being bombed again by Israeli warplanes. Flashes of light and thudding explosions created a dramatic backdrop. Then came a surreal scene. As a line of a dozen TV reporters trained their cameras on the airport, a crowd of cheering Lebanese came out of nowhere, including a Christian couple—she in her wedding dress, he in a dark suit with a boutonniere—who wanted to take their wedding picture with the airport going up in smoke behind them. Celebrating the destruction of their new airport by a foreign power showed how much some Lebanese hated Hezbollah, at least at the start of the hostilities.

The Lebanese people and their government were angry that Hezbollah had picked this fight just as the country was getting back on its feet after its civil war, a fifteen-year, multi-sectarian conflict that took 150,000 lives. The economy was booming, new roads were being paved, new bridges going up, and Lebanon was probably the most popular tourist destination for wealthy Arabs, and several Arab governments actually came to Israel's defense. Particularly gratifying, from an Israeli perspective, was Saudi Arabia's criticism of the "uncalculated adventures" that were exposing Arab states to "grave dangers." Fellow Sunni stalwarts Egypt and Jordan followed the Saudis' lead, making it a rare time that an important group of Arab states sided with the "Zionist foe" against other Arabs. The G8 leaders, meeting in St. Petersburg, blamed Hamas and Hezbollah for the crisis and said Israel had a right to defend itself. The United States cheered Israel on and ran diplomatic interference, which became increasingly important when Israel's conduct of the war came under criticism.

Israel's greatest military success was its first large operation, a thirty-four-minute air blitz in south Lebanon. The Israelis claimed to have knocked out fifty-nine stationary rocket launchers and two-thirds of Hezbollah's medium-range rockets, most of them supplied by Iran and concealed in and around the homes of Hezbollah activists.

But the second day of hostilities showed Israel's military intentions in a more disturbing light. Several miles to the east of my hotel in south Beirut, Israel dropped twenty-three tons of high explosives in the Dahiya neighborhood, on Hezbollah's headquarters in the capital. The stated aim was to kill Nasrallah and his high command in their underground bunker. The Israelis had dropped thousands of leaflets warning civilians to leave the area, and a good thing too: streets lined with apartment blocks were reduced to smoldering rubble. Hezbollah responded with an intensive rocket attack, for the first time hitting Haifa, twenty-five miles south of the border.

That evening, Nasrallah gave a live speech from his underground bunker in south Beirut. Accusing the Israelis of "changing the rules of the game," he said, "You wanted an open war, an open war is what you will get." An assistant handed him a note just as he was recalling that he had promised surprises during the war. He urged his listeners in Beirut to look out at the Mediterranean. "This is the first surprise. Right now, the Israeli warship at sea— look at it now, it's burning." An Israeli missile boat had been hit by an Iranian-made, radar-guided missile, disabling the vessel and killing four crew members.

Nasrallah was a savvy war leader, charismatic and smart. People in the Middle East sometimes made fun of him because he was pudgy and had a lisp, but he was well-spoken, even eloquent. When he made a threat, people believed it. Like Muqtada al-Sadr in Iraq, Nasrallah was a sayyid, a descendant of Mohammed. But Nasrallah had far greater gifts than Sadr. I always imagined that Nasrallah was the leader that Sadr dreamed of becoming.

In the first two days of the fighting, 73 Lebanese were killed and 200 wounded; 12 Israelis died and 150 were wounded. The Israelis imposed a total land, sea, and air blockade on Lebanon. To tighten its pinch, they attacked fuel depots, radar stations, ports and jetties, and even the new lighthouse near the Corniche. They blew up roads and bridges, as well as a power plant that supplied the electricity to most of south Lebanon. Hezbollah's rocket attacks only killed two Israelis, but they forced 220,000 people to seek refuge in shelters that were hot, unhygienic, and cramped after years of government neglect—the kind of indignity that proud Israelis thought was only suffered by the Arab side.

On July 16, a mere four days after the soldiers were kidnapped, I said on the *Nightly News* that parts of Lebanon were beginning to look like Baghdad. Israeli airstrikes were becoming increasingly indiscriminate, often with no apparent military purpose. I managed to get an interview with Lebanese prime minister Fouad Siniora, whose dismay at Hezbollah at the start of the war had turned to anger at Israel: "They talk about terror? They do terror every day." Siniora proposed a cease-fire, followed by a prisoner exchange, with Lebanese and UN troops replacing Hezbollah along the border. Nasrallah wasn't buying. The war, he said, was "just beginning."

With Hezbollah firing 150 to 180 short-range Katyusha rockets a day, Israel knew that its bombing campaign would not be enough to win the war and that ground action, perhaps even a full-scale invasion, would be needed to subdue the militants. But the Israelis were in for a rude shock. On July 19, eighteen men from the elite Maglan reconnaissance unit ventured less than a mile into Lebanon near a small village called Maroun al-Ras. They suspected that Hezbollah was using underground bunkers, but had no idea how sophisticated or numerous they were.

As they reached a summit next to the village, the Israelis found themselves surrounded by Hezbollah fighters. Two Maglan soldiers were killed and nine wounded, and after fierce fighting the Israelis killed five militants. An elite unit of paratroopers arrived in tanks to evacuate the Maglan soldiers only to get snared in another ambush. Surrounded and outnumbered, the Israelis got lucky: they captured a personal communication system from a Hezbollah fighter and, by listening to the militants' moves inside the village, were able to ambush and kill a number of Hezbollah fighters, sometimes at point-blank range. "We expected a tent and three Kalashnikovs—that was the intelligence we were given," said one soldier. "Instead, we found a hydraulic steel door leading to a well-equipped network of tunnels."

By the end of the first week, fifty-five thousand Lebanese had taken refuge in schools and one hundred thousand had crossed into Syria. British and French nationals, along with twenty-five thousand Americans, were being evacuated from Beirut by sea.

After reporting from Beirut for a week, I wanted to get to the southern part of the country to see the damage. Twice we turned back because the Israelis were targeting any vehicle on the roads, and we were virtually the only people driving. Bridges were out, highways were cut, and even a lot of side roads were impassable.

We finally made it to southern Lebanon on July 23. Our goal was to reach a town called Nabataea. Relentless Israeli airstrikes and shelling had turned it into a ghost town. Six square blocks had been reduced to rubble. Once there had been pharmacies and clothing stores, but only broken mannequins remained. At Nabataea's hospital, 115 residents had been treated for burns and shrapnel wounds.

The next day, following a trail of destruction toward the front line, we reached Tyre, the ancient Phoenician city a dozen or so miles up the coast from the Israeli border. Tyre was relatively safe, never carpet-bombed like south Beirut or the four-mile strip along the border, but dangerous enough that eighty thousand of its one hundred thousand inhabitants had fled. Along with other television journalists, we placed our camera at the Rest House hotel, which offered unobstructed views of the coastline.

I reported from there that US intelligence officials had told me that Israel had flown fifteen hundred combat sorties since the beginning of the war and fired more than twenty thousand rounds of artillery into south Lebanon. It was now estimated that seven hundred thousand people had fled their homes.

That same day, twenty miles to the southeast, Israel Special Forces launched an attack on Bint Jbeil, a town of twenty thousand. After a massive artillery barrage, Israeli troops made an inauspicious advance from the east. Five soldiers were wounded by friendly fire, and the two tanks sent to evacuate them were disabled by Hezbollah defenders—the first when struck by a missile, the second when it went over a remote-controlled mine. Then an armor-plated bulldozer attempting to rescue the tank casualties was repulsed after being hit by a missile. Two Israeli soldiers were killed and eighteen were wounded, and another two died when their attack helicopter, assigned to fly support for the ground forces, crashed on the Israeli side of the border.

The Israelis continued to get their noses bloodied in four days of fierce fighting at Bint Jbeil. They inflicted heavy casualties on Hezbollah, but the militiamen reportedly held four IDF divisions at bay with a company-size force of 100 to 140 men. The Winograd Commission, which at the behest of the Israeli government analyzed Israel's poor showing and the resilience of Hezbollah, said the failure to capture Bint Jbeil was "a symbol of the unsuccessful action of the Israel Defense Forces throughout the fighting."

The battles of Maroun al-Ras and Bint Jbiel revealed the massive failure of Israeli intelligence before the war. The IDF was unaware that southern Lebanon was catacombed with fortified bunkers and rocket launchers, "nature reserves" in the slang of Israeli soldiers. The Israeli air force needed only ninety seconds to pinpoint the spot from which an incoming missile was launched, but well-trained

Hezbollah firing teams needed less than a minute to fire rockets, lower the launching platforms back into the ground, and cover them with fire-retardant blankets to conceal their heat signatures.

All in all, it was a dismaying performance by the IDF, one of the world's most respected militaries: squabbling generals, senior officers who hunkered down in bunkers while their troops fought in Lebanon, lack of discipline even among well-trained regulars, reservists so unprepared for battle that commanders chose to hold them back. In a footnote of venality, Chief of Staff Dan Halutz, who was briefly hospitalized during the war, apparently due to stress, later admitted to selling $28,000 worth of his equities three hours after Hezbollah kidnapped the two Israeli soldiers.

Then came Qana. This small village in southern Lebanon is psychologically located at the intersection of Palestinian dreams and Israeli power. During the IDF's "Grapes of Wrath" offensive in 1996—a sixteen-day campaign aimed at stopping Hezbollah's shelling of northern Israel—the Israelis fired artillery shells at a UN compound in Qana, killing 106 Lebanese civilians and wounding 116 more.

On July 30, 2006, I was in Tyre with a bunch of other journalists when word came of another incident in Qana. My NBC crew was packed up and ready to leave, so we quickly headed for Qana, only eight miles away as the crow flies, arriving within a half hour.

We found a scene of anguish unlike any other I had seen in a war zone. Usually the victims of a bombing attack are mangled, too grisly to show on television. But in Qana, the victims were apparently killed by the percussive force of Israel's three-thousand-pound bombs or after suffocating in the wreckage. Twenty-eight people were killed, including sixteen children. I described the grim aftermath on *Meet the Press*:

"When we arrived, we saw this destroyed building. It was a three-story home under construction. There'd been dozens of people in the basement of this house, mostly women and children it appears. I counted eleven bodies of small boys, perhaps aged eight to ten. They were being carried out, some on stretchers; some being carried out wrapped in blankets, one body on top of the other. The bodies were intact, but had bled from their ears and from their noses. Then we went to the morgue and saw about twenty-two bodies lined up on the floor. They were wrapped in plastic, tied shut in packaging tape."

On the *Nightly News*, I reported that the "conflict may have reached a turning point with this single deadly attack." The war dragged on but international public opinion had turned sharply against the Israelis, shortening the time they had to achieve their war objectives. Siniora, the Lebanese prime minister, accused the Israelis of war crimes and asked, "Why, we wonder, did they choose Qana yet again?" The UN Security Council, following an emergency session, expressed "extreme shock and distress" at the bombing. Violent protests took place at UN offices in Beirut and Gaza, and thousands demonstrated in Israel, most of them in the Arab town of Umm al-Fahm but also in Tel Aviv and Haifa. The international reaction was harshly critical.

At first, Israel said it hit the building in Qana because Hezbollah was using it to fire Katyusha rockets across the border less than eight miles to the south, with villagers acting as "human shields," in the words of IDF chief Dan Halutz. Journalists and international observers emphatically disputed the claim, saying that Hezbollah was firing rockets from unpopulated areas off-limits to civilians.

The international outcry prompted Israel on July 31 to suspend airstrikes over southern Lebanon for forty-eight hours. Pressure was building for a permanent cease-fire and an end to the hostilities.

While the airstrikes were suspended, Israel sent thousands more troops into southern Lebanon to recapture the so-called security belt it had occupied between 1982 and 2000; this buffer, which reached several miles into Lebanese territory, was designed to create some space between Israeli civilians and militant groups north of the border.

By August 5, the IDF had ten thousand soldiers operating inside Lebanon, but they were mostly reservists who were undertrained, having spent the past few years on police duty in the West Bank and Gaza. They were poorly equipped and often lacked water, food, and ammunition. This was a far cry from the seemingly invincible IDF that had cowed Arabs in the past. Even so, the IDF announced on August 7 that it had completed plans for a full-scale ground invasion.

At the same time, the UN was feverishly working on the framework for a cease-fire. On August 11, Olmert reviewed the draft of the UN plan, which called for an international force of fifteen thousand peacekeepers to be deployed along the border and for an arms embargo to be imposed in order to prevent Hezbollah from acquiring more weapons. Significantly, however, the cease-fire was not conditioned upon the return of the two kidnapped Israeli soldiers, whose kidnapping had triggered the bloody conflict. The agreement was accepted by Hezbollah and the Lebanese government on August 12 and by the Israeli government on August 13.

By then, Olmert had launched the ground invasion, a last gasp to assert military superiority on the ground. Once again, the IDF got its nose bloodied by Hezbollah guerrillas. Two dozen tanks were sent to join paratroopers supposedly holding the high ground at a village called Ghandoriyah. The column ran smack into a Hezbollah tank trap and came under a barrage of Russian-made Kornet antitank missiles. The paratroopers, meanwhile, were getting an awful surprise of their own. They suddenly found themselves pinned down by Hezbollah fighters who had been lying low, waiting for an opportune moment to strike.

By the time the misbegotten incursion ended, twelve Israeli soldiers had been killed and fifty wounded. Eleven of Israel's supposedly indestructible Merkava Mark IV tanks had been hit. All told, thirty-three Israeli soldiers died in the war's last sixty hours, one-fourth of the IDF's fatalities in the conflict. At least five hundred Hezbollah militants were killed.

Critics would say Israel did itself no honor in another attempt to get in last licks before the cease-fire took effect at 8:00 a.m. on August 14, 2006. Both sides fired cluster bombs, but Israel was by far the greatest offender, showering Lebanon with nearly 4.2 million submunitions in the last seventy-two hours of the war, more than 90 percent of the total it fired during the whole thirty-four-day conflict. Some of the bomblets were newly manufactured, others were US munitions dating to the Vietnam War. Driving around south Lebanon after the cease-fire, I saw unexploded cluster bombs and other ordnance almost everywhere I looked.

The Lebanon war had been a debacle for the Israelis. The vaunted IDF destroyed towns but did not manage to actually *capture* one. It was even worse from a public-relations standpoint. For decades, Israel had claimed the moral high ground over its Arab enemies, taking pride in its "purity of arms."

In most countries, the performance of Israel's military would have been a disgrace, but in Israel it became a doctrine, named after the Hezbollah stronghold that was flattened in south Beirut. As articulated by Israeli general Gadi Eizenkot, the Dahiya Doctrine pertains to asymmetric warfare in an urban setting, in which the army targets civilian infrastructure to prevent the enemy from using it for military purposes. That's military-speak and doesn't reflect what Israel did in Lebanon in 2006. The object of the Dahiya Doctrine was to hit the enemy, and the civilians living nearby, so hard that the enemy dare not try to hit back, at least for some time. The idea is if you can't beat your enemy in urban battles, inflict so much suffering on the civilian population of the city, or the country, that the people turn on the enemy and demand that it not attack again.

The Dahiya Doctrine recalled the bombing of civilians in World War II to try to break the enemy's morale, a strategy whose efficacy is still debated. But when Israelis are asked how they can justify destroying more than a quarter of Lebanon—125,000 houses and apartments, 91 bridges, highways, and roads the length and breadth of the country—they have a ready answer: after 2006, Israel enjoyed years of peace and quiet from its northern neighbor. The doctrine of pain seemed to have bought peace for Israel, at least in the short term.

A big question is what will happen to the Dahiya Doctrine when Israel meets a foe that can match its military technology at least in terms of inflicting an equal or greater number of civilian deaths and infrastructure damage on the Israeli side.

For me, the Lebanon war was a milestone. It was a war that ended without even an attempt to resolve the core grievances. It was a war designed to be painful to dissuade a hostile group, in this case Hezbollah, from attacking again. It assumed that when conflicts are complicated—and hostilities ingrained—that they can only be resolved by the fear of more pain and death. It assumes a perpetual state of unresolvable hostilities in the Middle East.

SIX

I TURNED THIRTY-THREE SHORTLY AFTER I BEGAN SETTLING DOWN IN BEIRUT AFTER
the month-long Lebanon war. I was fulfilling my ambition, covering the biggest story of my generation, and I was being rewarded
with praise and promotions from my bosses at NBC. But I sure
wasn't living a normal life.

For years I had frenetically covered the fighting in Iraq, spending six or eight weeks in the war zone, then pulling out for a couple
of weeks of R & R at a hotel in Thailand or Italy, then returning
to the nerve-jangling violence of Baghdad. Then when I finally got
the go-ahead to set up a bureau in Beirut—which I thought would

bring a modicum of stability to my life—the Israelis and Hezbollah started killing each other.

The shooting finally stopped on August 14, 2006, and I found the apartment of my dreams in Beirut on a small, historic street near the Albergo Hotel. Ironically the apartment had been vacated by an Italian diplomat during the fighting. Israel was bombing Hezbollah strongholds in south Beirut both from the air and from the sea and at times the fighting was getting close to the center of the city.

So now I had a place to call home. I started dating again and had a lively social life, unremarkable for a single guy my age unless you're a single guy who had spent the past few years putting your mattress against hotel windows as a defense against car bombs.

I had a broader journalistic portfolio now, but Iraq was still at the center of the action. The triumphant US invasion had become a sectarian struggle that was far more savage and sinister and seemed to go on forever. To understand why, you have to go back to the debate over the American invasion. President Bush seemed obsessed with Iraq. He believed that if the United States got rid of Saddam Hussein and instituted democratic reforms, the Middle East—and the world—would be a safer and better place. He seemed to have no idea, however, how it would happen. The administration often used the analogy of planting the "seeds of democracy" in the Middle East, as if they'd sprout into democratic regimes as nature took its course. Democracy doesn't sprout like apple trees. Scattering the seeds isn't enough, no matter how many soldiers do it. To continue with the gardening analogy the Bush administration seemed to love (there were also many "seeds of terror" and "seeds of hope"), democracy is more like a fragile flower that requires constant attention and the right soil. Dictatorships and fascist regimes are hardy weeds that sprout on their own.

The casus belli, of course, was Iraq's purported arsenal of weapons of mass destruction (WMD). A secondary rationale was an alleged link between Saddam and al-Qaeda. "We've learned that Iraq has trained al-Qaeda members in bomb-making and poisons and deadly gases," Bush said on October 7, 2002, five months before the invasion.

I thought this was preposterous, as did most people familiar with the Middle East, but the supposed presence of WMDs made it a secondary concern. Saddam sometimes pretended he was a true-blue Muslim by commissioning a copy of the Koran purportedly written with twenty-eight liters of his own blood. In 2001, he burnished his Islamic-warrior image with the completion of the Mother of All Battles mosque in western Baghdad. It had minarets shaped like Scud missiles.

But Saddam was no Islamist and saw Islam mostly as a propaganda tool. He drank whiskey. He smoked cigars. He liked nice suits. He did not dream about the seventh century. He lived very much in the twenty-first century. A brutal dictator, he did not tolerate dissent, much less a bunch of extremists who wanted to topple him and restore the caliphate. Al-Qaeda was his enemy, not his friend.

Another factor in the decision to invade Iraq was that the war in Afghanistan, which began less than a month after 9/11, had been too easy. To use a phrase military leaders love, the US "overlearned" the lesson of Afghanistan. In just three months after 9/11, at a cost of only a billion dollars and one American life, US airstrikes, 110 CIA operatives, and 300 Special Forces scored a decisive victory. Working in concert with Afghan tribesmen, who were paid according to the amount of lethal force they used against the enemy, the United States toppled the Taliban and prompted a hasty retreat by al-Qaeda, which at the time only had several hundred fighters. The small American force in Afghanistan would likely have captured Osama bin Laden after the battle at Tora Bora in December 2001, but the Defense Department, pointing to its early success, rejected the request for eight hundred additional soldiers to chase down al-Qaeda in the rough mountainous terrain.

If those eight hundred troops had been sent in and bin Laden was captured or killed back in 2001, it is possible the United States would never have invaded Iraq. Perhaps the defense establishment, the Iraq war lobby, and the neocons around the president would have been satisfied that Washington got its revenge after 9/11 and had something to show for it, bin Laden's head. Instead, toppling the Taliban and sending al-Qaeda into hiding was a quick, mostly covert, and cheap affair. Washington had little to point to and tell the American people that 9/11 had been avenged. Ousting the Taliban should have been the end of the Global War on Terrorism, known by the ugly acronym GWOT, but the United States couldn't walk away from the blackjack table. Aside from Bush's personal, family preoccupation with Iraq, the generals at the Pentagon hadn't got their piece of the action. Afghanistan, at least at first, had been so easy and quick, many assumed Iraq would be just as simple, with far greater rewards. Iraq would be a *real* war, with troops in uniform, where officers could win medals and command men in battle, far different from the CIA-led mission that tossed out the Taliban in the blink of an eye. Even though the Iraq war would prove to be a failure, its proponents were right about a few things. How many generals did the American public know before 9/11? After the war, how many became presidential advisors, special envoys, lobbyists, consultants for arms manufacturers, and analysts for oil companies and hedge funds? So the United States went into Iraq, expanded its military operation in Afghanistan, rotated 2 million troops through the war zones, left seven thousand Americans dead, fifty-two thousand wounded, a million US veterans filing for some form of disability, caused the deaths of two hundred thousand Muslims—perhaps many more, depending on the estimate—spent a few trillion dollars, and created some choice real estate for hyperviolent extremists.

When the inspectors could not find WMDs, Iraq's alleged ties with al-Qaeda took on greater importance as a justification for military action. Then the American proconsul, Paul "Jerry" Bremer, dissolved the Iraqi army and gave Shiites control of the country for the first time in fourteen centuries, stripping the minority Sunnis of their self-respect, stoking their sectarian rage, and sending them into the arms of Sunni extremists.

Al-Qaeda flocked to Iraq like moths to a flame, making the claims of the Bush administration a self-fulfilling prophecy. Abu Musab al-Zarqawi, a protégé of bin Laden's, turned Iraq into a sectarian killing field.

I watched all this unfold while covering the aftermath of the invasion. The Sunni-Shiite civil war ushered in a level of brutality that was unrivaled even in a region known for bloody excess. To the dismay of al-Qaeda leaders holed up in Pakistan and Afghanistan, Zarqawi made Shiites the primary enemy, not Americans. And he understood how to use the Internet to spread the pornography of violence, digitally recruiting young Sunni men with visions of martyrdom and the solace of dark-eyed virgins in the afterlife.

Bin Laden never did this because he had neither the means nor the inclination. Bin Laden mostly released audio messages and the occasional low-quality video. But the United States had helpfully wired Iraq so everyone could use a cell phone—and, as an unintended consequence, get access to Zarqawi's gruesome videos. Which is why, in the historical accounting, Zarqawi and not bin Laden may be viewed as the transformative figure in Islamist terrorism. An American airstrike killed him in 2006, but he had by then created the template for ISIS. ISIS evolved over time, first as al-Qaeda in Iraq and then striking out on its own.

THE BUSH ADMINISTRATION KEPT CLAIMING THAT THE WAR IN IRAQ WAS MAKING American cities and towns safer. Fighting terrorism became the main rationale for the war after WMDs weren't found and the "seeds of democracy" didn't seem to be sprouting. I can't remember how many times I heard the president, US diplomats in Baghdad, and American troops quote the phrase: "fight them [the terrorists] over there [in Iraq], so we won't have to fight them over here [in the United States]." It became almost a religious mantra, defense by constant offense. Kill the monsters in their lair before they could come to the United States and kill us. US troops were told they were in Iraq to keep the terrorists from blowing up shopping malls back home and therefore saw most Iraqis as potential enemies, which complicated the fact that they were also told to build communities and win hearts and minds. In reality, by occupying Iraq for years and by reopening old religious wounds and upsetting the old order, the US invasion was making a terrorist attack in the United States more likely than it would have been otherwise. Iraq had nothing to do with 9/11 and wasn't a nest full of terrorists. By being "over there" we were making terrorists want to come "over here." At least that's what I suspected as the war dragged into its fourth year. I traveled to several countries to find out if the war in Iraq was feeding terrorism or, as the administration claimed, was keeping it at bay. Zarqa, a Jordanian city just across from the Iraqi border, was my first stop. It was al-Qaeda's principal stronghold in Jordan and the birthplace of Zarqawi. Rarely visited by uniformed police, Zarqa was a place where Sunni hard-liners barely concealed their activities.

I arranged an interview with a low-level al-Qaeda-in-Iraq operative called Abu Zaal, who sold songbirds from his pet shop. A dwarf of a man, bent by his hunched back, he launched a harangue against the United States with the villainous glee of a character in a James Bond movie. But his tone turned deadly serious when he talked about fighting for al-Qaeda in Baghdad, Fallujah, and Ramadi: "America is dirtier than the devil because they kill Muslims. There is going to be a day when all Muslims become al-Qaeda." In the meantime, he wanted to kill American soldiers. And Iranian soldiers. And Shiites, whatever their nationality. As for me, I was just an average American guy he was proud and happy to talk to. He was living in a great historic moment and reveled in what he was doing. He had punched his jihadist ticket. He was bubbling with the kind of energy I saw among many Sunnis during that period.

My next stop was Amman, to interview Abdullah al-Mujahir, who had been one of Zarqawi's henchmen. I would not have chanced a meeting with him in Zarqa; it would have been too dangerous. Abu Zaal was more of a fixer, a low-level logistics man. Al-Mujahir, as he called himself, was a stone-cold killer. In later years he probably would have ended up in ISIS, happily setting people on fire. The interview was set up by NBC's fixer in Amman and took place in a private home. As I look back, I'm thankful I met Mujahir in Jordan in 2007. If I encountered him in Syria in 2015, he probably would have been standing behind me with a knife at my throat.

He arrived (and left) with his face mostly covered, taking care not to be spotted by Jordan's efficient intelligence service. Thickly set, he was forty or so, but his weather-beaten face—I could see around his eyes—made him look older. I was particularly interested in him because I had heard that he'd produced a number of al-Qaeda's beheading videos. Tapping his laptop with gnarled fingers, he brought up some of the videos on the screen. Not only was he the producer, he was also an actor. He claimed to have participated in attacks.

He showed me how easy it was to make the videos. Point and shoot, and edit with the same software that you'd use to record your family sitting in front of the fireplace on Christmas morning. "The slaughter videos," he said, "are meant to show that we can kill who we want, whenever we want—and to terrify American soldiers who don't want to die this way."

Mujahir said he was unconcerned about having his videos tracked by US and other foreign intelligence agencies. "There are so many different ways to avoid them," he said, declining to be specific. In any event, he said, the Muslim warriors occupied the moral high ground: "Our death sends us to heaven; your death sends you to hell."

His companion that day was a barefoot man named Jaffar, who looked to be in his early twenties. He had seen "his brothers" fighting in the Palestinian territories and Iraq and decided he wanted to be a mujahid, a career choice supported by his family. He was, to be blunt, a moron. He was also a dreamer ("I will be married to maidens in Paradise") and had been thoroughly brainwashed. I asked Mujahir, in Jaffar's earshot, what Jaffar could possibly do since he didn't have any training and didn't seem very bright. "He will most likely be a suicide bomber," Mujahir said. "He could drive a car or wear a suicide belt. He won't be wasted." If Jaffar was disturbed by his expendability, he didn't show it.

My next stop was Tripoli, in northern Lebanon, to meet with Sheikh Bilal Baroudi, who had recognized early on that the conflict in Iraq was creating hundreds of video clips and photographs that could be useful in the jihad. If they were in the movie business, Mujahir would be running a movie studio and Bilal would be overseeing Netflix. While the two were pursuing the same end, they couldn't have been more different. In contrast to the grizzled fighter Mujahir, Bilal was so smooth that he could have been poolside at the Beverly Hills Hotel. He was a dandy. He kissed both my cheeks. He was well perfumed. He was friendly, jolly, and charismatic. He gave me tea.

Bilal and I talked in his basement media center where he was training young men to use jihadist websites and chat rooms without being traced or entrapped by foreign intelligence services. "The jihad has become open to everyone," he said. "Someone from Turkmenistan can come to a camp in Lebanon to fight. But at the same time, it is a weak point because [the Internet] causes young men to get excited about things without preparing, and then they are easily caught."

Images of Abu Ghraib prison, where the US Army tortured and abused detainees, and the Haditha killings of twenty-four unarmed Iraqis by US Marines, were immensely powerful propaganda. But al-Qaeda in Iraq figured out that the Internet could be more than a recruiting tool. Militants no longer needed to travel to Afghanistan or Pakistan for training. They could simply stay at home and train online. But as Bilal pointed out, digital training requires special caution: "There are many sites that claim to show how to make a bomb, but many of them are put up by intelligence services just fishing for young people."

After visiting Jordan and Lebanon it was already clear the Iraq war was both attracting Islamic extremists and radicalizing the new recruits. US troops, it seemed to me, were creating more enemies than they were killing.

To get another look at Sunnis who went to Iraq to join the al-Qaeda resistance, I went to Ain al-Hilweh, the largest—and probably most dangerous—Palestinian refugee camp in Lebanon. I found it revealing, and disturbing, that Palestinians were leaving the camp to fight in Iraq, their long grievances with Israel morphing into a hatred of the US presence in Iraq. It wasn't that their anger had shifted away from Israel—they still hated Israel—but there was little they could do to attack Israel, which tightly controls its borders. They could, however, go to Iraq to join the fight to defend Muslim pride, specifically Sunni pride—and through it their own pride. I thought it was dangerous that Palestinians and other aggrieved groups were finding a common cause in the Iraq war. If a Muslim was oppressed in Tunisia, Saudi Arabia, or Egypt by his own oppressive US-backed government, but couldn't express his anger, US troops in Iraq were an inviting and open path to vengeance, redemption, and if you believe the rhetoric, to Paradise. In the Internet age, Iraq was becoming a jihad meme, a trending topic for millions of Muslims angry for his or her own reasons.

It was even more predictable than the way al-Qaeda was created. Al-Qaeda was founded when jihadists were used and then abandoned by Muslim governments and the CIA, until they eventually found a home in Afghanistan under the Taliban. This time, a new breed of Islamists was being created because of the Iraq war and Sunni humiliation. I feared the consequences would be worse, and this new crop of extremists was forming under our eyes.

Established in 1948, when roughly seven hundred thousand Palestinians fled or were forced from their homes after Israel declared itself an independent Jewish state, Ain al-Hilweh was crammed with seventy thousand people.

The camp was seething with anger, mostly at Israel but also at the United States, Israel's patron. The refugees also resented the Arab states for not doing anything about the camps and not integrating them into their societies—a policy designed to keep the Palestinian "cause" alive. In short, the refugees hated everybody, and because Ain al-Hilweh was a tinderbox of splinter groups—Marxists, socialists, Palestinian nationalists, the PLO, Islamists, and countless groups that have died out everywhere else on the planet—they often hated one another.

So it was no surprise that militant leaders in the camp claimed to have sent at least fifty suicide bombers to Iraq, among the most from any single location in the world. I went to Ain al-Hilweh primarily to interview Munir Hadad, who was reputedly recruiting young people to fight in Iraq. A news outlet in Lebanon had called the camp the "zone of unlaw," and once I was inside, it was easy to see why. Our team would be safe in Munir's section, but getting there was a hair-raising affair. Every street seemed to be controlled by a different gang, with checkpoints between sections of the camp. Men walked around with rifles slung over their shoulders. Islamists with long beards rode motorcycles and gave us hard stares. Even the Lebanese Army steered clear of Ain al-Hilweh.

"You see mujahideen who are volunteering and going to Iraq by themselves," Munir said. "Iraq is the closest place they can go and fight Americans." He said they were aroused by the American "massacres" of Iraqis: "When they see these massacres on television, they cannot handle it. Violence creates violence. Terrorism creates terrorism."

One of the mujahideen was Asid Jabr, thirty-six, an unemployed security guard and father of four. As he walked down an alleyway to meet us, he carried a semiautomatic rifle. A gaggle of children skipped in front of him. He cleaned his gun as he explained why he was going to Iraq. "Our duty is to fight the occupation in any Arab country. God has given us the right to fight whether it is in Palestine or Iraq.

Fear goes with the job when you're covering this part of the world, and you depend on a sixth sense to make sure you go when the going is good. "We're leaving the camp," I said on my broadcast sign-off. "We noticed we were being followed. Men riding motorcycles who weren't affiliated with our contact were circling, watching us. We've decided to just pack it in and leave right now."

The more I traveled, the more it became clear that the fighting in Iraq was impacting the entire region, and not for the better. I went to Syria to gauge its effects, as reflected both in attitudes toward the United States and in tangible social consequences. Iraq and Syria share a long border drawn by the European powers after World War I. Despite their interwoven histories, the two countries have had long periods of disagreeable relations since their partition. But at the time of my arrival—four years before the onset of the Syrian civil war—the Syrians were sympathetic to their neighbor, holding the US government responsible for the bloodshed in Iraq.

The people I spoke with took pains to distinguish the American people from President Bush and his policies. When Bush called for a "crusade" against terrorism in the week after 9/11, the word passed almost without notice in the United States, but it struck a deep historical chord in the Middle East, where a thousand years of history vibrate in the collective memory.

THE WORD *CRUSADE* TRANSLATES IN ARABIC AS *HARB SALIBIYA*, OR A "WAR OF the cross," a reference to the seven major European incursions sanctioned by popes, kings, and princes for several centuries beginning at the end of the eleventh century. The object of these military campaigns was to gain control of the holy places in or near Jerusalem, save Byzantium, the Christian Roman Empire founded by Constantine, and destroy the Muslim infidels. They were clashes of civilizations long before political scientists started using the phrase. Many in the Muslim world believe the Crusades have never ended, and Bush's comments after 9/11 only reinforced their thinking. As I would hear over and over, from Zarqa to Lebanon and now in Syria, "The US war on terror is a war against Islam."

Another source of anger in Syria was the flood of Iraqi refugees, most of them poor. (Rich refugees tended to go to Jordan.) The social and moral consequences of the influx were visible in neon on the outskirts of Damascus. What had been desert was now a strip packed with dozens of sleazy nightclubs, each featuring fifty to a hundred young girls, almost all of them Iraqi refugees forced into the sex trade to support their families.

The owner of a place called the Lighthouse let us film inside his club because he thought it would be good advertising. The girls were barely pubescent (and some clearly weren't), and they wore belly-dancing costumes covered with sequins. They didn't strip and danced only occasionally. Mostly they marched around the stage like prisoners in a small exercise yard. They were displaying their wares for a few dozen men from Syria, Kuwait, and Saudi Arabia.

This was not the kind of prostitution bazaar you'd find in Moscow or in the lap-dancing emporiums in America. The Lighthouse was not a place for transactions. The men didn't offer the girls money to come home with them for the night. If a customer was interested in a girl, he would talk to her father or uncle or male guardian. They would haggle over price and terms the next day. If a deal was struck, the girl would become the man's sexual property for a week, a month, six months, or for as long as he was interested.

When a young Iraqi man watched his sister pimped out by his dad, the effect was grimly predictable. As likely as not, he would quickly be radicalized and eager to join the mujahideen. So the cycle of violence took yet another turn. Iraqis driven out of their country because of the fighting returned to their country to fight. The cycle of violence was a challenge for many countries in the region. A Sunni state might turn a blind eye to its nationals aiding the Sunni cause in Iraq, but the return home of battle-hardened veterans promised nothing but trouble.

Saudi Arabia caught on to the threat early on and, with its vast resources, was determined to prevent a new generation of extremists, battle-hardened in Iraq, from returning to the Saudi kingdom. The government set up a rehabilitation program for jihadists and released Gitmo detainees. The Saudi approach was similar to the kind of tough love used in alcohol and drug rehab facilities in the States.

We were given access to the program's "campus," which was a large walled-in compound that had once been a resort. The al-Qaeda veterans were free to swim in one of four pools, kick soccer balls around manicured lawns, and play video games. Meals of lamb and rice were served Saudi-style from communal bowls. There was even room service. The main gate was locked, and the outside walls were topped by barbed wire, but no armed guards were in sight.

The only requirement was that "patients" attend daily classes, most of which were taught by Islamic clerics. The goal was to convince them that al-Qaeda's interpretation of Islam was incorrect. *Jihad* is often translated into English as "holy war," but in Arabic it means "a struggle"—to purify a soul, for instance, or to defend the faith with arms or with words. The message of the rehabilitation program was that true Islam was the Islam of peace, not of beheadings. The other message was: once you come home, leave your jihad at the door and all will be forgiven.

Most of the men being treated had become unhinged by images they saw on the Internet or television. "It seems to us that the international conflicts in Israel, in Palestine, in Afghanistan, were the main motivator for them," said Dr. Abdulrahman Al-Hadlaq, the program's director. "So when they see those atrocities, they want to help, they want to do something."

Saddam Sagami, twenty, was making a sculpture for art class when I sat down next to him on the floor. "I heard about jihad and Palestine and how Muslims were being killed, so I went online and searched for *jihad* on Google," he said. "I started contacting jihadis, and we started sharing opinions until I decided I wanted to be part of the jihad and maybe go to Afghanistan or Pakistan." But those countries were too far away so Sagami went to Iraq instead, to fight US troops and the Shiite-led government. He was arrested and deported back to Saudi Arabia, where he spent two years in prison, and finally ended up in rehab. His story was typical. All the al-Qaeda members I spoke with at the clinic told me they felt it was their duty to defend oppressed Muslims anywhere: in Afghanistan, Chechnya, or Palestine, but that Iraq was easiest to get to. And there were American troops there, who were responsible for crimes like those committed in Abu Ghraib. And those things were being posted on the Internet. I've long believed in what I call the real estate law of terrorism: location, location, location. Afghanistan was far away from the Arab world, cold, mountainous, and its people spoke exotic and difficult languages. Iraq was close, Arabic-speaking, familiar to everyone in the Arab world, and had the great advantage of a US troop presence that was providing a steady supply of propaganda opportunities. A few years later, Syria would prove to be just as inviting to Muslims looking for a place to fight.

Dr. Turki al-Otyan, one of the program's forty psychologists, said the radicals were mostly "followers" who were often stirred into action by their feelings, not their intellects. "They are not confident. They feel depression, they see emotional things, they cry."

In short, they were hotheaded and broken men, and the program was trying to put them back together again. "It's very important to bring them back to society, to let them settle down, to let them live a normal life," Al-Hadlaq said. "We try to find jobs for them. We encourage them to get married—as a matter of fact, we help them financially with their weddings. . . . If a man gets married, he will be busy with his wife, with his kids, he will think of other needs. And we think that's very important emotionally."

The man I was most eager to see in Saudi Arabia had little to do with Iraq but everything to do with al-Qaeda. Now that bin Laden is much smaller in death than he had been in life, it's easy to forget that in 2007 anyone who had caught a glimpse of the terrorist historian was journalistic gold, and Khalid Sulayman was fourteen karat. (He is not to be confused with a man with a similar name who was arrested on terrorism charges in Australia in 2014.)

Sulayman, then thirty-two, was easily the best-known graduate of the rehabilitation program. He was drawn to Afghanistan in the 1990s by videotapes of Muslims getting killed in Bosnia, Chechnya, and the Philippines, and he arrived there with several important attributes. He had a Saudi passport, which meant he could travel anywhere. He had never appeared on the radar of any of the intelligence services so would not set off alarms when he crossed a border. And he had a background in engineering, which suggested an aptitude for making bombs.

Bin Laden had set up a network of training camps, each housing about forty men. "So you can call it the University of the Jihad," Khalid told me when we met in Jeddah. Al-Qaeda's heavy hitters were at the camps: the bloodthirsty Zarqawi and Ayman al-Zawahiri, the Egyptian surgeon who had by this time become bin Laden's personal physician and who would become al-Qaeda's leader after bin Laden's death.

Khalid was popular in the camps, and because he was young, fit, and smart, he was groomed for leadership. The duller men were trained as foot soldiers. Khalid went through one round of training, then went back before 9/11 for a refresher. "I got training on weapons, mines, explosives, electronics, all these things," he said.

Rumors were that al-Qaeda was trying to acquire nuclear weapons, and some of the camps were experimenting with chemical weapons on dogs and rabbits. In June 2001, Khalid picked up a buzz that something big was in the works. He was called to meet bin Laden, who offered him land and help in building a home so he could start a life in Afghanistan. Khalid asked bin Laden what he'd have to do in exchange for the leader's patronage. "You don't let us down," bin Laden said, "we don't let you down."

Three months later came the dramatic strikes against the World Trade Center and the Pentagon. "Even bin Laden was shocked when the buildings fell down," Khalid said. "He thought the planes would just hit the buildings and just make some damage." Khalid was surprised that so many of the hijackers were Saudis. They were not known in Afghanistan, which of course was why the 9/11 plotters selected them.

When the United States launched Operation Jawbreaker against the Taliban and al-Qaeda in Afghanistan, Khalid went with bin Laden and al-Qaeda's high command to Tora Bora, a cave complex in the White Mountains in the eastern part of the country. He stayed in bin Laden's bunker one night, then bin Laden moved everyone to another bunker. Two nights later the first bunker was destroyed by an American airstrike. An Afghan, apparently carrying a GPS locator chip, had met with bin Laden. "And that guy, he was killed because he was sleeping in that bunker," Khalid said.

With Tora Bora under attack, bin Laden simply left the camp on foot reportedly on or around December 16, 2001, accompanied only by one of his sons and a bodyguard. Zawahiri left too, taking a different route. The next day, Khalid and some small groups followed, and two days after that the rest of the al-Qaeda fighters left Tora Bora. Khalid's group trudged through the snow-covered mountains for six days. Then some Afghans, who had previously worked for bin Laden, said they would guide Khalid and his companions to Pakistan and hide them there.

It was a betrayal. They were arrested by the Pakistanis, handed over to the Americans, and taken to the US base in Kandahar, Afghanistan's second-largest city. Khalid said the treatment there was harsh. Stripped naked in the frigid detainment area, the al-Qaeda prisoners were given only one meal a day and were beaten while they were interrogated. "Many people lost their minds," Khalid said. "They became mental, you know."

In January 2002, Khalid and other al-Qaeda prisoners were taken to Guantánamo Bay. Again they were stripped of their clothes and beaten, he said, but it was better than Kandahar: "We at least had three meals. You could pray. You had water." And it was warm. Khalid was given an orange jumpsuit and an identification number: JJE 155.

Three years later, Khalid was repatriated to Saudi Arabia where he was held for eleven months in al-Ha'ir Prison twenty-five miles south of Riyadh. He underwent medical and psychological examinations, and his family came to visit for a week. It was the first time he had seen his relations in five years.

He was deemed ready for the rehabilitation program, probably because he said he had begun a critical examination of his life while still at Gitmo. He said he had come to understand that he had wronged his family, his country—and himself. The rehab program smoothed his reentry into society in a fairly lavish way. The Saudi authorities bought him a car, paid for his wedding, gave him $20,000 to rent and furnish an apartment, and provided a stipend of $800 a month until he could find a job.

When we met at his apartment, Khalid was not at all what

I expected from a man who'd once sworn loyalty to bin Laden. He was exceptionally friendly, even lighthearted. He was unfailingly polite, thanking me for coming to visit and bringing us cans of Pepsi and glasses on a metal tray. For the several hours we sat together, I can't remember a time when he wasn't smiling. That surprised me. Al-Qaeda doesn't normally attract happy people. Maybe Khalid changed in prison. Or maybe he was the lone happy-go-lucky warrior in al-Qaeda.

To get a final assessment of whether the invasion had made Iraq and the United States safer countries or were simply fueling al-Qaeda–style fanaticism, I visited the National Counterterrorism Center (NCTC) in Washington at the end of August 2007. The center had been established because a primary criticism after 9/11 was the lack of communication between America's intelligence arms. In the main hall of the NCTC, CIA analysts sat on one side and FBI agents on the other, supposedly so they could compare notes in the event of a terrorist threat.

The director of the center, retired admiral John Scott Redd, was clearly uncomfortable talking about Iraq, which seemed odd. Iraq was being billed by the White House as the centerpiece in a grand Global War on Terrorism, so important to keeping Americans safe that it was worth dozens of American lives and billions of dollars every month, yet the official in charge of counterterrorism in America didn't want to talk about it. When I suggested that Iraq had become a major recruiting tool for al-Qaeda, he conceded that "in the short term, that's probably true." I asked if the United States was safer than it had been before 9/11. "Tactically? Probably not," he said. "Strategically? We'll wait and see."

Redd said the United States was doing a far better job collecting, analyzing, and sharing information about terrorist threats and estimated that it had foiled a half dozen plots. "We've gone on offense," he said. "We haven't waited for another attack. We've gone after terrorists around the world." But Redd was under no illusion that the battle against terrorism would be quick or easy. "The Cold War lasted forty years. I suspect this one's going to last that long." It was a cop-out. Terrorism is an ancient tactic. It was used forty years ago and four hundred years ago. Weak enemies use terrorism to attack adversaries they cannot defeat. There will be terrorism forty years from now. My question was whether the Iraq war was helping would-be terrorists or hurting them. I was asking if it was true that we were "fighting them over there so we wouldn't have to fight them over here." After months of traveling and reporting I came to believe that Washington was trying to put out the fires of terrorism with gasoline.

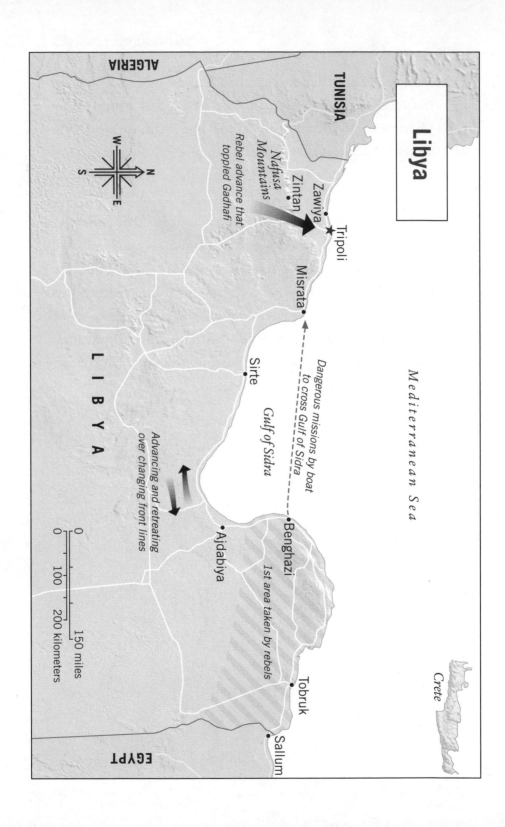

Libya

TUNISIA

ALGERIA

EGYPT

Mediterranean Sea

Crete

Zintan

Zawiya

★ Tripoli

Misrata

Sirte

Gulf of Sidra

Ajdabiya

Benghazi

Tobruk

Sallum

L I B Y A

Nafusa Mountains

Rebel advance that toppled Gadhafi

Dangerous missions by boat to cross Gulf of Sidra

Advancing and retreating over changing front lines

1st area taken by rebels

N
W   E
S

0   0
100   150 miles
200 kilometers

SEVEN

THE NEXT COUPLE OF YEARS WERE AN UNSETTLED TIME FOR ME. LIKE MOST companies, NBC retrenched after the financial crisis in 2008. The network downsized its bureau in Beirut, and I was called back to New York to cover the Middle East long distance, parachuting into the region when major stories broke. I gave up my dream apartment in Beirut and began living out of a suitcase in New York hotels.

I understood why NBC had to cut costs, but I wasn't happy about it. I grew up in New York, but after so many years abroad, I wasn't a New Yorker anymore, and I felt too far away from the action to stay ahead of the news. I didn't move to Cairo in 1996 and learn Arabic to do mop-up reports on stories that had already moved on the AP wire.

Staying in hotels also got old in a hurry, so in 2009 I bought a walk-up apartment in the West Chelsea neighborhood of Manhattan. The place badly needed renovating, which took almost a year. I went on a lot of long reporting trips so I could get away from the city. But New York was a blessing in one respect: I began a relationship with Mary Forrest, now my wife and mother of our child.

I didn't take much notice when a Tunisian street vendor named Mohamed Bouazizi set himself on fire to protest the confiscation of his produce by municipal officials. Tunisia, after all, is a small country (population 10.5 million), bounded on two sides by the Mediterranean and overshadowed by Libya, its large neighbor to the east, formerly led by the crackpot regime of Mu'ammar Gadhafi. There weren't a lot of reasons to go to Tunisia except to do a cultural documentary. Or so I thought.

Ironically, given the subsequent controversy over a nuclear treaty with Iran, I was in Tehran doing a story on a research reactor when the Arab Spring ignited. Wearing a protective suit to keep radioactive particles out of my clothing, I had spent the day touring the facility. I remember in particular filming a giant tank used to cool radioactive elements.

When I got back to my hotel, I turned on Press TV, the English-language station in Iran. The big story was that Tunisia's president of twenty-three years, Zine Al Abidine Ben Ali, had fled the country. Suddenly the protests against the man I had dismissed as a "little Mubarak" had become a big deal.

I flew to London the next day and filed the Iranian nuclear story. Then I caught a flight to Tunis, where the smell of tear gas was still in the air. I immediately started doing interviews with protesters who were busily ransacking Ben Ali's homes.

Much of their anger was directed at his wife, Leila Trabelsi, a onetime hairdresser notorious for her lavish spending. Before fleeing with her husband, Trabelsi reportedly took $65 million in gold bars from the central bank. Her family, often called Tunisia's Mafia, owned stakes in many of the country's largest businesses. The new government detained thirty-three of the ousted president's relatives.

The uprising in Tunisia was more than a colorful story. I felt certain that the resentments there would spread elsewhere in the Arab world. Rich countries such as Saudi Arabia and Kuwait could buy their way out of trouble by pumping money into the pockets of their people, but a big, poor country such as Egypt faced a severe reckoning.

Before I could dig deeper, I had a final obligation typical of the scattershot reporting I had been doing over the previous year—an interview in Washington with a Russian dissident who promised to expose corruption by Vladimir Putin. The Russian was visibly freaked-out during the interview, and by the end of the session I was pretty jumpy myself. I was getting phone calls and e-mails about massive demonstrations in Cairo. Protesters in Tahrir Square were clashing with police, who were responding with tear gas.

I rushed to Dulles Airport without stopping to pack, dressed in the same shoes and suit I had worn for the interview. I spent two days covering the riots in Cairo in leather-bottom shoes and suit trousers before I had time to buy rough-and-ready clothes.

This was a different Cairo from the one I knew fifteen years earlier. Back then, everyone was poor but with no dishonor in it, and violence was rare. Many Cairenes were villagers transplanted to the city, and they brought their rural values with them. Opposing the government often meant a beating at the local police station and maybe a stretch in one of Egypt's brutal prisons. But the abuses were nothing out of the ordinary in that part of the world, roughly the same as those meted out in Tunisia and Syria, and child's play compared to the iron-fist punishments in Iraq. Egypt then was a medium-grade police state where people could get hurt, but where everything just kind of rolled along. In many ways, Egypt in 1996 was similar to Egypt in 1986 or even 1976.

But the Egypt of the Arab Spring was an altogether different place. The wealth gap had grown enormously. Garden communities with golf courses had sprung up for the first time, and rich people drove their fancy new Mercedeses to fancy new restaurants, many of which served alcohol, usually anathema in Muslim societies.

Perhaps the biggest change, though, was something small and relatively cheap: the smartphone. Now poor people had a way of communicating with one another. If one man saw an expensively clad guy with a blond woman on each arm, a hundred of his friends soon knew about it too, and so did hundreds more of their friends. Economic resentments, not religious or ethnic divisions, had sent Egyptians into the streets. The Internet, Facebook, and Twitter didn't cause the revolutions, but like television in Eastern Europe in 1989, technology accelerated the pace of events.

By January 28, 2011, I was reporting that downtown Cairo was in open revolt. Protesters were throwing paving stones, bottles, and Molotov cocktails, amid shouts of "The people want to topple the regime." Al Jazeera, the Arab-language TV news network underwritten by the emir of Qatar, was pumping up the unrest. Its coverage was breathless and exciting, and guests would sometimes break into song. Al Jazeera became protester TV.

I reported the next day that Hosni Mubarak was under intensifying pressure to step down. I had thought him an old fool when he was in his late sixties, and now at eighty-two he was an even bigger fool. Even though he would have been able to leave the country a free man, he dug in his heels because he thought the whole thing was a conspiracy orchestrated by the emir of Qatar and journalists in general—and because he was determined to have his son Gamal, a conspicuous mediocrity, succeed him as president.

Islamic groups joined the protesters on January 29, and the day after that thousands of inmates, including thirty leaders of the Muslim Brotherhood, escaped from prison. Looting became widespread. "From police state to state of chaos," I said on the air. But Mubarak clung to power, launching a crackdown on journalists, dozens of whom were beaten, harassed, or detained. We used low light and minimal production touches when we filmed our nightly reports in order not to draw attention to ourselves. "If the protesters win, they believe they will win Egypt," I said on the *Nightly News*.

I have a theory about protests learned from covering a dozen of them from the Middle East to Ukraine: To be effective, demonstrators must pick the right square and make it the center of their activities. Tahrir Square was perfect. It was big, it was surrounded by lots of little streets and access roads, it was near a huge population of prospective protesters, and it was overlooked by several big hotels filled with journalists who were keeping an eye on things every minute of the day.

On February 5, Day 12 of the protests, Gamal gave up leadership of the ruling party, but his father hung on, with the encouragement of other Arab leaders who feared they would be next if he stepped down. The death toll had risen to three hundred by February 7. But the protesters sensed the tide had turned, and Tahrir Square was suddenly transformed from a battleground to a massive campsite. Crowds swelled into the hundreds of thousands on February 8 amid rumors that Mubarak was about to give up office. But in a speech delivered at 11:00 p.m. two nights later, Mubarak was still calling himself president, though he now described it as more of a symbolic role. But on February 11, Mubarak surprised everyone by fleeing to Sharm el-Sheikh—known as the City of Peace because of the numerous international peace conferences held there—at the southern tip of Egypt's Sinai Peninsula on the Red Sea.

"And so began the biggest, most joyful, wildest celebration in Egypt's modern history," I reported. The cleanup began the next day. "There is an energy, a can-do spirit in Egypt," I said on the *Nightly News*. "Egyptians realize they are setting an example—an example being watched across the Middle East, and Egyptians believe the revolution they have started will spread." The country was swept up in euphoria, with dancing, singing, and bonfires in the streets.

The most interesting and portentous day of the uprising may have been February 13, when Egyptians went back to work. Everyone felt a sense of empowerment, and grievances bubbled up everywhere. Men demanded seats on previously all-women subway cars, calling their exclusion unfair. Bus drivers demanded higher pay, and bank employees accused their CEOs of corruption. Journalists charged that their editor in chiefs played favorites. Even the police, who tried to crush the protests, demanded (and later got) a pay hike—but not before they held an apology march through Cairo. "Sorry, we were just following orders," they chanted.

It was the day when Egyptians learned they weren't just demonstrating against Mubarak but also against a million mini-dictators who drew power from him and did his bidding while overseeing state-run companies, state-run newspapers, state-run utilities, and state-run schools. These grievances, and the growing role of Islamic groups, were manifestations of the volatility that would rock Egypt in the months and years ahead. And all the while the new US president was cheering the demonstrators on.

Egypt's revolution was in my opinion one of the most decisive foreign events in President Obama's term in office. I suspect without realizing it, Obama—just like Bush before him—changed the direction that US policy in the Middle East had taken for decades. Since World War II, when the United States replaced Europe in the role of patron of the region, Washington's goal in the Middle East can be summed up in one word: stability. With the Eisenhower and Carter doctrines, and President George H. W. Bush's war to push Saddam Hussein out of Kuwait but not overthrow him, Washington had tried to maintain basic stability, keep the region's oil flowing, and uphold the cold peace with Israel. Suddenly, that all seemed out the window. First, President Bush toppled Saddam Hussein for no good reason except Washington, and the president personally, wanted revenge after 9/11 and wasn't satisfied with Afghanistan. Now President Obama was turning his back on America's oldest and closest ally in the Arab world.

President Mubarak was effectively a US lackey who controlled the biggest country in the Middle East. He was a key asset. If Washington wanted stability, it should have worked harder to keep him or transition him out smoothly, instead of having him thrown out by the military backed by an angry mob. President Obama unceremoniously threw Mubarak under the bus and watched him toppled in less than three weeks. Suddenly, Obama had a "doctrine" of his own. It was this: if you can get to a square, make a lot of noise, know how to use Facebook and Twitter, speak a smattering of English, and the police and/or army starts to beat you up, Washington is on your side. It was bold and revolutionary, perhaps even noble and correct, but it wouldn't last.

President Bush had been aggressive and reckless in the Middle East, attacking Iraq for no reason and then claiming to be fighting terrorism while actually creating more terrorists. I like to think of the Middle East of the Arab big men like a row of old rotten houses. They looked stable and imposing from the outside but were in fact full of mold and termites, which they both contained and created the way old houses do if no one opens the windows or cleans them out. President Bush knocked down the first rotten house by toppling Saddam Hussein, unleashing the anger, ignorance, and Sunni-Shia rivalry inside. President Obama, by turning on old friends, was now helping to knock down another house. Worse still, Obama would later fail to follow through on this new promise when the wave of protest reached Bahrain and then culminated in Syria. The Bush Doctrine was offensive defense: attack foreign nations before they attack you, even if you attack the wrong country for the wrong reason, or for no reason at all. The Obama Doctrine would turn out to be: help those seeking democracy when they are oppressed, except when you don't want to and prefer to promise help while not delivering it. The combined impact of these two policies—radical departures from decades of trying to find Middle East stability—would be devastating.

BY THE TIME THE ARAB SPRING ERUPTED I HAD MADE ISTANBUL MY HOME BASE. I bought an apartment there in 2007 as an investment and as a place to go on weekends because Istanbul is a cool city. I've since refurbished it, but back then it was pretty run-down. The ceiling leaked, there was no air-conditioning, and the kitchen was a joke. But at least I didn't have to shuttle back and forth to New York.

I had just left Istanbul for Egypt when authorities in Bahrain started cracking down on demonstrators there. Even before I got to the capital, Manama, I knew the odds were heavily stacked against the Shia protesters. Bahrain is tiny (pop. 1.2 million, 160,000 of whom live in Manama), 60 to 70 percent of the population is Shia, and it is in the backyard of Saudi Arabia, the powerhouse of the Sunni world. Bahrain's government is strong and rich. The country is also strategically important as the home of the US Fifth Fleet.

The protest began at 3:00 a.m. on February 17, 2011, with an Egyptian-style sit-in in Pearl Square. Riot police and soldiers fired tear gas canisters and rubber bullets. I went to Salmaniya Medical Complex and found the staff overwhelmed. The injured said many protesters dropped to their knees, bared their chests, and dared the soldiers to shoot. The soldiers obliged: at least four protesters were killed, fifty more were injured, and sixty were reported missing.

Bahrain is a case study in how to crush an uprising. The government tracked down people who were organizing protests online, arrested suspected rabble-rousers, and prevented crowds from forming. Determined not to have a repeat of Tahrir Square, the government simply bulldozed Pearl Square into rubble. By February 19, protesters were carrying flowers and shouting messages of peace. Unlike with Mubarak, President Obama said very little during Bahrain's violent crackdown. Inconsistencies in the president's policy were already emerging. Why was the United States sympathetic to demonstrators in Cairo's Tahrir Square, but seemed uninterested when Bahrain's monarchy bulldozed Pearl Square? People in the Middle East were left scratching their heads.

By now, all hell was breaking loose in Libya. From the start, this was not just a protest against economic inequality or religious discrimination, but a revolution aimed at toppling the regime of Mu'ammar Gadhafi. It was, in short, a real shooting war.

My crew and I gathered in Cairo. We didn't have visas to get into Libya, and we didn't know what to expect from the rebels who controlled the territory on the other side of the Egyptian border. I thought about hiring bedouin smugglers to get us into Libya. Crazy as it sounds, I even flirted with the idea of crossing the desert on camels. Not a lot of hands went up when I asked who was game for the trip. Fine, I said, I'll go by myself.

I know how to use a portable terminal that can connect to a satellite Internet network, but I didn't know how to edit video and upload it to the computer. The guys in my crew tried to show me, but with my primitive technological skills it must have been a pathetic sight. Finally a cameraman named John Kooistra, a good friend of mine, dismissed the tutorial as stupid and said he was coming with me.

We hired a taxi for the four-hundred-mile trip to Sallum, a village in northwest Egypt about ninety miles from Tobruk in Libya. When we arrived, we heard that CNN's Ben Wedeman had already crossed the border. That got my competitive juices flowing, especially because I had worked as Wedeman's freelance assistant when I was starting out in Cairo. The crossing point was a madhouse, with swarms of refugees coming into Egypt from Libya, but we finally got our exit stamps and headed for the no-man's-land separating the two countries. I tried to call NBC to tell my bosses that we were crossing, but I couldn't get any reception, which was probably just as well because New York would probably have said it was too dangerous. When we got to the Libyan side, the rebels waved us right in.

It was a bit harrowing at first because we got into cars without knowing for sure whether the drivers were kidnappers or friendlies. But the rebels and their sympathizers couldn't have been more helpful and considerate. They had seen how media coverage had helped the opposition in Tunisia and Egypt. If we had been the Al Jazeera team they would probably have carried us all the way to Tobruk on litters. As it was, we had to struggle to pay for drivers, a meal, even a cup of coffee. We hadn't yet heard a report by Wedeman, which suggested we were close on his heels.

We eventually made it to Tobruk, the scene of bitter fighting in World War II. Allied forces, mostly Australian, captured it in 1941, but Erwin Rommel, the famed Desert Fox, wrested it away for the Axis Powers the following year. I was reminded then of Rommel's observation that fighting in the desert was like fighting at sea. There were no population centers or strategic points, distances didn't mean much, and an army could gain or lose a hundred miles in a single battle. We saw this happen many times in the months ahead.

From Tobruk we traveled another 290 miles west to Benghazi, the second-largest city in Libya (pop. 700,000) and the rebels' capital. En route we heard a speech by Gadhafi on state radio. In a weird cadence, sometimes excited, other times slurred, Gadhafi claimed bin Laden and the United States were in cahoots and slipping hallucinogenic drugs into the rebels' Nescafé, making them crazy. (The Libyans, who were once colonized by the Italians, do amazing things with Nescafé. I became addicted to their sweet cappuccino served in plastic cups, but not because they had any drugs in them.) In my first report from Libya, I said Gadhafi "does not sound like a sane person."

In Benghazi, we stayed at the Uzo Hotel, where a media center had already been set up. The rebels had cleared the hotel of regular guests and allotted the rooms to military officers and journalists. A rebel office was downstairs, and if we wanted to go to the front lines, I only had to ask one of the commanders for a ride.

Most of the rebels were civilians, not trained soldiers, and they had captured Benghazi by acclamation of the populace, not in street-to-street battles with government forces. But like actors donning costumes, they immediately started dressing like Che Guevara—camouflage jackets, bandoliers, scarves, mirrored sunglasses, and, of course, berets. They swaggered around with guns, most of which hadn't been fired in anger. They fired a lot in the air.

After a week with the rebels in Benghazi, I wanted to get to Tripoli, the capital and site of Gadhafi's compound. But how? It was a 630-mile drive along the Mediterranean coast, roughly the distance between New York City and Detroit, but that was not the real problem. At the 350-mile mark lay Sirte, Gadhafi's hometown, which we figured would be unfriendly to foreign journalists arriving from the rebels' eastern enclave.

We considered crossing the Gulf of Sidra, a U-shaped body of water with Benghazi and Tripoli at opposite tips, but we couldn't find a suitable boat. So we drove twenty-four hours back through Tobruk to Sallum and finally to Cairo, booking a flight from there to Tripoli even though we still lacked visas for Libya. When the plane landed in Tripoli to pick up new passengers, we grabbed our gear and purposely stranded ourselves. We told immigration officials that we were expected at the press center at the Rixos Hotel. This cock-and-bull story bought us some time. After several hours, an immigration official called me into his office and shook my hand, slipping me a piece of paper with his name and phone number on it, then stamped us in. He was clearly hedging his bet on the regime, figuring a contact with an American journalist might come in handy later on.

When correspondents cover a civil war, they expect to live rough, but that was certainly not the case at the Rixos. This super-luxurious hotel had indoor and outdoor swimming pools, a Turkish bath, a gym with thirty brand-spanking-new treadmills, and a nightly buffet with roast meats and chicken, fresh vegetables, and a dozen different desserts.

After using all our ingenuity to get to Tripoli, it soon became apparent that we had arrived too soon. "We're in the eye of the storm," I reported on March 2. I said the city was more ready for tourists than war. Restaurants and hotels were open, and the markets brimmed with Mediterranean produce.

The same was not true twenty-eight miles to the west in Zawiya, Libya's fifth-largest city (pop. 200,000). When protests flared there, Gadhafi used airpower and dozens of tanks to pummel the city, leaving it in ruins. We tried to drive to Zawiya but were pulled off the road at a government checkpoint. As we waited to show our identification, I grabbed my BlackBerry and frantically deleted a hundred or so pictures I had taken of rebels in Benghazi, knowing they would probably have landed me in jail.

Pro-government demonstrations were staged every day in Green Square, adjacent to Tripoli's medieval old city, whose large port gave way to narrow streets with beautiful homes and courtyards, many of which had been converted to restaurants or hotels. I reported that the government was proclaiming the capture of towns that were still controlled by the rebels. "So people in Tripoli are being told to celebrate victories that aren't taking place."

After eight days in Tripoli, we flew back to Cairo. When you're covering a story like this, you always want to get to the next place. The grass is always greener. In Benghazi, you report on the rebels, you go to the front lines, you follow the ebbs and flows of the battle, and pretty soon you feel as if you're doing the same story over and over. Then you jump to Tripoli and find you're caught in a bubble. You turn on the television and see the competition getting good pictures of the fighting. So you say to yourself, "This battle is serious. Tripoli isn't cooking. I can hop over to Benghazi, catch some of the fight, and still get back to Tripoli if necessary."

We got to Cairo and made the long drive to Sallum to cross back into Libya. Our team was completely frazzled. On March 11, 2011, as we prepared to cross the border, a tsunami devastated Japan, killing fifteen thousand, destroying hundreds of thousands of homes, and causing meltdowns at three nuclear power plants. We knew that story would dominate the news for days, and we wouldn't be able to get our stuff on the air. So after a heart-to-heart talk, we decided to take a week's break.

When we finally returned to Tobruk, US and NATO planes had joined the rebel effort, and just in time. They knocked out government armored vehicles and artillery streaming toward Benghazi. If the heavy weaponry had reached its destination, the city would have fallen and the revolution would probably have come to an abrupt halt. President Obama had committed the US military to protect the rebels and the civilians around them from an advancing army. President Obama became a hero to the Arab street. First he refused to back Mubarak. Now he was saving Benghazi. Perhaps Bahrain where Washington failed to act was an anomaly. It was certainly overshadowed by Libya, where Washington and its European allies took direct action, sending jets in to support the rebels. It was dramatic, cheered by Arab television, and raised expectations among rebels and reformers all around the world, especially in Syria, where they would be bitterly disappointed.

We hung back in Tobruk to see how the US/NATO air campaign played out. Once we felt it was safe, we returned to Benghazi, passing destroyed armored columns by the side of the road. Gadhafi's forces had come within two miles of the rebel capital.

We found the rebel forces buoyed by the help from the air. Each day we would venture out from Benghazi and drive to villages along the ever-advancing front. The battle for Ajdabiya, a city of seventy thousand about 125 miles south of Benghazi, was considered crucial because it was the first test of the rebels' strength since the beginning of the Western air campaign. On March 24, my team and I were doing interviews with a rebel unit about five miles outside Ajdabiya when I encountered a fighter armed with a plastic toy pistol. I never got a chance to learn why. As I was describing the gun on camera, three incoming tank or artillery rounds exploded fifty yards away. We took cover behind a concrete block while the rebels scattered.

The next day government and rebel forces were fighting inside Ajdabiya. Ordinarily we stayed behind the rebels' front line, advancing only when they did, but this time we decided to risk moving forward while the battle was in flux.

Western airstrikes proved more effective than the rebels expected, obliterating dozens of Gadhafi's tanks and armored personnel carriers and creating a corridor of destruction that cleared the way for ground advances. By March 28 the rebels had followed it west for 340 miles, almost equal to the distance separating San Francisco and Los Angeles. They were more than two-thirds of the way to Tripoli, but they got bogged down at Sirte, Gadhafi's hometown and military bulwark.

Even with their successes, the rebels were still a ragtag army. They had virtually no lines of communication, and their commanders were woefully inexperienced. What they had were weapons—artillery, mortars, even surface-to-surface missiles. Unfortunately, they often had no idea how to use them. We were with a rebel unit outside Ajdabiya on March 30 when they were preparing to fire a rocket from a huge launcher. We set up our cameras to film the launch because this was the most advanced weaponry we had seen in rebel hands. When they fired it, the rocket went backward, landing not far from a hotel. By some miracle, no one was hurt.

Meanwhile, one of the longest and bloodiest battles of the war was intensifying in Misrata, Libya's third-largest city (pop. 500,000). Misrata's location—500 miles west of Benghazi (about 150 miles past Sirte) and only 115 miles east of Tripoli—made it strategically vital. The rebels had taken control of the city in late February, holding it even as Gadhafi solidified his control of the western part of the country all around it. On March 6, the government moved to reclaim Misrata, ultimately laying siege to the city by cutting off access to it by land, leaving its Mediterranean port the only way in and out. It was sometimes called Libya's Stalingrad because of the intensity of the fighting and the hardships endured by civilians.

We were stuck in Benghazi trying to find a boat that would take us there. Whenever we thought we had a way in, our editors back in New York thought it wasn't safe enough. One time we came upon a craft that looked seaworthy, only to find that it was laden with explosives. We didn't even mention it to the editors in New York because we knew the boat was a death trap. If someone dropped a cigarette, the boat would have been blown to smithereens.

But reporters from ITN, Al Jazeera, the BBC, the *Guardian*, the *Independent*, and, most gallingly, CNN did get into the city, usually on fishing boats. On March 29, CNN uploaded video of the horrific violence. Gadhafi units made daily forays into the city, stationing snipers in buildings. Then the main body of government soldiers would pull back so that heavy weapons—mortars, artillery, tanks, and truck-mounted rocket systems with forty launch tubes—could pound the city.

One of the problems about getting into Misrata was figuring out how to get back out. The fighting was not only heavy but, often, random. Hundreds, some claimed thousands, of people were killed, many of them noncombatants. The rebels would have been routed if it wasn't for NATO jets, which destroyed tons of Gadhafi's heavy weaponry and often kept his tanks at bay simply by flying overhead.

A government mortar attack on April 20 killed two journalists—British documentary filmmaker Tim Hetherington and Chris Hondros, an American photographer whose work had been nominated for a Pulitzer Prize. Not long afterward, Gadhafi's helicopters started dropping mines into Misrata's harbor. We were shut out for good. The rebels finally regained full control of the city on May 15, 2011.

As the battle for Misrata raged, I reported on April 1 that rebel forces had dug trenches 120 miles east of Benghazi and were holding their line. They probably did so at the behest of NATO, which knew the rebels could not fight their way through Sirte, circumvent Gadhafi's forces outside Misrata, and then mount a frontal assault on Tripoli.

What I had no way of knowing at the time was that yet another front was forming in Zintan, a city of fifty thousand in the

Nafusa Mountains, only eight-five miles southwest of Tripoli, not far from the Tunisian border. So now Gadhafi's forces were stymied in the east, embroiled in Misrata, and trying to fend off Zintanis, who had the advantage of fighting on familiar mountainous terrain.

You never know how big and turbulent the world is until you try to cover it. While I was in Benghazi on May 2, monitoring the escalating NATO air campaign, I got a frantic call from NBC in New York: "Get in front of the camera. There's going to be a presidential announcement coming up soon, and Obama is going to say bin Laden is dead." My crew and I muttered, "My God, we're in the middle of nowhere." But I knew bin Laden's history like the back of my hand and managed to put together a credible report from eastern Libya.

Benghazi became my watchtower on uprisings in Libya and Syria, where protests against Bashar al-Assad were turning bloody, and on the pincer movement beginning to threaten Tripoli.

All across the Middle East, events were now unfolding quickly and in completely interconnected ways. The uprising in Syria began while the war in Libya was still raging. All day long, people in Damascus, Aleppo, and Daraa watched NATO airstrikes on television. They saw Washington use its military might to defend those who went out in the streets to call for democracy. But already there were signs of what was to come. Egypt was starting to unravel. The protesters who overthrew Mubarak kept coming back to Tahrir Square. They returned with every grievance big or small. Egyptians found success once in Tahrir, and kept trying to repeat it, which made the country ungovernable. Egyptian protesters also expected the same amount of international interest and US support every time they started to cheer and hold up posters.

After Mubarak was overthrown, competing protests began, sometimes at the same time and in the same place. I was back in Cairo on July 15 reporting on a demonstration by one hundred thousand people in Tahrir Square who were protesting the hijacking of the Egyptian revolution by the military and Islamic groups. It was odd because some were standing against the growing influence of the military after Mubarak, while others were denouncing the military's old enemy, the Muslim Brotherhood, which was also gunning for power. Others were protesting against both groups, claiming they were in an alliance together. I saw people protesting against Israel too, for good measure it seemed. The Muslim Brotherhood would ultimately win the first round after Mubarak.

Within weeks of the revolution, the small apartment that served as the Muslim Brotherhood's headquarters was replaced by a palatial, six-story villa with chandeliers and gilded furniture. Their logo—crossed swords and the Koran—was prominently displayed on the outside of the building. The Muslim Brotherhood certainly felt confident back then.

I rushed off to Somalia to cover the famine there that took 250,000 lives by the time it eased in 2012.

I was back in western Libya in August amid reports that Gadhafi planned to flee. On August 20, 2011, the rebels waged an all-out assault on the capital, and residents began to celebrate—a bit too soon, at least judging by the sniper cross fire that kept us pinned down. Two days later I managed to get within a few hundred yards of Gadhafi's compound, which was still defended by loyalists with tanks and mortars.

I reported on August 23 that the final battle for Tripoli had begun that morning with NATO airstrikes. For five hours, loyalists maintained their fire from Gadhafi's compound. Then came

167

a noise we hadn't heard before: silence. I climbed down from the rooftop where we had been filming and drove rapidly to Gadhafi's compound. Rebels were already looting the place, mostly taking weapons but also furniture and cars. We drove down to Green Square, which was packed with thousands of rebels firing into the air. The din practically drowned out my report.

Only one piece was missing: Gadhafi, who had given a radio address urging his supporters to clear Tripoli "of all the rats." I reported that chaos was already setting in. The rebels had no central military command, and the political leadership was six hundred miles to the east in Benghazi. On August 25, I explored Gadhafi's compound and marveled at the maze of underground tunnels that stretched for miles. By then Gadhafi had become a figure of ridicule. At a checkpoint, rebels showed a picture of what he might look like dressed as a woman.

We stuck around for another couple of days to see if Gadhafi would be caught—September 1 would have marked the start of his forty-third year in power—but it didn't make sense to stay when other stories were growing more urgent. I was already seeing glimmers of the Arab Summer. Things were worsening in Syria and Yemen, where street fighting continued despite the overthrow of President Ali Abdullah Saleh, and Egypt seemed ever more addicted to revolution.

I still had high hopes for Libya. It had a thousand miles of beautiful Mediterranean coastline, abundant oil, an established trading partner in Italy, and a population of only 6 million, which should have made it manageable. This was not Egypt, with 80 to 90 million people, pervasive poverty, little oil, a polluted Nile, and a landmass consisting mostly of desert. As I said on the air, "If [the Libyans] can't get this one right, they have some serious problems."

But Libya's populism had a dark side that quickly became evident. Militias weren't disarming and were beginning to turn on each other. It was simply human nature. If a Libyan had been a hairdresser or potato farmer and suddenly became a commander of armed men, saluted and cheered by the locals, why would he want to go back to snipping hair or digging up potatoes?

I was in New York when Gadhafi was finally captured in Sirte on October 20, 2011. He was trying to slip out of the city when his convoy was hit by NATO warplanes and a US Predator drone. He crawled to a drainpipe under a bridge, where he was found by the rebels. They beat him, ripped off most of his shirt, propped him up on a car, and photographed him bleeding from his head. A photograph of his corpse showed an apparent gunshot wound to the left temple. There were reports, which were believed in many Arab capitals, that Gadhafi was also raped with a knife. True or not, by any account he died an awful death and it sent a strong message around the world about the Arab Spring and US policy. The message was Washington would not stick by its friends, old or new. Gadhafi had come out of the cold and made peace with Washington. He had agreed to give up Libya's nuclear program and pay reparations for the flight that exploded over Lockerbie, Scotland. His reward was to have Washington use force to back rebels who would tear him to pieces and put his body in a meat locker for public ridicule. The message certainly wasn't lost on Syria's president Assad. What incentive did he have now to compromise or trust Washington?

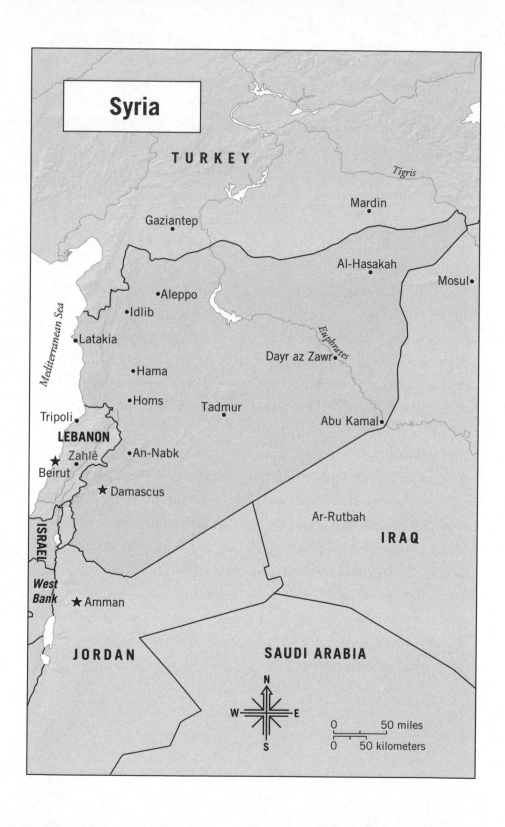

EIGHT

SYRIA MADE ME APPRECIATE LIFE MORE. THAT'S WHAT HAPPENS WHEN YOU'RE kidnapped and think you're going to die. To explain how I got into that fix, I need to double back to the belated arrival of the Arab Spring in Syria, and my subsequent trips into the country. I wish I had spent more time thinking about my border crossings and my travel companions on my trips into Syria in 2011 and 2012. Those gave me a false sense of security, and I guess I got greedy. In journalism, you never want to get greedy.

The Syrian uprising began on March 6, 2011, when fifteen boys from the southwestern city of Daraa, fifty-five miles south of Damascus, just north of the Jordanian border, painted the now-familiar slogan on a wall: "The people want to topple the regime." The boys were thrown in jail and tortured. They were released two weeks later. They had been beaten bloody; some had had their fingernails ripped out; the faces of others had been branded with hot knives. The people of Daraa were enraged.

When thousands demonstrated against the regime, Bashar al-Assad's government sent in soldiers and tanks to put down the protest. Witnesses said two dozen people were killed. The government kept tightening its grip, and by late April an estimated four thousand to six thousand troops had moved into Daraa.

Bashar learned about brutality from his father, Hafez al-Assad, who in 1982 crushed a revolt by Sunni Muslim activists in the city of Hama. The death toll there was placed somewhere between ten thousand and forty thousand, many of them members of the Muslim Brotherhood.

Born on September 11, 1965, Bashar al-Assad was an accidental president. He trained as an ophthalmologist in London and only returned to Syria after his older brother, Bassel, who was expected to succeed their father, died in a car crash. Like his father, Bashar was an Alawite, a Shia offshoot that made up only 12 percent of Syria's 22 million people, and he understood that there would be no mercy if he was overthrown in a country that was 70–75 percent Sunni, a point made even clearer after Gadhafi's death.

Western journalists, especially Americans, found it difficult to get into the country once the uprising began. But the news flowed out anyway, in videos uploaded on the Internet. They came first as a trickle, then as a flood. More than a million videos were uploaded between January 2012 and September 2013, documenting what the *Wall Street Journal* called the "YouTube war."

On May 19, 2011, President Obama said Assad should lead a transition to democracy or "get out of the way." The Syrian opposition, which had been watching the NATO airstrikes in Libya, assumed that Western help was on the way.

But Assad played his cards relatively well, especially in the early days. He continued to offer the prospect of change and reform, even as the crackdown intensified. Unlike Mubarak, who didn't seem to realize that what was happening was serious, or Gadhafi, who called on his loyalists to crush the uprising like cockroaches (when he didn't call his opponents rats, they were cockroaches), Assad offered both a stick and what appeared to be a carrot. In June he promised to prosecute the people responsible for the killing of protesters and said he would support a new constitution that could end his Ba'ath Party's monopoly on power. He formed committees of intellectuals to write down what the reforms would be, promising greater freedom of the press and political representation. He seemed to be offering an off-ramp. His critics say it was all a ruse, a ploy to confuse and divide his enemies and buy time. Either way, the promises of change came too late. Even after just a few weeks of protests, too much blood had been spilled, and the demonstrators were overconfident. I doubt that anything short of total capitulation by the Assad regime could have satisfied the crowds. They felt they had momentum. They felt they had Washington behind them. They felt they had the wind of history at their backs. They also had Al Jazeera's cheerleading coverage.

I had been spending most of my time in Libya covering the anti-Gadhafi rebels and monitoring the early days of the Syrian situation from there. I occasionally made my way to the Turkish-Syrian border, which was a babel of information about the uprising against Assad.

Turkey had become the home address for all things Syrian, especially the Syrian opposition. Prime Minister, and later president, Erdogan, a Sunni, was sympathetic to the cause. He let Syrian video activists cross the border to buy cell phones and USB sticks to get Wi-Fi connections for their computers. Turkey also boosted its cell-phone tower capacity so that calls and videos could reach deeper into Syria. Turkey turned a blind eye to Syrian rebels and activists, and would later turn a blind eye to ISIS extremists crossing the same border.

It was like Casablanca in the Bogart movie—Turkey was the place where all spies had come. State Department and CIA specialists operated almost openly on the Turkish border. They tutored cyberactivists on how to craft their messages, how to quickly erase everything on their phones in case they were caught, and how to use encryption software.

Because the Syrian rebels didn't initially hold any territory, they waged guerrilla war via social media. A couple of hundred people would turn up like a flash mob, hold a demonstration, then melt away when the police showed up and started firing tear gas. The video activists would record the scene and upload it on the Internet so Syrians and everyone else in the region could see the opposition to Assad in action.

I wanted to see the flash mobs for myself, but it was dangerous getting into Syria, and even more dangerous once you were inside. But after I conferred with two colleagues, Aziz Akyavas, a veteran Turkish journalist and an old friend, and John Kooistra, my trusted cameraman, we decided to give it a try in October 2011—more than a year before the fateful trip that led to our kidnapping.

We linked up with some Kurdish cigarette smugglers on the

border and set our sights on Qamishli, a Syrian city of 180,000 near the Turkish border. It had some flash-mob activity, and, significantly, its largest ethnic group was Kurds, who tend to be friendlier toward Americans than Syrian Arabs.

Our mission was a mixture of derring-do, slapstick, and some enterprising journalism, which was unfortunately overshadowed by the trip itself. Our plan seemed straightforward: The smugglers would take us across the border, skirting Turkish and Syrian watchtowers. Then we'd contact Syrian activists, film and interview them, and get out of Qamishli as fast as we could. After we were kept waiting three days in a dumpy farmhouse on the Turkish side of the border, we argued with the smugglers about the delay and finally went to their boss to complain.

Probably to show that he was in charge, he summoned his best smuggler and told us, "You're going now." It was three o'clock in the afternoon, and we were dressed like ninjas, all in black, expecting a night crossing.

We were dropped off in tall grass on the Turkish side and followed our smuggler on all fours. He spoke frequently on his cell phone with a compatriot on the Syrian side. We got to a clearing. There was a Turkish guard tower right in front of us. We sprinted for cover amid small trees and bushes. Then we came to another clearing and a barbed-wire fence—and a Syrian guard tower only a hundred yards away. We climbed through the barbed wire and started running again, diving into a gully in a farmer's field on the Syrian side.

We finally made it to the road where a car was supposed to be waiting, but there was no one there. Forty minutes later, two Syrian contacts arrived. Their car was tiny, and they were cockeyed drunk. Having no other choice, the four of us—me, Kooistra,

Aziz, and the smuggler who'd guided us through the bushes and fields—squeezed into the backseat. The radio was blasting, and the Syrians were smoking with the windows up—until one of them spotted a girl walking along the side of the road and rolled down his window so he could give her a catcall. Then the man at the wheel started driving to the music. He took a left, he took a right, he made the car dance a little as we sped into the city.

We sat in the back pretending we were invisible. The smuggler who'd brought us across yelled at the Syrians, calling them drunks and morons. I asked the Syrians to turn the radio down, and they turned it all the way up.

Finally we reached a "safe house." I described it on the air as a brothel, but it was more like a low-life flophouse, a disgusting, dirty basement apartment where men would bring prostitutes and drink and smoke dope. There was a mirror over one of the beds. The bathroom was so foul that I got the dry heaves. The first thing the Syrians asked us was whether we wanted beer and girls. I went nuclear: "We don't want any beer, we don't want any girls. We want you to stop acting like assholes. We're here as journalists."

Our smuggler gave them hell too, which seemed to get their attention. Over the next several days, we contacted a bunch of activists and persuaded them to come over for interviews. One of them took us to a small protest. We were with the flash mob when the Syrian police arrived and managed to disappear without getting arrested. If we had been caught, we would have been a propaganda prize for the Assad regime. I assumed we would end up on Syrian state TV with black eyes confessing to all sorts of things.

To leave Syria, we went through the same fields, only this time we ran into a farmer who was burning weeds and crop residue with a blowtorch. He asked us what we were doing, and our smuggler said, "Oh, nothing. We're just hanging out"—as if lots of Americans in ninja suits loitered around Syria in the middle of the afternoon. We asked him if he had a cell phone. He didn't, which meant we had twenty or thirty minutes to get back across the Turkish border. Our smuggler then told him we had gone to Syria for girls because they were cheaper there. The farmer smiled and nodded, either because he bought the story or because he was glad to be rid of us.

On November 16, 2011, I reported on the *Nightly News* that the death toll in Syria had reached thirty-five hundred, and that "hundreds if not thousands" of men had defected from the army. "This week something changed," I said. "The uprising in Syria became a revolution." The defectors formed the Free Syrian Army and attacked Syrian troops and destroyed tanks with rocket-propelled grenades.

I was on the Turkish border in February 2012 when the government mounted an attack on Homs, Syria's third-largest city, a hundred miles north of Damascus. "Witnesses described neighborhoods on fire, people living on shrubs and onions, bodies unreachable under the debris," I recounted on the *Nightly News*. The rebels were in desperate need of weapons, but US officials worried that the arms would end up falling into the hands of the Muslim Brotherhood or even more radical Islamic factions.

On May 25, 2012, government forces committed a horrific massacre in Houla, a cluster of three villages twenty miles northwest of Homs. A mass grave was found containing 108 bodies, 34 of them women and 49 of them children. We showed a video of the moment when Syrian forces had first started shelling the villages. "After that, witnesses say, government-backed militiamen called *shabiha* swept in and started stabbing and shooting children at close range." (The *shabiha* were organized as criminal gangs in the 1980s and were closely tied to the Assad family. They got out of control in the 1990s and were disbanded by Assad's father, only to make a comeback in the civil war.)

After the Houla massacre, the UN's peace envoy, former secretary-general Kofi Annan, said, "We are at a tipping point." But the Syrian government, I said on the air, was "pressing the same old line," and blaming the rebels for the violence. On June 12, 2012, with as many as fourteen thousand already dead in the war, I reported that Assad's regime was "trying to kill its way out of this crisis and stay in power at all costs."

I went back into Syria at the end of June 2012. It was entirely different from during my hair-raising expedition with the smugglers. I went in with Ali Bakran, an air-conditioner repairman turned rebel. We crossed the border at night, and I was shocked when we finally made our way to Jebel al-Zawiya, a region in Syria's northwest (think of Oregon), about forty miles southwest of Aleppo. Instead of Syrian soldiers, all I saw were rebels dressed in military garb. The government forces had lost control of the countryside and pulled back into the big cities.

It was like the Che Guevara period in Libya. The rebels bent over backward to be nice to us. They too had watched the Arab Spring unfold on television, and they believed the news media could help them topple Assad. We felt safe. There were no kidnappings at this stage. We operated completely in the open. If you were a white American riding on the back of a motorcycle without a helmet—well, you were hardly hiding.

We could feel a community spirit. Everyone picked up hitchhikers. You could stop at any house and spend the night. We ate like kings: chicken, fresh eggs, yogurt, olive oil, baby cucumbers, and slices of tomatoes that you'd dip in salt. I think one reason so many people died later is that they were seduced by this period. They couldn't see that it was fleeting.

But already signs were ominous. Ali Bakran had only 150 rifles for the 635 men he claimed to have under his command. He and his brigade were simple people, with no military experience beyond the two years of mandatory service all Syrian men were conscripted into. They were completely out of their league in a war against a professional army backed by Iran and Lebanon's Hezbollah. They were just average Joes who had taken up arms with the dream of bringing down a despotic regime.

On July 18, I was at NBC's studios in New York when four top Syrian officials were killed in a bomb blast. I tried to capture how shocking the attack must have been to Assad: "Picture this inside job. A meeting in Damascus earlier this morning of the top officials there to discuss how to continue the crackdown, how to keep the rebels from advancing on Damascus, when, suddenly, the room explodes." Killed were the defense minister and his deputy (who was also Assad's feared brother-in-law), an assistant vice president, and the director of the national security bureau. A dozen others in the meeting were reportedly injured. "Bashar al-Assad doesn't know who he can trust," I said on the air. "He doesn't know who has infiltrated his inner circle. It . . . could be a turning point." I kept seeing turning points. First the uprising. Then the creation of the Free Syrian Army, the FSA. Now a big assassination bombing in the heart of Assad's government. But the turn never came. It just got worse and worse.

With the fighting entering its seventeenth month and the death toll at nineteen thousand, I went back to Syria, to the village of al-Atarib, fifteen miles from Aleppo. The government had been mounting an offensive around Aleppo, and I was shocked at the destruction I found. This village of ten thousand was deserted, save for a handful of rebel fighters. "Syria is being destroyed one town at a time," I reported.

But the big show was the government's effort to recapture Aleppo. Damascus, Syria's political capital, and Aleppo, its commercial capital, had a Washington–New York style rivalry (and, coincidentally, were almost precisely the same distance apart), with both claiming to be the oldest continuously occupied city in the world. For a time I monitored the battle for Aleppo from its outskirts because the city center was too dangerous for civilians, especially American TV crews. Witnesses said the government was mounting a ferocious, all-out assault with tanks, helicopters, and artillery. Rebels counted one hundred armored personnel carriers joining the attack.

On August 3, 2012, the fifteenth day of the government offensive, rebels in the city said they were desperately low on ammunition and expressed dismay that the international community had not reacted when a huge massacre could be coming. Again, Libya was the example. Gadhafi threatened to overrun Benghazi and when he tried to do it, NATO started bombing. Now in Syria, Assad was threatening to crush the opposition in Aleppo and had already started doing it, but Washington's reaction was only hand-wringing. In my conversations with rebels it was clear they were becoming increasingly disheartened and desperate. (The rebels would usually communicate with each other on Skype, blending in with the billions of people using the Internet instead of going through cell-phone towers.) The United States was apparently still skittish about sending in arms because it feared they would end up in the hands of Islamic extremists, but that, like so many unintended consequences of US foreign policy in the Middle East, was a self-fulfilling prophecy. At this stage the rebels were numerous, strong, motivated, and moderate and I made that clear in my reports on the air.

"We've been on the ground here in Syria for nearly two weeks now," I countered, "and from what we've seen the rebels are not al-Qaeda. They are not extremists."

I do not think, however, that the United States could have saved Syria by intervening militarily at this stage. Based on what I witnessed during my years in Iraq, I think the United States would have entered another quagmire. Overturning Assad, an Alawite Shia, and replacing him with the Sunni rebels would have been Iraq in reverse. It would have been yet another historic reversal in the Shia-Sunni war that Washington had already proved itself unable to manage. But if the United States never intended to help, it shouldn't have built up the expectation. The false promise of help was cruel and inexcusable and it would only get worse over time. If a man is drowning and a boat drives past in the distance, the man accepts his death and goes down quietly. If a man is drowning and a boat pulls up beside him, dangles a life jacket, tells the world he wants to help, but then doesn't throw the life jacket, the drowning man dies crying and his family might take a blood oath to take revenge on the boat's crew. This type of anger was already starting to build in Syria and al-Qaeda would capitalize on it. That anger would, in particular, give al-Qaeda in Iraq, Zarqawi's monstrous group, a second lease on life, allowing it to become ISIS.

During our trip into Syria Ali Bakran, the brigade commander who had taken us in, told me that al-Qaeda had offered him money and weapons and that he was considering accepting them. His brother, the deputy commander of this little band of rebels, was arguing strongly for it. Without the help of Europe and the United States, Ali said he was a dying man willing to reach for any help he could get. I saw it as a pivotal moment, yet another potential turning point. This time I was right. On August 7, I reported that 262 al-Qaeda militants were operating along the Turkish-Syrian border, while others were living in a tent city outside Aleppo. Many rebel leaders—especially the ones outside Syria, holding conferences in luxury hotels—were worried that al-Qaeda was piggybacking off the Syrian uprising to advance its own agenda, which turned out to be depressingly true. But no one listened to what I was saying, or to the complaints of the well-fed, air-conditioned rebel leaders in Istanbul, Paris, and London. The change was coming from men such as Ali, field commanders with nothing left to fight with, and demoralized that the world, especially Washington, had apparently chosen to let them die. Clearly, Syria would not be Libya. The cavalry from the West wasn't coming. Instead, al-Qaeda was offering a helping hand.

Through the summer and fall, I reported that the rebels were worried that Assad was preparing to use chemical weapons. On July 13, US officials told me that Syria had moved its chemical arsenal, perhaps to more secure locations, and ten days later the government acknowledged for the first time that it had chemical weapons, threatening to use them against foreign aggressors but not against its own people.

In response to a question from NBC's White House reporter Chuck Todd, President Obama warned on August 20, 2012, "that a red line for us is we start seeing a whole bunch of chemical weapons moving around or being utilized." The Syrians didn't seem impressed. On December 7, I reported that US defense officials had told NBC News that the government had loaded precursor elements of sarin nerve gas into bombs but had not put the bombs on planes or other delivery systems. The president's red line looked like it was going to be tested.

For months I had been nibbling around the edges of Aleppo, going in and out of Syria, most often with Ali Bakran or his associates, and I finally got into the city itself in December 2012. The place was in dire straits, with widespread destruction and food shortages. Residents wrote numbers in red on their hands to indicate their place in bread lines; sometimes the numbers would reach into the five hundreds. It was sad to see a city so historic and beautiful getting ravaged.

Rebels and government troops fought at close quarters with automatic weapons and grenades. They also yelled at each other, hurling insults back and forth. It was too dangerous to stay long, and we'd go back to farming villages that were close enough to the Turkish border for us to get phone signals.

It was becoming harder to get Syrian stories on the air. The war had lost its novelty, and its growing complexity made it difficult to explain in a two-minute news segment. At first, it seemed new and clear: rebels were rising up just as they had in Egypt and Libya. By now the rebels were increasingly a mix of hard-core Islamists, criminals, and moderate fighters who were opposed to Assad and his allied Iranian and Lebanese militias. It was a mess. There were no good guys or bad guys anymore. These days, I no longer believe there ever are truly good guys or bad guys in war, at least in the Middle East. They're generally shades of gray. But that doesn't translate well on television. It was too complicated. Too remote. Too Middle Eastern. But on the ground, I was desperately interested. I was hooked by the most complex fight I'd ever seen, far more nuanced and complicated than Iraq or the Israeli-Palestinian conflict. The outcome seemed to be hanging in the balance, and I wanted to be close to the action. I think that's what made me greedy. I kept going into a conflict zone I knew had changed and where actors could no longer be trusted, at a time when my news organization was less and less interested. I got caught. My team and I all got caught.

On December 13, 2012, one of the local fixers—the guys who help journalists contact rebel leaders inside Syria—told us he had a story we might be interested in filming. I'll call him Mustafa. He mainly worked for CNN and had a good reputation. CNN couldn't make the trip for one reason or another, so he was offering it to me. He said the Sunni rebels were shopping around a trip to see six captured fighters—four Iranians and two Lebanese. All were Shiites, and their presence in Syria would allegedly show that the Assad regime was getting material support from coreligionists in the region. It would be proof of one of the rebels' biggest claims.

The rebel commander leading the expedition called himself Abdelrazaq. He had a bodyguard, whose name I never got, armed with an AK-47. We hired a driver named Taher, chosen by us at random, at Bab al-Hawa, one of the main crossing points between Turkey and Syria. I had never met any of them before.

I was bringing along a team of five: Aziz Akyavas, the well-connected Turkish journalist and close friend, who wanted to see the prisoners for himself; producer Ghazi Balkiz; cameraman John Kooistra; the fixer Mustafa; and a security consultant. I knew and trusted the first three; I had no experience with the security guy or Mustafa.

Ten minutes after we crossed into Syria, the road was blocked by about fifteen men who fanned out around our cars. They were dressed in black, wore black ski masks, and carried AK-47s. As they herded us into a nearby container truck, Abdelrazaq protested that he was from the Sunni-led Free Syrian Army. We assumed we were being captured by pro-Assad *shabiha*. They were dressed in all-black like *shabiha*. They spoke with the appropriate accent generally used by *shabiha*. They were praising the Assad regime. The kidnappers kicked Abdelrazaq in the face, then smashed a rifle butt into his back.

The kidnappers wrapped duct tape around our mouths, eyes, and wrists and stripped off our belts and shoes. Abdelrazaq's bodyguard was taken off the truck, and the leader of the kidnappers—who called himself Abu Jaffar—said, "Finish him." We heard bursts from an AK-47 and the thud of what sounded like a body hitting the ground.

Our captors took us to a farmhouse, where we stayed for several hours. Pro-Assad graffiti was sprayed on the walls in green paint. The kidnappers made a video of us saying more or less what they wanted us to say. All the while, Abu Jaffar bragged about how many Sunnis he planned to kill. He threatened to shoot Ghazi in the leg, but when he pulled the trigger, Ghazi didn't scream. Abu Jaffar had fired into the ceiling just to scare us. Then they took us to a house nearby and served us coffee in cups and saucers that had Shia logos on them.

For the next five days, we were moved from house to house, almost always blindfolded, tapping each other on the leg to make sure everyone was accounted for. On the second night we were given food and cigarettes. Then a new group of captors arrived. They seemed to rank higher than Abu Jaffar, who called them sir.

They showed little concern for our well-being. One day we were given only an apple to eat, and during one stretch I wasn't allowed to use the bathroom for thirty hours. They seemed to know what they were doing and have experience at moving prisoners. I was convinced they'd kidnapped people before.

I found that, at least for me, an effective way to cope with the stress of being a hostage is to think about something that takes a lot of concentration and drives out the dark thoughts. The dark thoughts come often. They bombard you. It's hard to keep the noise out of your head. Thoughts of torture, of relatives you'll never see again. I love to cook, so in my mind I invented a pasta meal I wanted to have when I got out. I followed it step-by-step, painstakingly chopping onions into a perfect mince, peeling garlic, and dicing mushrooms and plum tomatoes. I stirred the sauce with my favorite wooden spoon and took a sip of red wine. I could taste the red wine go down my throat. I could hear the clank of the bowls when I set the table. I could smell the truffle oil as I drizzled it over the pasta and let it cool before I sat down to eat. My then girlfriend (and now wife), Mary, set the knives, forks, and spoons on napkins on the table. I made ice cream for dessert. I concentrated on every detail, each fall of the knife, every stir of the pot, every sound and smell and smile from Mary. It took me away.

One of my biggest fears was that we would be separated and interrogated one by one. Then the kidnappers could use the old police trick: "Well, Ghazi says this and you say that. Which is it?" I knew we wouldn't be able to keep our stories straight for long. Ghazi and I were concealing that we spoke Arabic. If they found out that I did, I felt sure they would accuse me of being a CIA agent and force me to make confessional videos at the point of a gun, then kill me or sell me or trade me to another group. We were meat to be bought and sold. Speaking Arabic made me a curious and unusual product. I didn't want to be special. I didn't want them to be curious about me. I just wanted out.

On the first day, Abdelrazaq disappeared. On the fifth day, our driver, Taher, went missing. That left six of us: me, Kooistra, Ghazi, Aziz, Mustafa, and our British security consultant, who had clammed up and sat as rigid as a stone for most of the time we were held.

On the fifth night we were told we were going to Foua, a stronghold of the Shia militia Hezbollah. About seven minutes into the trip—I tried to count the seconds to keep track of distances—the driver slammed on the brakes and yelled, "Checkpoint! Checkpoint!" He jumped out and started firing his AK-47 in short, quick bursts, shots that seemed aimed to kill. We stripped off our blindfolds and looked for a way to get out of the van. Abu Jaffar jumped out of the vehicle and I watched him fire toward the checkpoint. The kidnappers' trail car behind us sped off, apparently not wanting any part of the fight.

Our security man clambered over Abu Jaffar's front passenger seat. Aziz got out through the driver's door, kneeling by what he said was a dead body and using the van for cover.

Our rescuers approached the van and said they were from a Sunni religious group. They would eventually take us to the Turkish border. There were just five of us now. Our security consultant had run off into the night. He walked for miles in flip-flops until he was driven back to the Turkish border by friendly villagers.

We later learned that the kidnappers had accidentally set off an emergency GPS beacon when they were going through our things. NBC had been alerted to the distress signal, pinpointing the farm where we were taken on the first day for several hours as a key location and circulating a satellite photo to sources around Washington and the Middle East. The network kept our families informed and asked for a news blackout, a request that was respected by major news outlets.

From Turkey on the day we got out, John, Ghazi, and I recounted the kidnapping on the *Today* show. I spent two days in Turkey, then flew to New York to see my family. I went to a psychiatrist (NBC insisted we all go) and told her I had been through traumatic experiences before and understood that the kidnapping would leave "fingerprints" on me for a while. The key was knowing what to expect. If you get blind drunk, you know you're going to wake up with a hangover. By the same token, I expected post-traumatic stress symptoms—anger, irritability, a sense of isolation—and I experienced those feelings, off and on, for several months. It's like having the monkey on your back again, and being self-aware helps shake him off.

For us the story of the kidnapping was over after we got out. We had survived and reported about what we had seen and believed to have happened. We moved on. About two years later, however, the story would come back into the news. I was contacted by a reporter from the *New York Times* who said the paper had information that we weren't in fact captured by pro-Assad *shabiha,* but by a criminal gang linked to the rebels, and that the Syrians who had rescued us actually had ties to the kidnappers. It was a total shock, but in Syria, and in all wars, strange and murky alliances are not uncommon.

An NBC producer and I immediately started checking with US law-enforcement and intelligence sources. We spent the next month trying to piece together events and interview everyone who might know anything about what had happened to us. Working with Syrian exiles in the United States and Turkey, we contacted dozens of activists and rebels inside Syria. We spoke to people associated with armed groups in Ma'arrat Misrin, the town where we were held. Many of the key players were dead or missing. Others didn't want to talk or couldn't be trusted. What we were able to piece together is that the kidnappers in all likelihood were Sunni criminals pretending to be Shiite *shabiha* so that if we ever got out we wouldn't have been able to identify them. The rebel group that rescued us did in fact have a past relationship with one of the kidnappers' ringleaders, but apparently had a falling-out in part because of our abduction. Like any reporter faced with new information, I updated the account of what had happened.

When I look back on our decision to take that trip, I see now that we were far too confident. We had grown so accustomed to traveling with Syrian rebels that we didn't give enough thought to the possible dangers.

All that changed afterward. NBC created a special team for me, including a producer with extensive experience in conflict zones. But I think Syria was becoming too dangerous to cover for any Western reporter. It would certainly become that once ISIS gained strength.

I went back to Syria for the first time after the kidnapping on June 25, 2013. I reported that a rebel commander outside Aleppo rarely saw Assad's forces anymore, just Shiite fighters from Hezbollah, Iran, and Iraq, and that a group of dangerous Sunni fanatics was growing. ISIS was coming into its own.

By this time, ninety-five thousand people had died in the civil war, but one attack made the others pale in comparison.

On August 21, 2013, we showed footage of what we said "may be the worst chemical attack anywhere since Saddam Hussein gassed Iraqi Kurds in 1988." The attack took place in Ghouta, a suburb of Damascus. The next day, we reported that the White House had called for an investigation. Some speculated online that the videos were fake. "But how can anyone fake rows of dead children?" I asked on the air. "No apparent injuries, no blood. Just lifeless bodies, their arms folded." The United States later estimated that upward of fourteen hundred people had died.

Almost exactly a year earlier, President Obama had made his "red line" warning. But by the time of the Ghouta attack, the situation on the ground had become even more complicated. Al-Qaeda and other radical Islamists had streamed into the country, and it was becoming almost impossible to distinguish between Syrian rebels and extremists exploiting their cause.

On August 30, 2013, back in Syria again, I described the dilemma facing Washington: "The US, frankly, faces bad choices for Syria: do too little and it looks weak; do too much and it could create chaos in the region." Two weeks later the United States decided it was not going to intervene in Syria—at least for the time being. The Syrian opposition felt betrayed and abandoned. Worse, Syrians were now completely without hope, which is the most dangerous human condition. A man or woman with no hope is capable of anything.

NINE

AFTER 9/11, TWO WORDS—AL-QAEDA—BECAME SHORTHAND FOR ISLAMIST
terrorism anywhere in the world. After that, US troops battled
Islamist fanatics in Iraq. In the media we called them insurgents
and terrorists and documented their horrors in Baghdad. With
the help of a huge troop surge and a seemingly unlimited budget,
the insurgents were ultimately overpowered. But they weren't
completely defeated. They found new life in Syria. The group
founded by Zarqawi was reborn in the crucible of Syria and had
three main goals: controlling Syria, restoring Sunnis to power
in Iraq, and establishing a Sunni caliphate. The wider world was
shocked into noticing the rise of ISIS in June 2014. The group

had captured Mosul, an industrial city in Iraq roughly half the size of Chicago. When Brian Williams, then the anchor of the *NBC Nightly News*, introduced my report, he was also introducing the American public to a fearsome new jihadist group.

"Tonight a heavily armed fighting force, in some cases using [captured] American arms and vehicles, is making lightning speed from city to city across the Iraqi countryside. . . . They are known as ISIS, standing for the Islamic State of Iraq and Syria, which happens to be their goal." On June 29, ISIS proclaimed a "caliphate" called the Islamic State, with Abu Bakr al-Baghdadi holding the title of caliph, or successor to the Prophet Mohammed. Abu Bakr was in fact Zarqawi's successor. ISIS now controlled broad swaths of territory and the lives of millions of people in both Iraq and Syria.

The capture of Mosul probably surprised ISIS as much as it did the Iraqi and US governments. Mosul, a large Sunni city 250 miles north of Baghdad, was once a bastion of the Iraqi army. It was where Uday and Qusay, the two sons of Saddam Hussein, went to hide and were ultimately killed by American soldiers after the fall of Baghdad. But when the United States ill-advisedly disbanded the Sunni-led Iraqi military after the invasion, the newly empowered Shiites ran roughshod over their former rulers. The people of Mosul came to hate the government and its security services.

When ISIS fighters arrived in Mosul, they were outnumbered by an enormous margin. Just hundreds of jihadists attacked two or three divisions of the Iraqi army, upward of twenty thousand men.

The ISIS gunmen were willing to die for their cause, but the Iraqi soldiers decidedly were not. They cut and ran, leaving behind uniforms, weapons, and thousands of Humvees. (Some of these were later packed with explosives and used as suicide vehicles when ISIS overran Ramadi, some seventy miles west of Baghdad, in May 2015.)

ISIS had tapped on the Iraqi army and found that it was as fragile as an egg. The group's leaders drew a reasonable conclusion: "This is easy. Let's keep going, we can take the whole thing." But even they couldn't have imagined the rot they had exposed. The Iraqi army crumbled in almost every early battle because it was corrupt, riddled with nepotism, and debilitated by ghost ranks. Ghost ranks are soldiers on the duty roster who don't show up. It's a kickback racket for officers. An officer will find a young recruit and say, "Okay, it's better if you go home. I'm going to keep you on the roster and you'll still be paid. But you go home and find another job as a taxi driver or a house painter or whatever. And I'm going to keep two-thirds of your salary. So you don't have to do any soldiering, but I'm going to still give you a third of your salary."

Imagine a US army platoon commander who's a lieutenant and has to give a percentage of his salary to his captain, who then kicks back a piece to his senior officer, and so on up the chain of command. Who's going to fight and die for that kind of army?

Mosul was a game changer, the moment when ISIS surpassed al-Qaeda as the region's dominant jihadist group. ISIS flaunted its newfound power. The group formally broke from al-Qaeda and even declared war on its affiliate in Syria, the Nusra Front. ISIS also wasn't content to embarrass the Iraqi army and take its weapons. It brutalized the soldiers it captured, lining up and executing seventeen hundred prisoners in a single incident. ISIS put the whole gory exercise online, and some Sunnis secretly cheered, as if they were saying, "Hey, our team won. Okay, it was our extreme team, but it was still our team." Some were cheering because ISIS, radical as it was, was marching toward Baghdad promising to re-plant the Sunni flag removed by the United States. The idea of the caliphate, even one stained in blood, also resonated with Sunni Muslims. It harked back to a time when the Islamic world, and Arabs in particular, were strong and leaders, instead of weak and divided as they have been for the last century.

Mosul was ISIS's break-out moment, but the group had been slowly building for months. We, and others, reported on its rise time and again. We reported how its fighters were slipping into Syria from Turkey's southern border. I'd seen them as far back as 2012 at the Istanbul airport and in Antakya, a city of 215,000 only a dozen miles from the Syrian border. (The ruins of the an-cient metropolis of Antioch, known as "the cradle of Christian-ity," lay on the outskirts of the modern, overwhelmingly Muslim city.)

The ISIS recruits were as conspicuous as college kids on their way to Cancún for spring break. I especially remember a group of them in Antakya, Arabs with beards, all in their twenties and thir-ties, with military builds, carrying backpacks and wearing sneak-ers or hiking shoes. So what were they doing walking through the middle of Antakya? They weren't there to pray at Saint Peter's Church. They weren't there to see the Byzantine mosaics. And they weren't there to look at the beautiful scenery or sample Antakya's famous cuisine. They were there for one reason: to cross the border and bring the fight to Syria. If a journalist could see them, Turkish intelligence and the CIA could certainly see them too.

Arab speakers often call the group Daesh, a tag rejected by ISIS because the Arab word *daes* means "crush underfoot."

ISIS follows Salafism (the Saudi version of Salafism is called

Wahhabism), but the group effectively stole al-Qaeda's ideology and expanded on it, embracing the most grizzly and brutal aspects of Islam's history like enslaving female captives and beheadings, while rejecting the faith's long traditions of tolerance. It would be like a group that claimed to act in the name of Christianity, but only accepted the worst practices of the Spanish Inquisition at the expense of all others. ISIS nonetheless proved to be appealing to a certain segment of Muslim society because it offered the possibility of living without modern rules. It appealed to psychopaths and to Muslims who felt outraged by the racism they encountered in Europe. It is a disturbing aspect of human nature that if there is a place where there are no consequences and where the most grotesque murders are tolerated in the name of a cult claiming to be a faith, a certain type of person will be attracted to it.

My first face-to-face meeting with ISIS recruits came in early December 2012, shortly before I was kidnapped. I was traveling with rebels in the Free Syrian Army in the vicinity of Aleppo, Syria's largest city, which is located in the northwest corner of the country close to the Turkish border. The rebels' system was communal and loose. We would hop from one safe house to another, spending a few hours at one and maybe a few nights at another. These houses provided a place to sleep, some food, and use of a bathroom—much-needed creature comforts when you're living rough.

One night we were at a house not far from Aleppo. It was cold. We'd been there for several days and were sleeping on blankets and rollout mattresses on the floor. We were comfortable and enjoying the company of our hosts, who were secular revolutionaries, moderates who wanted to overthrow the regime and create a more or less democratic and tolerant society. They were the kind of rebels the United States talked about supporting but never really did.

Then another group of opposition fighters turned up. In the rotating system of safe houses, this was not unusual. The newcomers were different, however, in their appearance, their behavior, and their attitude toward us. They all had beards and wore more military-style uniforms. They carried their guns with them inside, all the time, instead of leaving them at the door as the other fighters did. They were deadly serious, not at all like the Free Syrian Army rebels, who would slap everyone on the back, take off their shoes, plop down on a pillow, and light cigarettes. Their beards made it clear they were Islamists. They didn't introduce themselves.

Our host brought out plates of food, and we all sat down on the floor, on our legs or with legs crossed Indian-style, a typical communal meal in Syria. The Islamists who had just arrived weren't talking to us, apparently because we were Westerners. They weren't rude to us, but they were hard-eyed and aloof. I was sitting next to one of them, a man in his late thirties or early forties, heavyset, built like a construction worker. He eventually started speaking to me, if only because I was next to him. He harped on the coming of a new caliphate.

I said, "Oh, why do you say that?"

"We're building it. It's happening. The caliphate will return, and will return soon." Then he looked in my eyes and said it again. "Soon. The caliphate is coming back, imminently." He was sure about this—in December 2012.

When the bearded gunmen finished their meal, they got up and left. I got the feeling they didn't feel comfortable there because of our presence. If that meal had been a year later, I'm sure we would have ended up leaving with our hands tied behind our backs, kidnapped.

But at the time, ISIS was relatively weak. It was in re-formation. The moderate rebels still had the upper hand, and since we were their guests, these hard-core guys couldn't hurt us. They didn't call themselves ISIS fighters yet. They just described themselves as warriors for Allah. They had a quiet fierceness common to true fanatics.

I was kidnapped less than two weeks later, and in retrospect it seems clear that if I had been held longer, I probably would have been sold to or taken by guys like this, whether they called themselves ISIS or not. James Foley, a freelance correspondent, was kidnapped thirty miles from Aleppo three weeks before the Sunni-connected criminal gang grabbed me.

I went back into Syria in June 2013 with Salim Idris. At the time, Salim Idris was chief of the Free Syrian Army. I had a good relationship with him. He was secular, eager for American support, and happy to have me tag along. I think he wanted to show me that the FSA was still in charge. But what he ended up showing me was that the FSA was not in charge, not by a long shot. He had two protection vehicles when he went into Syria, one in front of his SUV and one in back. The three SUVs were packed with gunmen. Probably seven armed guys were in the front vehicle, six in the trail car. Another three rode in his car with him. So we had sixteen or seventeen guards, all heavily armed, all fully trusted by Salim Idris.

On the road from the Turkish border to just outside Aleppo, about a forty-minute drive, we passed seven checkpoints, none of them controlled by the FSA. Some were manned by independents keeping an eye on their villages. Some were controlled by

ISIS. Remember, this was only six months after my dinner with what I presumed were ISIS fighters. Back then they were keeping a low profile. Now they seemed to be advertising their affiliation. They had black flags and wore ski masks. Salim Idris was trying to say, "Hey, look, I'm still in charge. I'm still the big guy. I can take you into Syria." Frankly, I was worried he wouldn't be able to get me out.

At one ISIS checkpoint, the militants stopped us and started talking to the driver. You could see them trying to figure out what to do: "Do we take these guys on? Do we remove Salim Idris and his Western journalist and crew from the car?" I'm not a mind reader, so I can't be 100 percent sure what they were thinking. But judging by their body language, the tone of their questions, and the spirited conversations they had among themselves, it sure looked like a kangaroo court had been convened.

They eventually waved us through. A few months later, I don't think we would have made it. By then, the FSA was no match for ISIS. Salim Idris no longer had any clout. We would have just been taken. And ISIS wouldn't have been concerned about the consequences. There would have been little if any political backlash, just pleas from NBC and the US government to let us go. I know this sounds melodramatic, but anyone who's crossed a lawless border—in Pakistan, Somalia, Afghanistan—knows the feeling. You can simply disappear and no one would be the wiser.

When I went into Syria again in August 2013, this time to collect soil samples to test for evidence that Assad had used chemical weapons, the first person I saw was an ISIS gunman with a ski mask and a headband with an Islamic slogan written on it. The ISIS fighters were sending a message to the FSA and al-Qaeda and everyone else in Syria that they were now in charge. ISIS evolved in plain sight, right under the world's nose and often in front of our camera. ISIS is not a virus that came from nowhere. It started in Iraq, and then expanded in Syria, cannibalizing the rebel movement and capitalizing on Syrians' dashed hopes and growing anger.

ISIS also learned to market itself. The group is obsessively concerned with its public image, knowing that it's key to recruiting and to its jihadist preeminence. So it reacts swiftly to any development that raises doubts about its control of its caliphate in Iraq and Syria. In late June 2015, for example, Kurdish fighters stirred ISIS's ire when, with the help of US warplanes, they captured the Syrian town Tal Abyad. This was not just any town. It sits astride a key supply line for arms and fighters bound for Raqqa, ISIS's command center in Syria. Raqqa, a city of 220,000, lies fifty-five miles south of the Turkish border and a hundred miles east of Aleppo.

ISIS responded with a barrage of snuff videos. In one, five men described as spies were put in a cage and lowered into a swimming pool while a camera captured their drowning throes. A second group was crammed into a car that was then blown up by a rocket-propelled grenade; the scene was made all the more gruesome when the car burst into flames. In the third, seven men were decapitated simultaneously by an explosive cable strung around their necks.

When ISIS captured the ancient city of Palmyra in May 2015, the world rightly feared for its archaeological treasures. Under ISIS's austere monotheism, human statues and memorials constitute idolatry forbidden by Sunni Islam.

ISIS had grander plans for Palmyra, a UNESCO World Heritage site located 135 miles northeast of Damascus. On July 4, 2015, a date perhaps chosen for its resonance in the United States, ISIS released a ten-minute video whose cinematic style resembled the early epics of Cecil B. DeMille. In a meticulously choreographed death pageant, ISIS fighters led twenty-five Syrian soldiers into an ancient Roman amphitheater. The Syrians, dressed in dark green fatigues, were lined up on the stage and forced to kneel. Then an equal number of ISIS teenagers, wearing sand-colored clothes and tan headscarves, filed past the stage, with a soundtrack of musical chants giving them a heroic air. They mounted the stage, each taking a place behind one of the soldiers, pointed handguns at the Syrians' heads, and pulled the triggers at the same time.

ISIS had become more than a savage terrorist group; it had also become a state of mind, a place off the grid of humanity where only ISIS rules mattered. While most of the horrific acts given an ISIS label were committed by "core" members in the caliphate, a growing number were carried out by "branches," "offshoots," or "affiliates" inspired by ISIS—or lone-wolf copycats turned on by ISIS snuff videos.

On June 26, 2015, which ISIS called "Bloody Friday," four attacks were carried out on three continents in the wake of the group's call for "calamity for the infidels" during Ramadan. In a beach rampage in Sousse, Tunisia, a lone gunman killed thirty-eight people, most of them British tourists. ISIS claimed responsibility, but investigators believed the killer belonged to a separate network of Salafis. The gunman, twenty-four-year-old Seifeddine Rezgui, trained with an extremist group in Libya, along with two other militants who killed twenty-two people at the Bardo National Museum in Tunis in March 2015.

In Kuwait, a branch of ISIS claimed responsibility for an attack on a Shiite mosque. (The same group had previously claimed responsibility for killing twenty-four in attacks on two other Shiite mosques, both in eastern Saudi Arabia, in May 2015.) In Somalia, a radical group called Al-Shabaab, which several years ago pledged allegiance to al-Qaeda, killed dozens of Burundian soldiers at an African Union base. Al-Shabaab ditched al-Qaeda in favor of an allegiance to ISIS, partly because al-Qaeda was demanding kickbacks from the Somali group and partly because ISIS was the hot new brand in the terror business.

Perhaps the most disturbing ISIS-related attack on Bloody Friday only took one life. A worker at a US-owned industrial plant in southeastern France killed his boss, then decapitated him and put his head atop a fence outside the factory. He also took pictures of the victim's body draped with an Islamist flag. The suspect had visited Morocco, Saudi Arabia, and Syria, was thought to be connected to a Salafist group, and had been under surveillance by French authorities off and on for the last decade. Yet his stated motive for the atrocity was chillingly banal: he wanted to get back at his boss for chewing him out for dropping a pallet of valuable material.

Watching the ISIS videos is disturbing. Meeting the group's victims in person, however, leaves a mark.

In the summer of 2015, I met Mohammed, fourteen, in the southern Turkish city of Sanliurfa, an ancient city of stone walls and canals filled with fish from a sacred pond. The city looks more like Aleppo than cosmopolitan Istanbul. I met Mohammed in a small apartment where he lived with his brother and a friend of the family who was acting as his nurse. Mohammed was using a wheelchair to move around the apartment on the third floor of a dilapidated walk-up building. It had no air-conditioning. The doorways in the apartment were narrow. His wheelchair didn't fit through all of them, so Mohammed, originally from eastern Syria, often pushed himself out of the chair and hopped around the apartment on one foot.

ISIS had chopped off Mohammed's right hand and left foot two weeks before I met him. ISIS tried to turn Mohammed into a child soldier. The group disfigured him because he refused to cooperate.

Although Mohammed looked like a typical young teenager, pimples and all, he had been part of the Free Syrian Army, fighting against the Syrian regime and ISIS. Mohammed worked as a spotter, using binoculars to help the rebels locate their targets.

"First we were going to [anti-government] demonstrations. Later on we got armed with the Free [Syrian] Army, and we fought the al-Assad regime for three years," Mohammed said with obvious pride in his voice.

The balance of power shifted in eastern Syria when ISIS took over Mosul and captured stockpiles of American-made weapons. Mohammed went into hiding. He knew the rebels couldn't defeat ISIS after Mosul.

"I stayed at home for seven months," Mohammed said. "Later on, ISIS started arresting members of the Free [Syrian] Army. One of the detainees told them I was also a member."

Mohammed didn't know he'd been informed on until a group of ISIS fighters showed up at his door to seize him.

After Mohammed was discovered and arrested, he was locked in an ISIS jail for two months. He says he was in a room with seventy-five other boys and men. He says they were all tortured savagely, his shins beaten with bats and electric shocks to his genitals.

"Many people died there. No water, no electricity. They

provided water twice a day. We used the toilet once a day," Mohammed said.

Mohammed was released from prison and also sentenced to repent by going to an ISIS indoctrination school. But Mohammed was convinced that if he went to the school, he'd be sent to the front lines to die or used as a suicide bomber. Mohammed decided to try to escape with a group of friends.

One of them turned him in.

Within a few hours, Mohammed was brought before an ISIS judge. His crime was trying to escape ISIS-held areas, thereby choosing to leave the realm of "true Islam" for the land of the infidels, which ISIS considers everywhere else.

"He said to me 'This is the judgment of Allah. You were going to the land of the infidels . . . so you are like them. Your leg and arm must be cut off.'"

The punishment was carried out the next day.

The "chopping" ritual was carried out in a carnival-like atmosphere with an assembled crowd cheering and jeering as the condemned were brought to a city square. A section of honor in the square was reserved for the children of foreign fighters.

The sons of foreign fighters were expected to cheer and jeer the loudest. They were being trained, Mohammed said, to be elite members of ISIS's next generation of suicide bombers and foreign terrorists. Sometimes the sons of foreign fighters carried out executions themselves, erasing their respect for human life while they're still impressionable.

Mohammed's punishment was to have his opposing limbs cut off: his right hand (considered in Islamic culture to be the "clean" hand) and his left foot. ISIS attempts to make the horrific ritual appear hygienic. The ISIS members who held Mohammed's limbs in place wore surgical gloves and squirted iodine on his hand and foot. Mohammed said he was given an injection. He didn't know what it was but said he was told it would calm him down.

ISIS members tied Mohammed's arm and leg with tourniquets to cut off the blood flow to his hand and foot. The purpose of the amputations was not to kill the victim, but maim him forever. The tourniquets were left on for about fifteen minutes. Then, Mohammed's arm was stretched out on a block of wood. A large meat cleaver was placed on top of his wrist at the point where the cut would be made. A man with a mallet smashed the back of the cleaver so it would cut straight through bone and flesh. Mohammed and others identified the man who carried out the punishment as an Iraqi from ISIS's "chopping committee," known by the nickname "the Bulldozer."

The first chop was met with celebratory cries of *Allahu Akbar*. The ritual was repeated to cut off his foot. Mohammed was then taken to an ISIS clinic where his skin was stretched and sewn over the stumps.

Mohammed's mother picked him up from the clinic, brought him home, and smuggled him into Turkey a few days later.

"They are fooling children with money," Mohammed said. "They are fooling them to bomb themselves. They give a boy some money, or a bicycle, and after two days they take him in a car to bomb himself. They target children the most. They focus on children, because children are unaware of anything in this life."

In Turkey, Mohammed didn't have enough money for medical and psychological care. His brother and the family friend who nurses him did the best they could with the help of a few generous Turks. Mohammed cried every time his bandages were changed. He was having nightmares, wet his bed, and often got confused.

One time, he forgot his foot was missing and tried to walk out, falling down the stairs of the building where he was living. His brother took him outside every day to get some fresh air.

"I can only sleep after I take sleeping pills," Mohammed said. "The most difficult time is when I go to sleep. The pain starts. In the daytime, I sit in the street and watch the people passing by to forget the pain."

But Mohammed said what hurt more than falling down the stairs was when a Turkish man approached him and gave him fifty Turkish lira, the equivalent of about $15. Mohammed wasn't begging. He was just sitting in his wheelchair, as he said, to forget the pain.

When he looked at the money in his lap, he started to cry. It dawned on him that he'd become what in Arabic is called a *miskeen*, someone who deserves pity. That's not how Mohammed saw himself, but he realized that's how others saw him.

What was even more disturbing was that ISIS, even while bragging about and showing off its brutality, continued to grow. General James Clapper, director of National Intelligence, told Congress in February 2015 that ISIS had as many as thirty-one thousand fighters. Based on conversations with US military officials, I think the number of fighters was probably double that, and well over one hundred thousand if the ISIS support network is included.

Who are these would-be jihadists? In simpler times most jihadists were motivated by idealism, misguided or not. In Antakya in September 2013, I interviewed a Tunisian man who called himself Abu Abdul Rahman, not to be confused with Zarqawi's deputy of the same name, as he waited for a smuggler to take him across the Turkish border into Syria. (Tunisia had by mid-2015 sent upward of three thousand fighters to Syria, more than any other country, despite having a population of only 10.8 million, little more than half the 20.1 million people who live in the New York metropolitan area.)

Abu Abdul Rahman, a twenty-two-year-old college student who had never fired a gun in anger, thought he was volunteering for al-Qaeda, but his contact across the border was ISIS. The lines between the two groups were still blurry back then. Regardless, his motives were typical of recruits for both groups. "This was a dream for me, to wage jihad for Allah's sake, because this is one of the greatest deeds in Islam, to lift aggression off my brothers, to bleed for Allah and no other," he said in my report on the *Nightly News*.

He was going to Syria to defend Muslims who Assad's regime was killing with barrel bombs. He was going to Syria because no one else was helping. He called his mother on the way to the border. She asked him to wait for her so she could come to Turkey to say good-bye in person. He lied to her, saying he was already in Syria and it was too late. "I am happy," he told me. "People say that by coming here I might die, there is shelling and so forth. . . . I did not come for money, I only came for Allah's sake and to support my Muslim brothers."

By 2015, ISIS was attracting not only idealists but also a grab bag of off-kilter types: sociopaths aroused by bloodlust; loners and misfits who craved a sense of belonging; thrill seekers who wanted to test themselves in combat; Muslims in Europe and America who felt they were excluded from Western prosperity or demeaned by Western permissiveness; people who resented authority in any form; naïfs seduced by slickly produced propaganda that gave violence a romantic patina.

The ISIS economy was healthy. The group controlled roughly 9 million people, a sizable tax base. The jihadists also had significant earnings from the sale of artifacts and oil pumped in areas it controlled. Plunder from conquests was another profit center: after taking Mosul, ISIS stole hundreds of millions of dollars from the central bank and several small banks. Kidnappings provided a steady revenue stream. Between 2008 and 2014, according to US government estimates, radical Islamist groups received $200 million in ransom payments.

ISIS also tried to show it could be a functioning government. In Mosul, ISIS fixed roads, spruced up gardens, installed streetlamps, and swept up cigarette butts. But it also blew up iconic shrines, shut down cell-phone towers and the Internet, and limited outside travel. In May 2015, when ISIS captured Ramadi, tens of thousands of residents had already fled. After killing opponents and seizing weapons, ISIS set about repairing roads, distributing fuel, maintaining the electrical grid, and ensuring the markets had food.

After the adrenaline rush of combat, sweeping streets and picking up garbage is pretty humdrum stuff. It could be argued that Saudi Arabia was born in a similar way, with Ibn Saud conquering four regions and proclaiming them a kingdom in 1932. Saudi Arabia became a major oil producer and a modern country with a court system, albeit one that condemns prisoners to beheadings. But I don't see ISIS becoming another Saudi Arabia. It's too radical and too intolerant. And its fighters have drunk too much blood. Saudi Arabia was born with ISIS's zeal and intolerant Sunni vision, but it wasn't run by a collection of murderous maniacs who'd come specifically to a place so they could carry out war crimes.

SOME US SECURITY EXPERTS STRESS THAT ISIS IS MORE INTERESTED IN CONSOLI- dating power in the Islamic world and less focused than al-Qaeda on attacking the United States and other Western countries. I don't agree. ISIS has made no secret of its interest in going global. In 2014, the group's principal spokesman, Abu Mohammad al-Adnani, issued a manifesto in which he said Allah had called on Muslims to "punish in similar fashion as you were afflicted." Adnani claimed that US aggression had taken close to 10 million Muslim lives in recent decades. "So if a bomb is launched at them that will kill ten million of them, and it will burn their land as they burned Muslim lands, this is therefore permissible." In a video released on February 15, 2015, showing ISIS militants executing twenty-one Egyptian Christians on a Libyan beach, one of the gunmen pointed across the Mediterranean and declared, "We will conquer Rome, by the will of Allah."

The rivalry and competition between ISIS and al-Qaeda is also a concern. If al-Qaeda is going to catch up with ISIS and regain its leadership of the international jihad, it needs to strike at the heart of the West as it did on 9/11. Another troubling scenario is one in which ISIS and al-Qaeda sort out their differences and realize they're on the same team.

When I arrived in 1996, a state system was in place in the Middle East: Saddam Hussein in Iraq, Gadhafi in Libya, Mubarak in Egypt. The Assad family, first Hafez and then Bashar, in Syria. Ben Ali in Tunisia. The Jordanian and Saudi monarchies. These regimes or their predecessors had survived the shock of the 1967 Arab-Israeli war. They were not the most enlightened leaders around, they were corrupt and thuggish, but the Arab world was at least a functioning place. The Middle East house may have been rotten, but it was standing.

But between President Bush's misguided military action and President Obama's inconsistent and confused action, the United States managed to destroy the status quo in just fifteen years, plunging the region into chaos and exposing the rot that had long been festering within. The combined and contradictory actions of the Bush and Obama administrations pushed over the row of rotten houses in the Middle East, unleashing the bitterness stewing inside, and it will be difficult to erect them again. I suspect people will eventually get fed up with the chaos, as they did in Egypt amid the turmoil that followed the Arab Spring. After a year in office, Mohammed Morsi, a leading member of the Muslim Brotherhood and the first democratically elected head of state in Egypt's history, was deposed by Abdel Fattah el-Sisi in a military coup. At this writing, Morsi is in jail, sentenced to death. Egypt always leads the way in the Middle East, so what happened there is instructive.

I started my career at the peak of the Arab big men in the late 1990s. I watched the region change with the death of the Israeli-Palestinian peace process. I followed its descent into chaos in Iraq. I saw the rise of a cynical new type of war in Lebanon where only violence mattered. I watched the zigzag policies of the Obama administration, the hopes and anguish of the Arab Spring and the madness that followed. I can only guess what will happen next. I suspect that over the next several years, we'll see strongmen back in power in all or most Middle East countries. Out of the chaos, new dictators will offer themselves as an alternative to the horrors of ISIS, the Sunni-Shia bloodshed, Turkish-Kurdish enmity, and Arab-Persian proxy wars. Once in power, the new dictators—the ones to establish a new status quo—will likely be worse than the old strongmen because they'll be able to use new technologies to identify and hunt down their enemies by their digital fingerprints. They will have the ability to point to the ugliness of recent history as a justification for taking their citizens' rights. "Give me your freedoms unless you want to return to the way things were," they might say.

But these would-be strongmen face a difficult path ahead. Many dictators will try to assert themselves. Not all will survive. The chaos that has been unleashed by the breaking of the old status quo won't easily be contained. ISIS supporters will fight to the death to retain the foothold they've taken for themselves. A lot of killing remains to be done before leaders of stature emerge—and before the fires of chaos are tamped down once again.

EPILOGUE

TWENTY YEARS HAVE PASSED SINCE I HEADED TO CAIRO TO COVER WHAT I SENSED would be the story of my generation, just as reporters before me had gone to Vietnam and Moscow to cover the big stories of their times. It turned out the train of history would pass through the Middle East's station, but who would have guessed that the United States would fight two of the longest ground wars in its history and plunge the Muslim world into a frenzy of violence and revolution. My ambition was to ride the train of history, and the train came rumbling right at me.

I arrived in Egypt before suicide bombings and beheadings and mass executions became almost daily occurrences in the region. It

seems corny to say now, but Cairo had a kinder and more generous spirit back then. People didn't like being poor, but since everyone was poor, they felt more or less in the same boat.

As I moved beyond Egypt, Syrians, Yemenis, Jordanians, Palestinians, and others welcomed me into their homes too, and I went
from place to place without concern for my physical safety. I was
a vagabond, free to wander and absorb my surroundings. When I
began to study Arabic on my own and with tutors, Cairenes were
delighted that I would take the time to learn their language. I
would go to cafés, and people would bring out papers and pens to
help me with my grammar.

Living in Egypt and exploring the Middle East was magical. I rode on horseback around the seventeen pyramids on the
Saqqara plateau south of Cairo, including Egypt's first, the step
pyramid of Pharaoh Djoser, completed forty-seven hundred years
ago. I luxuriated in the lush garden on Elephantine Island in the
Nile off Aswan, Egypt's southern gateway four thousand years
ago. I wandered through the temple complex at Karnak, a forest
of columns seemingly built by giants for giants but actually the
work of a succession of thirty pharaohs beginning five thousand
years ago.

The Parthenon in Athens is often held up as the epitome of
man-made beauty, but for me nothing compared to Petra in Jordan, where a hidden canyon cuts through rock that seems red
from afar but is swirled with blue, yellow, and pink and leads to
perfectly proportioned and harmonious tombs. Dating to 312 BC
and mysteriously abandoned and just as mysteriously rediscov-
ered, Petra was once a city of thirty thousand but its location was
unknown to Europeans until 1812. I loved walking through the
shaded alleys in the Old City of Jerusalem and visiting the Church

of the Holy Sepulchre, where the site of Christ's crucifixion is up a steep flight of stairs and where his tomb has long been covered with scaffolding because no one can agree on who should carry out badly needed renovations.

I always smiled as I walked alone through the souk Al-Hamidiya inside the old walled city of Damascus. It was famous for its furniture (notably mother-of-pearl inlaid chests), brass pitchers and candlesticks, antique globes and doors—and vanilla ice cream with crushed pistachio nuts on top. The old city of Sana'a in Yemen was a serendipitous bazaar offering curved-blade daggers (*jambiya*), spices (frankincense), dates, qat (a mild stimulant everyone chewed), and all manner of objects from tiny artisanal workshops.

Sana'a is a symbol of what has happened to the region over the last two decades. I used to go there often, sitting in cafés and chatting with Yemenis in a relaxed and friendly way. On one trip I stayed in Sana'a for weeks, going out every day reporting without a plan or a safety network. I bumbled into stories and learned by accident. Today I might be able to go once or twice a year and not feel nearly as safe wandering the streets. To be seen in the same place for too long could make me a marked man—for kidnapping or an AK-47 round. Given the choice, I'd prefer the latter. Kidnapping these days could mean being beheaded, drowned, or burned alive. When the Furies were released in the Middle East, an evil emerged beyond my worst imaginings.

The joy of the Middle East has been replaced by fear, pervasive in Iraq and Syria and darkening the lives of people throughout the region. This is why refugees have been flowing out of the Middle East by the millions for Europe. If President Bush's seeds of democracy or the Arab Spring had bloomed, these families wouldn't be risking everything to leave. Many in the region have simply lost all hope, which is understandable. If you lived in Libya after the fall of Gadhafi, you'd be terrified. You can't work, you can't sell your goods, your children can't go to school, you can't even drive around without fear of being kidnapped by bandits or terrorists. It's not a place where people can be happy and even marginally prosperous. It's pure chaos. It's worse in Iraq and Syria.

When the strongmen I suspect are coming try to claw their way to power, they will confront a generation of young people shaped by this chaos—uneducated, inured to violence by ISIS videos and the atrocities they have seen firsthand, and dehumanized by squalid refugee camps in Turkey, Jordan, and Lebanon and from living in train stations and in fields on the long march to Europe. In one notorious ISIS video, a Chechen militant hands his pistol to his son, and the boy shoots several prisoners kneeling in front of them. Can kids like these regain their appreciation of human life? They will be in their twenties and thirties when people my age are in their fifties and sixties. They will not be like convicted murderers in the United States, who are released from prison as old men, usually too broken and tired to commit another crime. These young Muslim men will be in the prime of their killing years.

When I came to the Middle East, journalists had a kind of immunity that allowed us to travel freely and meet with militants who hated Israel and the United States. In 2000, when I was working for Agence France-Presse, I didn't feel fearful when I went to Gaza to meet with Hamas leaders or to the West Bank to speak to Palestinian gunmen. These men didn't much like me. We didn't have anything in common. But they felt that they had to treat me with common decency and a modicum of respect because I was a journalist and I was writing about them. They wanted to spin me so that I would give the world their version of events. They were never completely happy, of course, because my pieces didn't make them look as perfect as they looked to themselves. But they needed to talk to me and other reporters because we were the only way they could get their story out.

Now jump ahead to 2006. Zarqawi was on his killing spree in Iraq, and suddenly the Internet had become ubiquitous, and uploading videos on YouTube and other platforms was literally child's play. So Zarqawi and his henchmen said to themselves, "Why should we let reporters interview us and filter what we say? We can go straight to the Internet and say exactly what we want, for as long as we want to say it, and we can post videos that Western journalists would never show."

Journalists became worthless, at least as megaphones. But we became valuable as commodities to be stolen, bought, and sold, traded for prisoners, or ransomed for millions. As a correspondent for a major American network, I began to feel like a Ferrari in the worst neighborhood in the world. The policy of the United States (and the United Kingdom) is not to pay ransoms for kidnapped nationals, although security agencies develop intelligence on their whereabouts and Special Forces have sometimes carried out rescue raids, most of which were deadly failures. European governments do pay ransoms, however, making journalists from the Continent prime targets for ISIS and other extremist groups.

The next ten years in the Middle East promise to be extremely violent, but I suspect the fighting will be mainly local and sectarian, nothing like the US invasion of Iraq—and probably of little interest to Americans. In 2015, when I went back to the States or to an international conference, I found that people didn't much care anymore. They saw the Middle East awash in blood, beyond redemption, and didn't want to read about it or see it on the evening news. They just wanted to keep away from it.

But American eyes returned to the Middle East because of the Iran nuclear deal. The agreement, which restricts Iran's nuclear capacity for fifteen years, was signed on July 14, 2015, by Iran and six world powers—the United States, China, Russia, Britain, France, and Germany. It was unanimously endorsed by the UN Security Council on July 20.

It is at the time of this writing too early to predict how it will work out. In principle, the deal makes sense. The United States, as a superpower, should use diplomacy to protect itself from hostile powers and to strike strategic alliances. Any attempts to bring more peace in the world should be encouraged. But I would add a note of caution. Keeping track of nuclear materials and centrifuges may prove to be the easy part. The deal, which reintroduces Shia Iran to the world economy, alters the global power dynamic between Sunnis and Shiites, and our history in Iraq and Syria has proven that the United States doesn't seem to know how to strike that balance. In the end, it isn't Washington's responsibility to make amends between Sunnis and Shiites. From the US perspective, the deal limits Tehran's ability to make nuclear weapons and that's good for Americans. But the Middle East has proven to be a dangerous hole US administrations continue to slip into. If the Iran deal unravels or leads to an arms race, the United States could find itself slipping back in again. The Saudis could embark on a nuclear program of their own or buy nuclear weapons from another state, most likely Pakistan. A major ISIS attack could upset the balance of power or create a humanitarian crisis. A large-scale strike by ISIS or an al-Qaeda attack could renew calls for the United States to launch another war in the Muslim world. The Middle East is a magnet, and America could easily be pulled back in.

On July 20, 2015, the day of the Security Council vote, the US ambassador to the UN, Samantha Power, said, "This nuclear deal doesn't change our profound concern about human rights violations committed by the Iranian government or about the instability Iran fuels beyond its nuclear program." Which was exactly why governments of Israel, Saudi Arabia, and Egypt were unnerved by the deal. They worried that the infusion of billions of dollars and the freedom to buy and sell sophisticated conventional weapons—surface-to-air missiles from Russia, advanced ballistic missiles from China—would make Iran the muscleman of the region, stirring dreams of Persian glory and hegemony.

DESPITE MY KIDNAPPING, AND BOMBS BLASTING OUT MY HOTEL WINDOWS IN Baghdad, and getting caught in cross fires in Aleppo and other places, I don't have many professional regrets. I don't sit around saying, "Jeez, I've been a dentist for twenty years and I really wanted to be a ballet dancer." I've had more excitement than I thought possible when I was a thirteen-year-old in Marrakech with dreams of becoming a foreign correspondent who wore white linen suits and smoked cigarettes in a bone holder.

When I was at Stanford, I lived in a house with a lot of football players. They were always injured, limping around in braces or casts. If you play football, you know you're always in danger of knee and neck injuries. It's the price of playing the game. By the same token, dealing with trauma is part of being a foreign correspondent. I know what to expect, and I know I'm going to deal with post-traumatic stress symptoms in the months and years after an ugly incident. After my kidnapping, I wanted to go to Syria as soon as possible to prove to myself I was all right. And when I got back in, I said, "Ha! I'm still standing. I'm not barking at the moon. I'm okay."

The effects of my abduction actually settled in later. I got occasional flashbacks, and now I take more seriously what happened to me—and appreciate more fully how lucky I was. A friend recently asked me where I went on a family vacation after my release. "Turks and Caicos," I blurted out, but I knew that wasn't right. "Oh, I'm sorry, that's not it," I said. "It was an island. Where in the hell was it? I'll have to check." It was actually Virgin Gorda. I'm blessed with a good memory, and if I couldn't remember a week in Virgin Gorda, I must have been more shook up than I thought.

As a foreign correspondent, which often means a war correspondent, you have to embrace the risks. I'm not addicted to them in the way some gamblers are addicted to losing because it hurts them and touches them deep in their souls. When I take risks now, I do so only when I have to and with every precaution. I used to prospect for news, dropping into places to see what was up. Well, I could go to parts of Libya today and find lots of good stories, but I probably wouldn't be around to tell them.

I did some soul-searching after my kidnapping. I felt I had seen history up close and lived life to the fullest—except in the most elemental way. I was forty years old, unmarried, and childless. That aspect of my life was a void.

Mary and I had grown serious about each other over the previous year, and I asked her to move in with me. When she did, I made her that pasta meal I'd pictured cooking while in captivity.

It was fantastic and she looked as beautiful as I pictured under my blindfold. We started talking about spending our lives together and starting a family. Now we have a wonderful son. I used to think having a child was more frightening than running through a minefield. I thought it would crush the romantic spirit I wanted for my life. I was wrong. Being a husband and a father is pretty romantic too.

I look forward to doing more stories in China, Russia, and other places that have taken a backseat to the Middle East during most of my career. But the story of my generation may also be the story of the next generation.

With its tangled history and politics, the Middle East has a way of sucking in great powers—and journalists. I bought my ticket on this train of history in 1996, and what a wild ride it's been. I plan to stay on the train until I have to get off one way or another.

ACKNOWLEDGMENTS

I'D LIKE TO THANK STEPHEN G. SMITH, WHO HELPED AT EVERY STEP OF THE WAY AND without whom this book would never have been completed. Ben Plesser, who provided insight and raised questions I hadn't considered. Mary Engel, whose support and love are deeply appreciated. Ali Zelenko, whose advice is always valuable. And of course the great master of editing and publishing, Alice Mayhew. There are too many colleagues to mention by name, but I'd like to recognize Aziz Akyavas, John Kooistra, Randy Brown, Madeleine Haeringer, Bredun Edwards, Wajjeh Abu Warefah, Mohammed Ajlouni, Zohair Beyati, Ghazi Balkiz, Ammar Sheikh Omar, Charlene Gubash, Mohammed Muslemany, and many others. Thank you to all of you.

INDEX

ABC, 52, 78, 79, 104
  Engel's work for, 63, 66, 73–75, 78, 86, 91
Abdelrazaq, 184, 185, 187
Abdul Hamid II, 32
Abed Rabbo, Yasser, 53
Abu Bakr, 92
Abu Ghraib, 135, 142
Abu Salim Prison, 7–8
Abu Zaal, 133
Adnani, Abu Mohammad al-, 208
Afghanistan, 45, 46, 104, 131, 142, 143, 155
  al-Qaeda in, 46, 130, 131, 137, 144

Kandahar, 145
Taliban in, 46, 130, 137, 144
Tora Bora, 130, 144
war in, 129–30
Agence France-Presse (AFP), 49–53, 58, 63, 214
Ain al-Hilweh, 136–38
Aisha, 92
Ajdabiya, 163, 164
Ajlouni, Mohammed, 73–74
Akyavas, Aziz, 174–76, 184, 187
Al-Aqsa, 55–58, 63
Al-Aqsa Mosque, 56
Alawites, 172, 181

Aleppo, 166, 178, 180, 182, 183, 189, 195, 197, 217

Al-Gama'a al-Islamiyya, 22

Al-Hadlaq, Abdulrahman, 141, 142

al-Ha'ir Prison, 145

Al-Hamidiya, 213

Ali (cousin and son-in-law of Mohammed), 2, 91–92, 103

Ali (driver and friend), 75, 76, 78, 79, 81, 106

aliyah, 51

Al Jazeera, 79, 111, 152, 159, 165, 173

Allah, 3, 7, 20, 28, 36, 38, 41, 92
    Jews and Christians and, 44

Allawi, Ayad, 97, 100

al-Qaeda, 27, 35–36, 67, 106, 131, 133, 146, 181–82, 190, 191, 193, 201, 208, 216–17
    in Afghanistan, 46, 130, 131, 137, 144
    beheadings by, 134
    founding of, 136–37
    in Iraq, 8, 98, 129, 131–33, 135, 181
    ISIS and, 193–95, 198, 206, 208
    in Jordan, 133
    prisoners from, 145
    rehabilitation program for veterans of, 140–43, 145
    rise of, 46
    Saddam and, 129
    Sulayman in, 143–46
    weapons of, 144
    Zawahiri and, 28

al-Rais, 7

Al-Rashid Hotel, 69, 73, 74, 76

Al Shaab, 19

Al-Shabaab, 201

Amish, 41, 42

Amman, 133

Amn al-Dawla, 19

Annan, Kofi, 178

Annas, Abu, 77, 84

Antakya, 194, 205

Antioch, 194

Arab caliphate, 20, 29, 31, 33–36, 39, 43, 44, 91–92, 194, 196

Arab-Israeli war, 208

Arab leaders, 5–9, 53, 87, 156, 194, 208–10

Arab Spring, 150, 156, 169, 178, 209, 213
    in Egypt, 152–56, 166–67, 209
    in Syria, 138, 156, 163, 166, 171–90

Arafat, Yasser, 55, 61–63, 112

Aristotle, 29

Arnett, Peter, 78, 82

Ashrawi, Hanan, 53

Assad, Bashar al-, 6, 8, 166, 169, 172–74, 176, 178–85, 198, 202, 206, 208
    background of, 172
    Obama and, 173

Assad, Bassel al-, 172

Assad, Hafez al-, 8, 172, 208

Assad family, 5–6, 87, 178, 208
Aswan, 212
Atarib, 179–80
Aziz, Tariq, 81–82

Ba'ath Party, 76–78, 81, 94, 173
Baghdad, 31, 60, 64, 67, 73, 74, 99, 102, 104, 133, 217
   Al-Rashid Hotel in, 69, 73, 74, 76
   Australian embassy bombing in, 89–90, 97, 98
   bombing attacks in, 89–90, 96–98, 103–4
   Canal Hotel in, 96
   Engel in, 69–86, 89–91, 98–101, 103, 105, 115, 127
   Flowers Land Hotel in, 69–70, 71
   Hamra Hotel in, 89–90, 99, 101, 103, 105
   Imma Bridge stampede in, 103
   Kazimiya district in, 102–3
   lawlessness in, 95
   Mansour neighborhood of, 69
   Mother of All Battles mosque in, 129
   Palestine Hotel in, 76, 79–81, 83–85
   sandstorm in, 79–80, 82
   Shaab neighborhood of, 80
   US bombing of, 70, 77–80, 82–84, 115
   US capture of, 93
Baghdadi, Abu Bakr al-, 192
Baghdad International Airport, 83
Bahrain, 4–5, 93, 156, 157, 162

Bakran, Ali, 178, 179, 181–83
Balkiz, Ghazi, 184–88
Barak, Ehud, 55, 56, 60
Barbary Pirates, 3
Bardo National Museum, 200
BBC, 52, 63, 78, 165
beheadings, 96, 107, 134, 141, 195, 211
Beirut, 114, 123, 125
   Dahiya neighborhood in, 117–18
   Engel in, 107, 109, 115, 120, 127–28, 149
   Israeli bombing of airport in, 114, 116–17
Bekaa Valley, 114
Ben Ali, Zine Al Abidine, 6, 7, 87, 150–51, 208
Benghazi, 159–66, 168, 180
Berg, Nick, 96
Bethlehem, 54, 62
Bilal Baroudi, Sheikh, 135–36
bin Laden, Osama, 27, 28, 34–39, 130, 143, 159
   death of, 28, 143, 166
   as historian, 28, 33–35
   Saddam and, 8
   speeches of, 28, 132
   Sulayman and, 144–46
   Taliban and, 46
   training camps of, 143
   Zarqawi and, 96, 98, 107, 131–32
   Zawahiri and, 27–28, 143
Bint Jbeil, 121
Bloody Friday, 200–201

Bosnia, 45, 143

Bouazizi, Mohamed, 150

Brahimi, Rym, 78

Bremer, Paul "Jerry," 94, 131

Britain, 5, 33, 216

  Egypt and, 4

  Iraq and, 4, 70, 77, 79, 80

  Jordan and, 4

  in Middle Eastern border
    creation, 1, 4

  Palestine and, 5

Burundian soldiers, 201

Bush, George H. W., 155

Bush, George W., 7–9, 30, 94, 139,
  209, 213

  "crusade" statement of, 30, 139

  Engel's meeting with, 108

  Saddam and, 64, 75–76, 87, 128,
    129, 156

  speech on Iraq, 75–76

Bush administration, 8, 113

  Iraq and, 8, 60, 64, 86–87, 128,
    130–32, 156

Bush Doctrine, 156

Byzantium, 29–32, 139

Cairo, 9, 14, 18, 21–22, 45, 51, 52,
  66, 151–52

  Engel in, 11–17, 36, 50, 53, 107,
    149–50, 158, 160–62, 167,
    211–12

  Mit Ouba neighborhood of,
    11–15

  Tahrir Square demonstrations
    in, 151–54, 157, 166–67

  Tahrir Square shooting in front
    of Egyptian Museum, 23–27,
    51

  Zamalek neighborhood of,
    16–17, 23

Camp David Summit, 51, 53,
  55–56

Carroll, Jill, 105

Carter Doctrine, 5, 155

Catholic Church, 30

Cefalù, 65

cell phones, 152, 174, 180

censorship, 21–22

Cervantes, Miguel de, 3

Chechnya, 45, 104, 143

China, 10–11, 216, 217, 219

Christ, 2, 44, 213

Christianity, 28, 29, 195

Christians, 1–3

  Allah and, 44

  in Crusades, 3, 4, 30, 31, 33–35,
    139

  as religious minority, 44

  tourists, 26

Christian Science Monitor, 105

Church of the Holy Sepulchre,
  212–13

CIA, 46, 129, 130, 137, 146, 174,
  194

Clapper, James, 205

Clinton, Bill, 55, 56

CNN, 52, 63, 78, 82, 158, 165, 184

Cold War, 5, 11, 35, 46, 147

Columbus, Christopher, 32

Constantine the Great, 29, 30, 139

Constantinople, 4, 29–32, 35
Crusades, 3, 4, 30, 31, 33–35, 139
   United States and, 30, 34, 139

Dahiya, 117–18
Dahiya Doctrine, 125–26
Damascus, 139, 166, 171, 177, 179,
   180, 190, 199
   Al-Hamidiya souk in, 213
Dante Alighieri, 2
Daraa, 166, 171–72
Dark Ages, 29, 30
democracy, 166
   in Iraq, 93, 94, 98, 104, 132
   in Middle East, 113, 128–39, 213
Divine Comedy (Dante), 2
Dome of the Chain, 56
Dome of the Rock, 56
Dulaimi Hotel, 75

Egypt, 5–7, 11, 13–14, 20–22,
   35, 38, 43, 45, 51, 117, 136,
   151–52, 158, 159, 168, 182,
   208, 209, 211–12, 217
   Aswan, 212
   Britain and, 4
   Cairo, *see* Cairo
   censorship in, 21–22
   Karnak complex in, 212
   Luxor attack in, 27, 36, 51
   Nile in, 14, 17, 23, 45, 168, 212
   prisons in, 45–46
   pyramids in, 212
   revolution in, 152–56, 166–67,
   209

Egyptian Museum, shooting at,
   23–27, 36
Eisenhower Doctrine, 5, 155
Eizenkot, Gadi, 126
electromagnetic bombs, 70
Elephantine Island, 212
El Manial, 17
Engel, Richard:
   at ABC, 63, 66, 73–75, 78, 86,
   91
   in Baghdad, 69–86, 89–91,
   98–101, 103, 105, 115, 127
   in Beirut, 107, 109, 115, 120,
   127–28, 149
   in Cairo, 11–17, 36, 50, 53, 107,
   149–50, 158, 160–62, 167,
   211–12
   divorce of, 91, 111
   first trip to Saudi Arabia, 38–39
   first wife of, 50, 64–65, 91
   as freelancer, 38, 49, 63, 65
   in Iraq, 50, 46–67, 69–86, 89–91,
   98–101, 105–7, 109, 127, 181
   ISIS members met by, 195–98
   ISIS victim met by, 201–5
   in Istanbul, 156–57
   in Jerusalem, 50, 51, 53, 58,
   63–65
   kidnapping of, 171, 184–89, 195,
   197, 217–19
   in Lebanon, 109–11, 114
   in Libya, 158–68, 173
   at *Middle East Times,* 16, 19,
   21–22, 38
   mother of, 75

Engel, Richard (*cont.*)
  Muslim Brotherhood and,
    16–21, 36
  at NBC, 91, 97, 100, 103, 104,
    109, 111, 115, 122, 127, 149,
    158, 166
  as NBC bureau chief, 107, 109,
    115, 127–28, 149
  in New York, 149–50
  as Palestinian-affairs
    correspondent for AFP, 49–53,
    58, 63
  Sicily house of, 65
  at Stanford, 10–11, 50, 217
  in Syria, 114, 138, 171, 174–90,
    195–98, 218
  Tabligh wa Dawa and, 36–38
  video journal of, 89–90
  visa of, 50, 65–66, 71, 73–74, 75
  wife of, *see* Forrest, Mary
England, *see* Britain
Erdogan, Recep Tayyip, 174
Erekat, Saeb, 52, 53
Erez Crossing, 112
Euphrates River, 94
Europe, 32
  in Dark Ages, 29, 30
  industrial revolution in, 32
  Middle East borders created by,
    1, 3, 4, 6, 33–35, 138

Fallujah, 96, 133
Fatah, 61, 112, 113
Fatima, 92
FBI, 146

First Intifada, 58, 63
Flowers Land Hotel, 69–70, 71
Foley, James, 197
Forrest, Mary, 150, 186, 218–19
Foua, 187
Fox, 78
France, 5, 33, 216
  Lebanon and, 4
  in Middle Eastern border
    creation, 1, 4
Free Syrian Army (FSA), 177, 179,
  185, 195–98, 202

G8 leaders, 117
Gadhafi, Mu'ammar, 6–9, 87, 150,
  158–61, 163, 165–68, 173,
  180, 208, 214
  capture and death of, 169, 172
  speech by, 159
Gaza, 51, 111–14, 123, 124, 214
Geneva Convention, 79
Genghis Khan, 30
Germany, 3, 33, 216
Ghandoriyah, 125
ghost ranks, 193
Ghouta attack, 190
Gizbert, Richard, 104
Global War on Terrorism, 130,
  146–47
Great Britain, *see* Britain
Greece, 22
Green Square, 161, 168
Guantánamo Bay (Gitmo), 140,
  145
Guardian, 165

Gulf of Sidra, 160
Gulf War (1991), 8, 60, 64, 82, 86,
    93, 155

Haditha, 135
Hagia Sophia, 32
Haifa, 61, 118, 123
hajj, 28, 39, 41, 42
Halutz, Dan, 113, 116, 122, 123
Hama, 8, 172
Hamas, 61, 63, 112, 113, 117, 214
    Israeli soldier kidnapped by,
        111–13
hawza, 97, 101
Hawza (newspaper), 95, 97
Hebron, 54
Herzegovina, 104
Hetherington, Tim, 165
Hezbollah, 113–14, 179, 187, 189
    Israeli soldiers kidnapped by,
        113, 122, 124
    Israel's cease-fire with, 124–25
    Israel's war with, 114–26,
        127–28
Holy Land, 2, 30
homosexuality, 20, 43, 44–45
Homs, 177
Hondros, Chris, 165
Houla massacre, 177–78
Hurricane Katrina, 102
Hussein (Ali's son), 92–93
Hussein, Qusay, 75–76, 77, 86, 192
Hussein, Saddam, *see* Saddam
    Hussein
Hussein, Uday, 75–76, 77, 86, 192

Ibn Saud, 4, 40–41, 207
Idris, Salim, 197–98
Ikhwan, 41
Imma Bridge stampede, 103
Independent, 165
India, 4
Inferno, L', 2
Inferno (Dante), 2
International Herald Tribune, 10
Internet, 131, 135–36, 141, 142,
    152, 155, 172, 180, 215
Iran, 35, 64, 93, 105, 107, 108,
    109–11, 113, 114, 150, 189
    nuclear capacity of, 150, 216, 217
    Shiites in, 93, 108
Iraq, 1, 4, 6, 7, 11, 29, 34, 69–87,
    89–106, 128, 184, 189, 208,
    209, 213, 214, 215
    al-Qaeda in, 8, 98, 129, 131–33,
        135, 181
    American POWs in, 79
    army of, 94, 131, 192, 193
    Ba'ath Party in, 76–78, 81, 94
    Baghdad, *see* Baghdad
    Britain and, 4, 70, 77, 79, 80
    Bush administration and, 8, 60,
        64, 86–87, 128, 130–31, 156
    civil war in, 96, 98, 102, 131
    Coalition Provisional Authority
        in, 100
    Constitution of, 104
    Council of Representatives in,
        104
    democracy in, 93, 94, 98, 104,
        132

Iraq (*cont.*)
  elections in, 97–98, 100, 102,
    104–5
  Engel in, 50, 64–67, 69–86,
    89–91, 98–101, 105–7, 109,
    127, 181
  in Gulf War (1991), 8, 60, 64, 82,
    86, 93, 155
  Haditha, 135
  Information Ministry of, 77, 79,
    80
  insurgency in, 97, 98, 106
  ISIS and, *see* ISIS
  journalists in, 95, 97, 99
  journalists' departure from, 73,
    75, 76, 78, 82
  journalists killed and taken
    hostage in, 105–6
  looting in, 93, 95
  map of, 68
  Mosul, 191–94, 202, 207
  oil fires in, 79
  Ramadi, 133, 193, 193
  refugees from, 139
  Shiite population in, 93
  Syria and, 138
  US invasion of, 50, 70, 72,
    76–87, 93, 95, 102, 107, 108,
    115, 128–30, 132, 146, 215
  US military presence in, 95, 136
  veterans in, 140
  weapons of mass destruction in,
    64, 86, 129, 131, 132
Iraqi Peace and Friendship Society,
  65–66

Iraq war, 9, 72, 74, 87, 99, 107,
  109, 115, 130–33, 136, 137,
  141–42
  common cause found in, 136
  terrorism and, 146, 147
ISIS, 9, 40, 107, 132, 174, 181, 189,
  191–210, 216–17
  al-Qaeda and, 193–95, 198, 206,
    208
  beheadings by, 96, 107, 195
  Bloody Friday attacks of,
    200–201
  as Daesh, 194
  economy of, 207
  Engel's meeting of members of,
    195–98
  Engel's meeting of victim of,
    201–5
  evolution of, 198–99
  as government, 207
  growth of, 205
  Iraqi army and, 193
  kidnappings by, 207, 215
  marketing of, 199, 206
  Mosul captured by, 191–94, 202,
    207
  Palmyra captured by, 199–200
  Ramadi captured by, 193, 207
  as Salafist, 194–95
  Shiite mosques attacked by,
    200–201
  Sousse rampage and, 200
  videos of, 96, 199–201, 208, 214
  Zarqawi and, 96, 107, 132, 191,
    192

Islam, 14, 20, 34, 141
  afterlife and, 38, 131
  Allah in, *see* Allah
  birth of, 1, 28, 35
  Koran in, *see* Koran
  Mohammed and, 2, 3
  orthodox, 92
  Ottomans and, 39
  reform of, 47
  Saddam and, 129
  and separation of church and
    state, 7, 28
  spread of, 28–30
  superiority of, 44
  see also Muslims
Israel, Israelis, 5–7, 11, 20, 34–36,
    111, 114, 137, 155, 167, 217
  aliyah and, 51
  Arab-Israeli war, 208
  Beirut airport bombed by, 114,
    116–17
  Dahiya Doctrine of, 125–26
  Lebanon's cease-fire with, 124–25
  Lebanon's war with, 114–26,
    127–28
  military service in, 111
  PR operations of, 52
  Zionism and, 19–21, 51, 77
Israel Defense Forces (IDF), 113,
    116, 121–25
Israeli-Palestinian conflict, 52–64,
    184
  A-B-C districts and, 54–55, 62
  Camp David Summit and, 51,
    53, 55–56

First Intifada in, 58, 63
Israeli bombing of Palestinians,
    113
kidnappings of Israeli soldier,
    111–13
Operation Defensive Shield in,
    62
Oslo II Accord and, 53–54
Palestinian prisoners, 112
peace process and, 53, 62, 63,
    209
Second Intifada in, 50, 56, 60,
    62–64, 115
suicide bombers in, 60–62
West Bank in, *see* West Bank
Istanbul, 29, 156–57
Italy, 159, 168
ITN, 165

Jaafari, Ibrahim al-, 100
Jabr, Asid, 138
Jaffar, 134–35
Jaffar, Abu, 185, 187
Japan, 162
Jebel al-Zawiya, 178
Jenin, 61, 62
Jericho, 54, 62
Jerusalem, 4, 11, 30, 32, 50, 56,
    66–67, 115, 139
  Americans in, 51
  East vs. West, 57–58
  Engel in, 50, 51, 53, 58, 63–65
  Mahane Yehuda market in, 50,
    61
  Nachlaot area of, 51

Jerusalem (*cont.*)
  Old City in, 50, 55–56, 212–13
  Temple Mount in, 55–58, 63
Jerusalem Capital Studios (JCS), 52
Jesus, 2, 44, 213
Jews, 27, 35
  aliyah and, 51
  Allah and, 44
  Al Shaab and, 19
  anti-Semitism and, 18–20,
    43–44, 45
  Palestine and, 5, 34
  as religious minority, 44
  Zionism and, 19–21, 51, 77
jihad, meaning of word, 141
jihadists, 36, 45, 46, 135–37
  in Egyptian prisons, 45–46
  mujahideen, 138, 140, 141
  rehabilitation program for,
    140–43, 145
  Salafi, 35–36, 38, 45, 46, 194–95
  see also al-Qaeda; ISIS
Jordan, 1, 5, 11, 73–74, 111, 114,
    117, 134, 136, 139, 208, 214
  al-Qaeda in, 133
  Britain and, 4
  Petra, 212
  Zarqa, 133

Kabul, 18
Kandahar, 145
Karbala, 40, 92–93, 96
Karnak, 212
Kazem, 71, 75
Kazim, Musa al-, 102–3

Kenya, 27
kidnapping and hostage-taking, 3,
    105–6, 111, 213, 214
  of Engel and crew, 171, 184–89,
    195, 197, 217–19
  by ISIS, 207, 215
  of Israeli soldiers, 112–13, 122,
    124
  ransoms and, 3, 207, 215
Kooistra, John, 158, 174–76, 184,
    187, 188
Koran, 3, 13, 20, 28, 44, 91–92, 98
  Saddam and, 129
Kufa, 92
Kurds, 4, 9, 34, 175, 190, 199,
    209
Kuwait, 4–5, 86, 87, 151, 155
  ISIS in, 200–201

Laos, 82
Lebanon, 4, 107, 109–26, 136, 209,
    214
  Ain al-Hilweh refugee camp in,
    136–38
  Bint Jbeil, 121
  civil war in, 117
  Engel in, 109–11, 114
  Hezbollah in, *see* Hezbollah
  Israel's cease-fire with, 124–25
  Israel's war with, 114–26,
    127–28
  map of, 110
  Maroun al-Ras, 119, 121
  Nabataea, 120
  Qana, 122–23

Tripoli, 135
Tyre, 4, 120, 122
Lebanon War (1982), 57
Libya, 6, 9, 150, 158–69, 180, 182, 183, 208, 214, 218
  Ajdabiya, 163, 164
  Benghazi, 159–66, 168, 180
  Engel in, 158–68, 173
  map of, 148
  Misrata, 164–66
  NATO airstrikes in, 162, 163, 165–67, 169, 173, 180
  Sirte, 160, 163, 164, 169
  Tobruk, 158, 159, 162, 163
  Tripoli, 160–68
  Zawiya, 161
  Zintan, 165–66
Lighthouse, 139–40
Likud Party, 56, 57
Livni, Tzipi, 116
Lockerbie, flight over, 169
Luxor, attack in, 27, 36, 51

Ma'arrat Misrin, 189
Madaen, 102
Mahdi Army, 102
Manama, 157
maps:
  Iraq, 68
  Lebanon, 110
  Libya, 148
  Middle East, 25
  Ottoman Empire, 24
  Syria, 170
  West Bank, 48

Marines, 135
Maroun al-Ras, 119, 121
Marrakech, 10, 16, 217
Mashhur, Mustafa, 17–18
Mecca, 28, 32, 39–42
Medina, 39–42
Meet the Press, 122–23
Mehmed II, 31–32
Mesopotamia, 93–94
Middle East, 1–2, 8, 9, 11, 183, 211–19
  democracy in, 113, 128–29, 213
  Europeans' creation of borders in, 1, 3, 4, 6, 33–35, 138
  history and, 29, 33
  instability in, 34, 35, 155, 156
  journalists in, 214–15
  leaders in, 5–9, 53, 87, 156, 194, 208–10
  nation-state system and, 34, 35, 36, 208
  oil in, *see* oil
  map of, 25
  refugees from, 213–14
  US policy in, 5, 35, 155, 156, 157, 169, 181, 209, 216–17
Middle East Times, 16, 19, 21–22, 38
Misrata, 164–66
Mohammed (hacker), 71
Mohammed (ISIS victim), 201–5
Mohammed (Prophet), 2, 3, 28–31, 36, 39–42, 44, 91–92, 100, 118, 192
  cartoons of, 2
Moldova, 71

Mongol invasions, 30–31, 33, 34, 36

Moon, Sun Myung, 16

Morocco, 10

Morsi, Mohammed, 209

Mosul, 191–94, 202, 207

Mu'awiyya, 92

Mubarak, Gamal, 153

Mubarak, Hosni, 6, 7, 9, 12, 14, 21, 22, 53, 87, 153–55, 157, 166–67, 173, 208
  Obama and, 155, 162

mujahideen, 138, 140, 141
  see also jihadists

Mujahir, Abdullah al-, 133–35

Munir Hadad, 137–38

Muslim Brotherhood, 8, 14, 21, 22, 43, 45, 153, 167, 172, 209
  Engel and, 16–21, 36
  logo and slogan of, 20, 167

Muslims, 1–3, 20, 29, 131
  Crusades and, 3, 4, 30, 31, 33–35, 139
  fundamentalists and extremists, 26–27, 35, 36, 38, 45, 76–77, 87, 136–37, 140, 181, 190, 191
  golden age of, 29, 33, 47, 194
  jihadists, see jihadists
  Mongol invasions and, 30–31, 33, 34, 36
  nation-state system and, 34, 35, 36
  Ottomans and, 31
  pirates, 3
  reformers, 47

Salafi, see Salafi Muslims
Shia, see Shia Muslims
Sunni, see Sunni Muslims
  see also Islam

Mustafa, 184, 187

Nabataea, 120

Nablus, 51, 54, 58, 61, 62

Nachlaot, 51

Nafusa Mountains, 165–66

Najaf, 92–93

Napoleon I, Emperor, 3

Nasrallah, Hassan, 116–19

Nasser, Gamal Abdel, 6

National Counterterrorism Center (NCTC), 146

National Intelligence, 205

National Security Council, 94

NATO, 162, 163, 165–67, 169, 173, 180

NBC, 78, 82, 104, 133, 149, 198
  Engel at, 91, 97, 100, 103, 104, 109, 111, 115, 122, 127, 149, 158, 166
  Engel as Beirut bureau chief at, 107, 109, 115, 127–28, 149
  and kidnapping of Engel and crew, 187–89
  Meet the Press, 122–23
  Nightly News, 103, 114, 119, 123, 153, 154, 177, 192, 206
  Syria and, 182–83
  Today, 188

Netanya, 61, 62

New York, 149–50

New York Times, 188
Nightline, 83
Nightly News, 103, 114, 119, 123, 153, 154, 177, 192, 206
Nile River, 14, 17, 23, 45, 168, 212
9/11 attacks, 8, 30, 60, 63–64, 129–32, 139, 143, 144, 146, 155, 191, 208
Noble Sanctuary (Al-Aqsa), 55–58, 63
North Korea, 64
nuclear power, 144, 169
    Iran and, 150, 216, 217
Nusra Front, 193

Obama, Barack, 7–9, 209
    Assad and, 173
    Bahrain and, 157, 162
    Benghazi and, 162
    bin Laden and, 166
    Mubarak and, 155, 162
    Syria and, 182–83
Obama Doctrine, 155–56
oil, 1, 5–7, 72, 155, 168, 207
    in Saudi Arabia, 41–42, 47, 207
Olmert, Ehud, 116, 124
Operation Defensive Shield, 62
Operation Jawbreaker, 144
Operation Southern Focus, 64
Operation Tailwind, 82
Oslo II Accord, 53–54
Ottoman Empire, 3, 31–35, 39, 40, 44
    European powers' division of, 1, 3, 4, 6, 33–35, 138
    map of, 24
    Wahhabi movement and, 39–40
Ottoman Wahhabi War, 40
Otyan, Turki al-, 142

Pakistan, 46, 131, 145, 216
Palestine, Palestinians, 5, 52–53, 214
    in Ain al-Hilweh refugee camp, 136–38
    Britain and, 5
    Engel as Palestinian-affairs correspondent, 49–53, 58, 63
    Gaza, 51, 111–14, 123, 124, 214
    Hamas, *see* Hamas
    Israeli conflict with, *see* Israeli-Palestinian conflict
    Jews and, 5, 34
    in Lebanon War, 57
    prisoners, 112
    PR operations of, 52
Palestine Hotel, 76, 79–81, 83–85
Palestinian Authority, 63
Palmyra, 199–200
Parthenon, 212
Pashtuns, 46
Pearl Square, 157
Pentaki, Efi, 76
Peretz, Amir, 116
Persian Gulf, 5
Petra, 212
Phalanges, 57
Philippines, 143
pirates, 3
Power, Samantha, 217

Press TV, 150
Prussia, 33
Public Radio International, 63
Putin, Vladimir, 151

Qalandia, 58
Qalqilya, 62
Qamishli, 175
Qana, 122–23
Qatar, 4–5, 152, 153
Queen Boat, 45

Rahman, Abu Abdul (Aarqawi's deputy), 106, 205
Rahman, Abu Abdul (Tunisian man), 205–6
Ramadan, 200
Ramadi, 133, 193, 193
Ramallah, 51, 54, 58, 62
Raqqa, 199
Redd, John Scott, 146–47
Republican Guards, 76, 82
Rezgui, Seifeddine, 200
Rixos Hotel, 161
Robertson, Nic, 78
Roman Catholic Church, 30
Rommel, Erwin, 159
rubber bullets, 50, 58–59
Russert, Tim, 107–8
Russia, 4, 33, 45, 151, 216, 217, 219
Ruzicka, Marla, 99–100

Sabra, 57
Sadat, Anwar, 6

Saddam Hussein, 6–8, 11, 70, 72, 75, 77, 79, 83, 84, 86, 100, 108, 190, 208
    al-Qaeda and, 129
    Ba'ath Party and, 76–78, 81, 94
    bin Laden and, 8
    capture of, 86, 87
    George H. W. Bush and, 155
    George W. Bush and, 64, 75–76, 87, 128, 129, 156
    Islam and, 129
    statue of, 85
    Sunnis and, 8, 86, 93, 94, 97, 101
Sadr, Mohammed Sadiq al-, 85–86
Sadr, Muqtada al-, 95, 102, 118
Sagami, Saddam, 141–42
Sahhaf, Mohammed Saeed al-, 77–78, 84, 95
Salafi Muslims, 35, 40–42, 200
    ISIS and, 194–95
    jihadis, 35–36, 38, 45, 46
    Wahhabi, see Wahhabis
Saleh, Ali Abdullah, 168
Sallum, 158, 160, 162
Salmaniya Medical Complex, 157
Sana'a, 213
Saracens, 3
Satanism, 45
Sattar, Abu, 75
Saud, Amir Abdullah bin, 40
Saud clan, 40–41

Saudi Arabia, 4, 9, 35, 36, 45, 46,
117, 136, 151, 201, 207, 208,
216, 217
Bahrain and, 157
Engel's first trip to, 38–39
oil in, 41–42, 47, 207
rehabilitation program in,
140–43, 145
Wahhabism and, 40–42, 47
sayyids, 92, 118
Second Intifada, 50, 56, 60, 62–64,
115
September 11 attacks, *see* 9/11
attacks
sex trade, 139–40
sexuality, 15, 18, 38
homosexuality, 20, 43, 44–45
shabiha, 177–78, 185, 188, 189
Shalit, Gilad, 111–12
sharia law, 44
Sharm el-Sheikh, 154
Sharon, Ariel, 56–57, 58, 60, 63
Shatila, 57
Shia Muslims (Shiites), 2, 4, 9, 29,
34, 85–86, 91–98, 102, 107,
131, 156, 184, 209, 216
Alawite, 172, 181
in Bahrain, 157
elections and, 105
Hezbollah and, *see* Hezbollah
in Iran, 93, 108
ISIS attacks on mosques of,
200–201
and kidnapping of Engel and
crew, 189

minority status of, 93
Saddam and, 8
shabiha, 177–78, 185, 188,
189
Sicily, 65
Sidon, 4
Siniora, Fouad, 115–16, 119,
123
Sirte, 160, 163, 164, 169
Sisi, Abdel Fattah el-, 209
Sistani, Ali al-, 94, 95, 97, 102
smartphones, 152, 174
Somalia, 167, 201
Sousse rampage, 200
Soviet Union, 5, 45
Spain, 3
Spanish Inquisition, 195
suicide bombings, 99, 135, 137,
193, 211
Palestinian, 60–62
Sulayman, Khalid, 143–46
Sunni Muslims, 4, 9, 22, 29, 34,
72, 86, 91–98, 101, 102,
106, 107, 111, 117, 131,
133, 136, 137, 140, 156,
157, 172, 174, 181, 184,
189, 207, 209, 216
elections and, 105
ISIS and, *see* ISIS
and kidnapping of Engel and
crew, 189
in Mosul, 191–94
Saddam and, 8, 86, 93, 94, 97,
101
Wahhabis, *see* Wahhabis

Syria, 1, 4–6, 9, 11, 34, 134, 142,
    152, 169, 171–90, 206, 208,
    213, 214
  Aleppo, 166, 178, 180, 182, 183,
    189, 195, 197, 217
  chemical weapons in, 182–83,
    190, 198
  Damascus, see Damascus
  Daraa, 166, 171–72
  Engel in, 114, 138, 171, 174–90,
    195–98, 218
  Engel and crew kidnapped in,
    171, 184–89, 195, 197, 217–19
  Free Syrian Army, 177, 179, 185,
    195–98, 202
  Ghouta attack in, 190
  Homs, 177
  Houla massacre in, 177–78
  Iraq and, 138
  Iraqi refugees in, 139
  ISIS and, see ISIS
  Lebanese in, 114, 120
  map of, 170
  Obama and, 182–83
  officials killed by bomb in, 179
  Palmyra, 199–200
  Qamishli, 175
  Raqqa, 199
  Tal Abyad, 199
  uprising and civil war in, 138,
    156, 163, 166, 171–90
  US intervention and, 181, 190

Tabligh wa Dawa, 36–38, 43, 45
Ta'e, Uday al-, 71, 78, 84

Taher, 184, 187
Tahrir Square:
  demonstrations in, 151–54, 157,
    166–67
  shooting in front of Egyptian
    Museum, 23–27, 51
Tal Abyad, 199
Taliban, 17–18, 46, 130, 137, 144
Tanzania, 27
technology, 152
  Internet, 131, 135–36, 141, 142,
    152, 155, 172, 180, 215
  phones, 152, 174, 180
Tehran, 150
Tel Aviv, 61, 123
Temple Mount, 55–58, 63
terrorism, 27, 67, 87, 132–33, 138,
    146–47
  Iraq war and, 146, 147
  real estate law of, 142
  war on, 130, 139, 146–47
Tigris River, 76, 78, 84, 94, 103
Tobruk, 158, 159, 162, 163
Today, 188
Todd, Chuck, 182
Topkapi Palace Museum, 39
Tora Bora, 130, 144
Trabelsi, Leila, 151
Transjordan, 4
Tripoli, Lebanon, 135
Tripoli, Libya, 160–68
Tulkarm, 51, 62
Tunis, 150–51
  Bardo National Museum in,
    200

Tunisia, 6, 136, 150–52, 159, 166, 205–6, 208
  Sousse rampage in, 200
Turkey, 173–75, 188, 194, 206, 209, 214
  Istanbul, 29, 156–57
Tyre, 4, 120, 122

Umayyads, 92
Umm al-Fahm, 123
Umm Qasr, 79, 83
Unification Church, 16
United Arab Emirates, 4–5
United Nations (UN), 62, 64, 97, 119, 178
  and war between Israel and Lebanon, 122, 124
  Security Council, 123, 216, 217
  UNESCO, 199
United States, 5, 6, 9, 11, 35, 36, 38, 91
  in Afghanistan war, 129–30
  CIA of, 46, 129, 130, 137, 146, 174, 194
  Crusades and, 30, 34, 139
  Fifth Fleet of, 157
  in Gulf War (1991), 8, 60, 64, 82, 86, 93, 155
  Middle East policy of, 5, 35, 155, 156, 157, 169, 181, 209, 216–17
  Iran nuclear deal and, 216
  Iraq invaded by, 50, 70, 72, 76–87, 93, 95, 102, 107, 108, 115, 128–30, 132, 146, 215
  in Iraq war, *see* Iraq war
  Marines of, 135
  State Department of, 174
  Syrian uprising and, 181, 190
  veterans in, 131
Uthman, 92
Uzo Hotel, 159–60

Vietnam War, 125
Vikings, 29

Wahhab, Mohammed Ibn, 40
Wahhabis, 4, 21, 36, 38–43, 195
  jihadists, 45
  Ottomans and, 39–40
  Saudi Arabia and, 40–42, 47
  spread of, 41–42
Wailing Wall (Western Wall), 56
Wajjeh, 112–13
Wall Street Journal, 172
weapons of mass destruction (WMDs), 64, 86, 129, 131, 132
Wedeman, Ben, 158, 159
West Bank, 11, 53–55, 58, 60, 61, 64, 124, 214
  map of, 48
  Operation Defensive Shield in, 62
WGBH, 63
Wilhelm II, Kaiser, 3, 33
Williams, Brian, 192
Winograd Commission, 121
witchcraft, 45
women, 15, 18, 20
World, The, 63

World War I, 32–34
   Middle East reorganized
      following, 1, 3, 4, 6, 33–35,
      138
World War II, 5, 35, 105, 126, 159
Wye River Memorandum, 53

Yazid, 92–93
Yemen, 168, 213
Yom Kippur War, 57
Young Turks, 3, 32–33
YouTube, 172, 215

Zarfar, 71, 72–73, 75
Zarqa, 133

Zarqawi, Abu Musab al-, 96–98,
   102, 105, 133, 143, 181, 205,
   215
   bin Laden and, 96, 98, 107,
      131–32
   death of, 106–7, 132
   Internet and, 131
   ISIS and, 96, 107, 132, 191,
      192
   videos of, 96, 132
Zawahiri, Ayman al-, 27–28
   bin Laden and, 27–28, 143
Zawiya, 161
Zintan, 165–66
Zionism, 19–21, 51, 77

PHOTO CREDITS

ABOUT THE AUTHOR

RICHARD ENGEL is the award winning Chief Foreign Correspondent for NBC and has been reporting on the Middle East for twenty years. He is the author of *War Journal* and *A Fist in the Hornet's Nest*.